POWER

POWER

Oppression, Subservience, and Resistance

RAYMOND ANGELO BELLIOTTI

Published by State University of New York Press, Albany

For information, contact State University of New York Press, Albany, NY
www.sunypress.edu

Production, Eileen Nizer
Marketing, Kate R. Seburyamo

Library of Congress Cataloging-in-Publication Data

Belliotti, Raymond A., 1948–
    Power : oppression, subservience, and resistance / Raymond Angelo Belliotti.
        pages cm
    Includes bibliographical references and index.
    ISBN 978-1-4384-5955-4 (hc : alk. paper)—ISBN 978-1-4384-5956-1 (pb : alk. paper)
    ISBN 978-1-4384-5957-8 (e-book)
    1. Power (Philosophy)   I. Title.

    BD438.B44 2016
    303.3—dc23   2015010176

10 9 8 7 6 5 4 3 2 1

To Marcia, Angelo, and Vittoria

∾

L'onuri chi si perdi 'ntra un minutu,
'Ntra cent' anni nun è ricumpinzatu.

("Honor that is lost in a minute
is not won back in a hundred years.")

Contents

Part Three

Abbreviations

As is the common practice, when I have cited from the writings of some prominent authors, the references in all cases have been given immediately in the text and not in the notes. I used multiple versions of the texts in some cases. Unless otherwise indicated, all references are to sections or chapters, not page numbers. I have used the following abbreviations:

For Nietzsche

BGE	*Beyond Good and Evil* (1886)
EH	*Ecce Homo* (1908)
GM	*On the Genealogy of Morals* (1887)
GS	*The Gay Science* (1882)
TI	*Twilight of the Idols* (1889)
UM	*Untimely Meditations* (1873–76)
WP	*The Will to Power* (unpublished notebooks, 1883–88)
Z	*Thus Spoke Zarathustra* (1883–85)
GS 125	*The Gay Science*, Section 125
Z I	"Zarathustra's Prologue," 5 = *Thus Spoke Zarathustra*, Book 1, "Zarathustra's Prologue," section 5
BGE 13	*Beyond Good and Evil*, section 13
EH	"Why I Am So Clever," 9 = *Ecce Homo*, "Why I Am So Clever," section 9
GM II, 12	*On the Genealogy of Morals*, Book 2, section 12

WP 1067   *The Will to Power*, section 1067

UM   "Schopenhauer as Educator," 8 = Untimely
                 Meditations, "Schopenhauer as Educator," section 8

TI   "Maxims and Arrows," 12 = Twilight of the Idols,
                 "Maxims and Arrows," number 12

For Epictetus

EN   *Encheiridion* (Manual for Living)

EN 12   *Encheiridion*, sec. 12

For Plato

R   *Republic*

G   *Gorgias*

R 368b–369b   *Republic* 368b–369b (Stephanus numbering)

G 480a–522e   *Gorgias* 480a–522e (Stephanus numbering)

For Machiavelli

AW   *The Art of War*

D   *The Discourses*

FH   *Florentine Histories*

Ltr.   Machiavelli's letters

P   *The Prince*

AW 2 45   *The Art of War*, Book 2, page 45 (Wood edition)

D I 55   *The Discourses*, Book I, chapter 55

FH I 3   *Florentine Histories*, Book I, section 3

Ltr. 247: 1/31/15   Letter 247: January 31, 1515 (Atkinson and Sices
                 edition)

P 18   *The Prince*, chapter 18

Preface

Power is the ultimate aphrodisiac.

—Henry Kissinger

I was discussing our respective academic disciplines with a colleague who was a political scientist. The dialogue was quite predictable until he suddenly blurted out, "But we study *power*!" To describe with words the glee with which he uttered this sentence is beyond challenging. On a scale of passion from one to ten, my colleague earned a score of twelve. To label his enthusiasm "deranged avidity" would not overstate his mindset. It was as if he were convinced that to study and try to measure "power" were enterprises that by themselves amplified the personal significance of practitioners and elevated their profession.

When another philosopher passed by and offered, "Well, we search for truth," his bromide received the derision one might anticipate. "Truth," it appeared, was abstract, contestable, and elusive. "Power" was real, indisputable, and registered expansive, discernible effects. The political scientist unknowingly echoed the conclusions of the character Callicles in Plato's *Gorgias*: philosophy is a project for babies. Engaging in it may help shape a child's mind, but real men seek glory in the political arena pervaded by power (G 484c–484d).

The conversation ended and everyone went their separate ways. But I was haunted by my colleague's words. I was convinced that throughout the history of philosophy many thinkers had reflected productively on the concept, consequences, and structures of power. Perhaps by explaining and critically examining these efforts I could combine the search for truth with a more profound understanding of power. Perhaps I could even go beyond being a baby and experience the visceral delight embodied by my colleague. Maybe in my seventh decade of life I could finally become a "real man." Such is the genesis of this work.

Acknowledgments

Numerous people contributed to this work directly or indirectly. As always, my family comes first. Thanks to Marcia, Angelo, and Vittoria for being my one, true thing.

Thanks also to Michael Rinella, a first-rate acquisitions editor, who added expertise to the production process and who dealt patiently and considerately with an author who is consistently impatient. Thanks to Joanne Foeller, an expert of book formatting who corrected my numerous errors and prepared the final manuscript with unmatched efficiency and grace.

Finally, I am deeply grateful to the following publishers who have granted permission to reprint, adapt, or revise some of my previously published work:

1. Part of my explanation of Marxism was first published in *Justifying Law: The Debate over Foundations, Goals, and Methods* (Philadelphia: Temple University Press, 1992).

2. A version of my analysis of Gramsci is included in *Watching Baseball, Seeing Philosophy: The Great Thinkers at Play on the Diamond* (Jefferson, NC: McFarland Publishing, 2008).

3. My rendering of Machiavelli reflects material from *Niccolò Machiavelli: The Laughing Lion & The Strutting Fox* (Lanham, MD: Lexington Books, 2008).

4. My interpretation of Stoicism adapts arguments from *Roman Philosophy and the Good Life* (Lanham, MD: Lexington Books, 2009).

5. Portions of my description and examination of Nietzsche were first published in *Jesus or Nietzsche: How Should We Live Our Lives?* (Amsterdam, Netherlands, Value Inquiry

Book Series: Ethical Theory and Practice, Rodopi Publishers, 2013).

6. A few paragraphs of the chapter on Habermas are revisions of material from "Radical Politics and Nonfoundational Morality," *International Philosophical Quarterly* 29 (1989): 33–51.

Introduction

When most people initially hear the term *power* they conjure images of domination and oppression: totalitarian political leaders dictating to the masses and enforcing their will because they monopolize the military forces of their country; or radically unequal relationships where one party enjoys privilege of place and prerogative; or the tragic effects of the distribution of widely unequal material resources among different social classes in society. At first blush, then, power strikes us as the means by which certain individuals or groups are able to assert their wills and attain their ends to the detriment of other, less-powerful individuals and groups.

While this understanding captures, in a simplistic fashion, one use of one type of power, it does not define the term. In its most general rendering, we all enjoy expansive power to do a variety of things and participate in a host of activities. In addition, even the exercise of power over another party can be in service of advancing the interests of the subordinate in the relationship. Thus, we should not identify power with oppression too facilely.

Furthermore, even oppressive power relations are more complicated than they first appear. We are inclined to assume that superiors in such relationships benefit abundantly while subordinates suffer gravely; that these relationships are static and ongoing; and that the possibilities for reversal are few if any. Also, power is typically understood as a commodity, object, or transferable substance that operates on antecedently constructed human beings. All such assumptions require refinement.

To deepen our understanding of power, a cluster of questions animates this work: How are we to judge appropriate from inappropriate exercises of power and acceptable from unacceptable relations of power? What normative standards permit us to justify acts of rebellion and efforts to transform extant power relations? Why would we undertake such acts and efforts? How would we do so? And for what end? How and why is resistance implicated in power's basic constitution? To what extent do relations of power constitute

1

the human subject? What is the relationship of power to knowledge? What is the relationship of power to our normative notions of morality and justice? Is it possible to pontificate about power from a vantage point not already contaminated by the effects of oppression? How much and what types of power facilitate human fulfillment?

The book is not designed to track the linear history of the philosophical literature on power. Instead, the work is organized by themes related to different aspects of power. Like ancient Gaul, this book is divided into three parts.

Part One includes four chapters. In the first chapter, I explain why and how the concept of power has proven to be uncommonly intriguing and maddeningly elusive. I then sketch a general notion of power that is broad enough to cover numerous types of power, but whose generality weakens its usefulness for analyzing specific relations of power; distinguish between power-to and power-over; catalog competing notions of what constitute a person's interests and how they connect to invocations of power; briefly discuss passive power and distinguish exerting influence from exercising power; introduce ideas about social power; and define and illustrate three major uses of power-over (oppressive, paternalistic, transformative). This chapter informs the analyses in the remainder of the book.

After my introduction on the concept of power, Part One links Thrasymachus and Socrates, Machiavelli, and Nietzsche because these thinkers address common aspects of power: Does might make right? What is the normative status of moral and political principles? How is the impulse for power connected to human personality? What process energizes reversals of power relations?

In chapter II, I introduce the vexing question of the relationship between power and the development of morality and our sense of justice. The character Thrasymachus in Plato's *Republic* insists that our general normative understanding is nothing more than the effect of exercises of power exerted by those who rule society. Might (power) makes right (what we take to be morally appropriate) in the sense that those who have disproportionate say in setting the terms of social life incorporate into law imperatives that serve their personal interests. Through habit and ideological distortion, these conventional ideas gain an aura of objectivity that reinforces their authority. What is in fact merely conventional, partial, and self-serving comes to be understood as natural, appropriate, and even necessary. The character Socrates disputes Thrasymachus's analysis and insists that our normative understanding must conform to impersonal, impartial, moral imperatives in order to earn our allegiance: power cannot of itself establish moral truth. The Platonic characters Thrasymachus and Socrates set the stage for a wide-ranging debate about the nature, effects, distribution, and exercise of power that endures.

In chapter III, I examine the work of Niccolò Machiavelli, the prince of power (apologies for the pun). Given the numerous plausible interpretations of his work, Machiavelli should be taken to be *the* classical philosopher of power. Not because the popular or any single interpretation of the *Prince* is definitive, but because when filtered through centuries of interpretive scholarship, we can reasonably view Machiavelli as having exemplified, both through his writing style and the content of his works, virtually every nuance of power considered important by contemporary thinkers: the three major ways power-over can be exercised (oppressively, paternalistically, transformatively); the development of power-to in countless dimensions; the uses that power-to can be put in service of power-over; the relationship between power-over and normative validity; and the possibilities for reversals of extant power relations. I conclude by paraphrasing what Alfred North Whitehead said about the relation between the European philosophical tradition and Plato: "The safest general characterization of the Western philosophical tradition on the nature of power is that it consists of a series of footnotes to Machiavelli."

In the concluding and fourth chapter in Part One, I introduce the thinker who has issued to date the most imaginative footnotes to Machiavellian power: the nineteenth-century German philosopher Friedrich Nietzsche, who insisted that "the world is the will to power and nothing else" (BGE, 36). Here I advance what I take to be the best understanding of Nietzsche's Will to Power; connect that notion to his ideal of perfectionism, which I critique; distinguish happiness understood as hedonistic fulfillment from Nietzsche's conception of happiness as increased feelings and experiences of personal strength; illustrate Nietzsche's conception of power in the context of his narrative of the struggle between master and slave moralities; and discuss how Nietzsche joins cause with Marx in arguing that the most invidious power is that which can conceal its own workings. Under certain circumstances, human beings can promote ideologies and social practices that have the effect of seducing other human beings into using their own minds to collude unwittingly in their own subordination. Nietzsche goes beyond Marx in that his account of the slave morality portrays ideology as constitutive of oppression, as a fundamental means of establishing oppressive relations. Nietzsche also anticipates Gramsci in his conviction that the formation of an ideology that opposes the existing set of dominant relations can be a means of rebellion and an instrument of social change.

Part Two joins Stoicism, Hegel, Marx, and Gramsci because they all confront the relationship between human will and the dynamics of power: How can those in subservient positions in power relations undermine the authority of those in superior positions? How do those in superior positions lure subordinates into acquiescing to their own oppression? What are the effects of power relationships on the characters of superiors and subordinates? What results occur when power relations distance parties from creative, productive labor? How do social structures solidify unequal power relations?

Part Two begins with an analysis of Stoicism in chapter V. At first blush, the Stoics seem poor candidates for the title of philosophers of power. Their lifestyle is designed to minimize wants, strictly define needs, and meticulously discipline inner lives. They neither brandish nor celebrate a will to power. Stoics seek the good life through limiting desires and identifying well-being with careful attention to and control of only those things fully under our control. But Stoics are probably the best teachers of the relationship between subordination and yearning. Theirs is a negative power in that they are able to not only resist oppression, but make it irrelevant to their lives. As such, a successful Stoic would not *experience* subordination in the way most victims would. More precisely, by refusing to recognize suffering or subordination as an infringement of their good, Stoics remove themselves from the power superiors might think they have over them. Moreover, Stoics do this without being prey to false consciousness. They would argue that they can identify their genuine interests—defined by taking control of their attitudes, judgments, choices, and ensuing actions—and that they cannot truly be harmed by those who inflict suffering, material deprivations, and even death upon them. Stoics also use what they take to be their genuine interests to inform their current desires and long-term preferences. Thus, successful Stoics do not experience a conflict among the different senses of interests commonly invoked. To be harmed one must endure a thwarting or setback to one's interests. By defining their genuine interests narrowly, Stoics apparently nurture the power to undermine what the rest of the world would perceive as the power over them possessed by superiors. Finally, Stoics parry the capability of others to control or limit their choices and actions. Accordingly, Stoics provide a stunning example of how those typically taken to be subordinates in relations of power can unilaterally diffuse oppressive exercises of power.

In chapter VI, I unravel Hegel's complicated, insightful analysis of oppressive, dyadic power relations. Within Hegel's depiction are numerous lessons about the phenomenology of power. First, within an oppressive relationship are the seeds of transformation and even reversal: relations of power-over are neither static nor one-sided. Second, exercising power over others oppressively can frustrate the superior party's personal development and fulfillment, which can trigger the transformation or reversal of the power relationship. Third, when superiors fail to develop and exercise their higher human capabilities outside of power relationships—for example, by failing to engage in robust, creative labor—they become overly dependent on subordinates for their sense of identity and self-worth. Fourth, human beings are dependent upon one another to gain a salutary sense of identity, but overly emphasizing one's presumed status as a master or superior unwisely heightens the master's dependence on subordinates: the master becomes a slave to his own oppressive power relationship because he relies too extensively on his subordinates for assertion and recognition. Fifth, through the exercise of creative labor, subordinates can gain self-reliance and a form of independence (perhaps even under alienating conditions). Sixth, human beings do not win freedom and self-worth by oppressing others of their kind. Most important, Hegel's paramount message is that human flourishing requires mutually validating, equal self-consciousnesses that preclude structures of oppression. Only union and solidarity with another of one's kind can generate full consciousness of freedom and full, salutary self-consciousness. Accordingly, the most important message of Hegel's lordship-bondsman narrative is that human flourishing and genuine freedom require both asserting the self and affording recognition, in its fullest sense, to others. Hegel teaches that the pernicious use of power-over often generates unwelcome surprises for the supposed superior party.

Chapter VII discusses the work of Karl Marx and Antonio Gramsci. Marx invokes ideology and false consciousness as methods that deepen and reinforce oppression that is already in place because of the needs of an economic system. Thus, Marx stresses the roles ideology and socialization assume in reflecting and sustaining power regimes. Marx recognizes the structural basis of power-over, the mutual dependence of the constitutive parties, and the ongoing nature of negotiation between them. Thus, Marxism highlights class struggle and how power is reproduced and transformed within it. Marx underscores why and how classes, as opposed to discrete individuals, are the engines of social change, the loci of social conflict, and the constituents of society. The actions of members of classes are comprehendible only with reference to ongoing structural relationships of power.

Gramsci presents a clear alternative to the historical materialism of Marx. He underscores the democratic impulses in Marxism: the need for workers to nurture and express their own critical consciousness; the importance of liberating ourselves from the constraints of false necessities; the practical advantage of viewing revolution as a series of human, active political events; and the role of consent in both sustaining and unsettling dominant political arrangements. Gramsci distances himself from the scientism of Marxism: his historical bloc and ensemble of relations analysis alters the economic base and ideological superstructure model; he does not believe in the historical inevitability or clear predictability of communist revolution; and he views history as indeterminate. As a result, Gramsci's philosophy embodies insights for social revolutionaries positioned on all points of the ideological spectrum.

Part Three connects three contemporary thinkers and movements in the philosophy of power, Habermas, Foucault, and Feminism. Thinkers in these movements ask questions such as the following: How pervasive are power relations? How, if at all, can normative principles be purified of the wrongful influences of oppression? How can we distinguish salutary power relations from debilitating power relations? Can subordinates in power relations nevertheless construct alternate understandings of power in service of collective, positive transformation?

Part Three begins with an analysis of the work of Michel Foucault in chapter VIII. Foucault's linkages between power, knowledge/truth, and the constitution of human subjects are instructive in a host of ways. First, he reminds us that in modern societies power is less frequently exercised by individuals with special prowess and status and is, instead, more commonly exercised through impersonal administrative systems that operate in accordance with abstract rules. Disciplinary sexual practices, psychoanalysis, and other normalizing techniques employed by criminology, medicine, and sociology nurture human subjects that are both docile and productive. Second, the exercise of power requires the production of knowledge and truth claims that become widely accepted. The most effective power is embodied within a network of relations that secure the consent of subjects by luring them into internalizing dominate norms and values. Third, genealogical and archeological examinations demonstrate that dominant ideas and practices arise from specific historical origins that lack objective or foundational justifications. Fourth, disciplinary power is a set of techniques for governing human beings that simultaneously amplifies their capabilities (their power-to) and their controllability. Fifth, even power relations of dominance cannot extinguish the possibility of resistance and reversal. Sixth, in order to transform the self, human subjects must detach themselves from extant modes of being and behaving, and create new ways that are at least somewhat detached from the disciplinary order. The end sought is the loosening of the constraints of power relations of wrongful dominance. Finally, although much of Foucault's work is anticipated by the likes of Nietzsche, Marx, Freud, and Wittgenstein, Foucault's specific applications and development of their thinking—in domains such as sexual practices, prison punishments, conceptions of madness, and psychiatric counseling—illuminate and amplify their insights in concrete situations.

In chapter IX, I examine the prolific writings of Jürgen Habermas. He uses Hannah Arendt's notion of communicative power as the springboard to outline how social and administrative power can be legitimated through public discourse that embodies normative standards. Communicative power is grounded in collective agreement, a consensus attained through the formation of the collective will guided by communicative rationality. The resulting norms provide a framework within which strategic social and administrative power can be exercised less oppressively than otherwise. Communicative power exercised from within a public arena that is organized fairly can soften oppressive social power differentials. For Habermas, the moral norms arising from the process of communicative rationality embody context-transcending validity and should be institutionalized in the political and legal structures that frame social action. These norms, again, arise from intersubjective communicative rationality conducted under proper conditions. Although I argue that Habermas's project fails, he nevertheless contributes significantly to the literature on power in several ways. First, he highlights the need to filter administrative and social power through the prism of valid norms in order to soften the possibilities of oppression. Second, he amplifies Hannah Arendt's insights and constructs a theory of communicative rationality that underscores the "noncoercive coercive" power of sound arguments grounded in good reasons. Third, he refuses to succumb to the seductions of an insipid relativism that tolerates too many conflicting positions on the theoretical level but acts quite differently on the practical level. Fourth, he offers a rationale for resistance to purveyors of oppression who distort the conditions required for communicative rationality. Thus, Habermas exemplifies an enduring spirit that animates the search for more wholesome forms of human association.

In chapter X, I identify four distinct but overlapping feminist themes regarding power: ending patriarchal oppression, redistributing power, using power-to for collective transformation, and using power-over for empowerment. The four themes converge on a critical point: most feminist thinkers agree that relationships should offer opportunities to empower and transform others in positive ways. The paramount issues surrounding patriarchal oppression form the launching pads for social transformation:

How might we distinguish legitimate from illegitimate exercises of power? What social practices and policies are patriarchally oppressive and why? How do such practices and policies arise? How can they be identified? How can they be changed? What concepts and exercises of power are compatible with feminism's ideal of an egalitarian society? In addressing such questions, what began as an obvious opposition to oppression becomes a complicated process of identification, explanation, and reformation.

In addition, a host of underlying matters makes the answers to the questions posed more complex. For example, assuming most, if not all, extant societies are patriarchal in a pejorative sense and that they have and do disadvantage women significantly, it follows that our notions of "power" themselves may be contaminated with male-bias. Also, under this assumption, the reformist programs of feminists are hatched in a patriarchal context. Will such "reforms" genuinely pave the way to gender equality? Or, given the context of their genesis, are they more likely to either reinforce or, at least, only repackage existing privileges and prerogatives?

The chapter continues by addressing the paradox of identifying genuine interests and outlines some of the suggested causes and remedies of gender oppression. In so doing, the distinctive contribution of feminist thought to the theory of power becomes manifest: an egalitarian quest of exercising power-to for purposes of collective transformation.

Chapter XI completes the work with a brief summary of the main issues discussed, conclusions reached, and some final words about the problems attending specifying the standards of normative validity required to distinguish justified from unjustified exercises of power. Identifying such standards is critical if we aspire to not merely describe but to evaluate various exercises of power.

PART ONE

I

Concepts of Power

Power is a word the meaning of which we do not understand.

—Leo Tolstoy

The concept of power is uncommonly intriguing and maddeningly elusive. In this chapter, I sketch a general notion of power; distinguish between power-to and power-over; catalog competing notions of what constitutes a person's interests and how they connect to invocations of power; briefly discuss passive power and distinguish exerting influence from exercising power; introduce ideas about social power; and define and illustrate three major uses of power-over.

A General Notion of Power

We use the term *power* appropriately to refer to a host of different, sometimes overlapping concepts.[1] At its most general, *power is the capability to produce or contribute to the production of outcomes.* Understood at this level, power is not necessarily relational—that is, it does not require at least two parties one of which is superior in capability to the other; power does not necessarily require a social setting to gain its meaning or to animate its structure; power does not necessarily generate resistance or opposition or a conflict of interests that the agent must overcome; nor does the exercise of power require a demonstrated intention.

For example, imagine an adult human being, Muffin, shipwrecked alone on a deserted island. Muffin will have numerous powers antecedent to arriving on the island. To name only a few: the power to walk; to lift weight of certain poundage; to speak a language; to sing; to write; to conceive countless ideas; and to interact with the environment in a variety of ways. Moreover, Muffin may develop any of these powers further while residing on the island. Our stranded mariner may also discover powers that she was previously unaware of possessing. Imagine Muffin stubbing her toe on a sharp object and shrieking maniacally. With no intention to do so and unaware that she could do so, the shriek amounts to a musical high C note, whose sound waves smash a nearby tumbler that Muffin had carried to the island. The result was unintended and Muffin was unaware of her power to produce such a note, but at this point she discovers the power. Thus, Muffin literally did not know her own power, at least in this regard.

Also, we may have power utterly independent of or even at odds with our immediate desires and long-range preferences. Thus, a person may have the power to sing well but be indifferent to exercising or even possessing that power. Another person may have the power to compose poetry while thoroughly disdaining that art form.

Finally, power at this level can be possessed by inanimate forces. Hurricanes have tremendous power to produce outcomes unwelcomed by human beings, as do various types of weather upon the crops of farmers. Thus, Muffin not only possesses certain powers but is also subject to a host of environmental powers while on the island.

This nonsocial rendering of power is crushingly uninteresting, probably because it is the most general concept connoted by the term. But it does illustrate several useful aspects of power: that power is a capability or disposition, thus someone can possess a certain power but not exercise it; that possessing power implies the actualization of a potential—we learn to walk, to speak a language, to sing, and the like by developing our potentials; that power does not automatically translate to domination, oppression, or subordination; that power is something almost every living and some nonliving things possess to some extent; and that to have power is typically to attain a good in some respect (e.g., the capability to produce or affect outcomes).

The Concept of Power-Over

But those who study, write about, and argue about power are most concerned with the concept of one entity having *power over* another entity (dyadic relational power) or a significant institution having power over an individual or a class of individuals (general social power). The concern focuses on the effects of domination, oppression, and subordination in setting the terms of social life—in identifying the agents of power and those whose lives are diminished as a result of the exercise of power.

Intentionally Changing the Behavior of Others

Here is one characterization of the relationship of power-over: "The superior has power over the subordinate when the superior successfully achieves his or her intended result by making the subordinate perform an action which the subordinate would not have done but for the superior's desire that the subordinate do it. Although the subordinate was reluctant, the superior overcomes that reluctance."[2]

Such a rendering will not do. First, the superior may possess power over the subordinate without ever exercising that advantage. Conflating the *ability* to exert power with its *exercise* is a mistake. Second, the superior can exercise power over the subordinate without any conscious intent. The most invidious examples of wrongful domination may be those in which the superior does not need to manifest a conscious intent in order to control the subordinate. Furthermore, exercises of power often have unintended effects for which the superior is nevertheless responsible. Third, the superior need not induce the subordinate to perform an action in order to exercise power. For example, the superior can exercise power by inducing the subordinate to refrain from acting or by constraining the subordinate's options by mystifying the subordinate's genuine interests or by limiting the number of alternative actions. If the subordinate's freedom is limited because the underling cannot perceive his or her objective well-being or situated interests or even long-term preferences because of ideological conditioning, then the superior who is responsible for this situation has exercised power without necessarily inducing the subordinate to perform a particular action. To mold the subordinate's perception of his or her interests wrongfully is an especially dangerous form of power because if successful the superior does not need to monitor the everyday activities of the underling closely in order to exert power. Fourth, even where the superior does exercise power by inducing the subordinate to perform an action it does not follow that the subordinate would not have so acted but for the superior's desire that the subordinate do so. For example, the superior in a particular circumstance may be unaware of the specific situation and thus have no desire about how the subordinate might act; yet the subordinate, unable to identity his or her interests, voluntarily does precisely what the superior would have wanted done had the superior thought about it.

Also, there is a technical problem with simultaneous causation. Suppose two independent superiors both possess power over the same subordinate. They both act simultaneously to induce the subordinate to perform a particular action. In this hypothetical, even if the first superior had not exerted power the subordinate would still have acted as he or she did because of the power exerted by the second superior, and even if the second superior had not exerted power the subordinate would still have acted as he or she did because of the power exerted by the first superior. Thus, it cannot be said of either superior that the subordinate would not have acted as he or she did but for *that* superior's desire that the subordinate do so.

Finally, the rendering of power-over at issue assumes that the subordinate will be reluctant to do as the superior desires and will offer resistance of some intensity and kind. But subordinates who cannot identity their genuine interests or who are naturally submissive or who are intoxicated by the spell cast by their superiors may willingly and enthusiastically perform actions that their superiors desire. In such cases, acquiescence and consent replace resistance and conflict.

But this characterization of power-over implicitly embodies a paramount truth: superiors can exercise power over subordinates without oppressing them. Nothing in this characterization of power-over implies that the exertion of power must be *against* the interests of the subordinate party. On the contrary, superiors can exercise power over subordinates in ways that advance the interests of underlings. This may occur through paternalistic intervention—when a superior exerts power over a subordinate that advances the subordinate's interests in circumstances where the subordinate cannot identity his or her genuine interests through no fault of the superior. The ignorant subordinate may even resist mightily doing what is in his or her interests but the superior's power may win the day. Thus, wise parents may exercise power over their children and induce them to eat more nutritiously or gain needed bed rest despite the protestations of their offspring.

Moreover, superiors may exert power over subordinates in order to develop the talents of the subordinates to the point where the influence of superiors is no longer required. Again, nurturing parents aspire to transform their children into fully functioning, capable, powerful adults; caring teachers tend to their students with the aim that their tutelage will be rendered obsolete as their pupils become their own best teachers. Although power-over is intuitively understood as wrongful domination or oppression, that should not obscure the fact that power may be exerted over a subordinate in ways that advance their genuine interests or transform their characters beneficially.

Exercising Power to Change the Behavior of Subordinates

Consider an intuitively appealing, closely-related definition of the *exercise* of power-over: One party exercises power over another party to the extent that the first gets the second to do something that the second party would not otherwise do.[3] Although plausible, this is also unsuccessful as a satisfactory definition of power-over. First, subordinates experience the lash of power not only when they are compelled to do certain things but also when they are prevented from pursuing particular projects. Superiors can exert power over subordinates in ways other than by explicitly changing the behavior of subordinates. For example, superiors may be able to prevent an issue tightly connected to the well-being of subordinates from being deliberated and acted upon. Although the overt behavior of subordinates has not been altered, the superiors may well have exerted power over them. On this account, a superior party exercises power over a subordinate party when the superior's preferences prevail over the contrary preferences of the subordinate, but also when the superior is able to control "the agenda, mobilizing the bias of the system, determining which issues are 'key' issues, indeed which issues come up for decision, and excluding those which threaten the interests of the powerful."[4]

Second, often subordinates misidentify their own interests and willingly comply with the prerogatives of power. Thus, power is not exercised only where the subordinate would have done otherwise but for a superior's exercise of power. Power is most forceful when it is able to secure the acquiescence of its victims or when it suppresses latent conflict. Third, there is again the technical problem of simultaneous causation (see above). Fourth, this definition presupposes the existence of (at least) latent conflict, which may in fact be absent where the superior party has secured the consent of the subordinate party through broader exercises of power. Finally, determining what the second party would otherwise have done, how he or she would have acted but for the invention by the first party, will often be problematic if not impossible.

In sum, the suggestion that getting someone to do something that the person would not otherwise do is also an inadequate definition because often that effect can be realized without the capability or exercise of power. For example, someone without any power over another may sway their behavior through the use of persuasive arguments or nonthreatening requests or by pointing out previously unforeseen consequences of the action that the other had contemplated. Thus, getting someone to do something that they would not otherwise do is not a sufficient condition of another person exercising power over that someone. In addition, a person could exercise power over another person without changing their behavior. For example, a prison warden has power over prisoners and may issue orders that they be subject to harsher treatment and fewer privileges, but those decrees do not automatically change the future behavior of the prisoners. Thus, getting someone to do something that they would not otherwise do is not a necessary condition of another person exercising power over that someone.

To expand on some of these objections: The effectiveness of power cannot simply be measured by intentional actions that produce outcomes wherein superiors prevail in policy or zero-sum choice situations in which the interests of superiors and subordinates conflict. Power is most effective where it is least transparent. For example, social structures that limit decision making to trivial matters permitting only marginal adjustment and incremental change foster a sense of consensus at the cost of truncating genuine, possibly fruitful, conflict. By shaping community values and procedures for dispute resolution, such institutional structures stifle latent power conflicts by promoting obstacles to public deliberation. The result is a fragile consensus that appears to be genuine but is in fact the outcome of a social process that masks potentially serious differences.

In that vein, the greatest power is that which secures the consent of subordinates to their own oppression. Here conflict, resistance, and rebellion do not arise, because those who are oppressed embody false consciousness: they are unable to identify their genuine interests and what would nurture their objective well-being and, instead, become unwitting collaborators in their own miserable situation. Of course, this is a familiar theme in Marxist thought: the dominant class has control over the ideological apparatus that supports the economic structure in place; culture and ideology disseminate messages that the underclass internalizes; and in this fashion, the ideological superstructure domesticates the potentially revolutionary impulses of the oppressed. The oppressed are largely unaware of their genuine interests because of the mystification and repression of the dominant ideology and the lack of available alternate ideological frameworks. The dominant ideology socializes oppressed people to internalize values and practices that legitimate their own subordination. The status quo is portrayed as appropriate, natural, and even necessary. By masking the true sources of its own messages—the needs of an economic system and the prerogatives of the dominant classes—the prevalent ideology mystifies the process and encourages the oppressed to misidentify their own genuine interests. Moreover, inertia and force reinforce the status quo, as the dominant class also controls military and police forces. Also, the material condition of the oppressed is just comfortable enough to encourage their acquiescence, but not so robust as to yield equal and opposite power to that held by the dominant class. Finally, rebellion and resistance are costly, and the oppressed typically lack the required resources to mount significant rebellion.[5]

Through this process, the dominant class shapes the perceptions, social circumstances, and preferences of the oppressed and facilitates false consciousness. With their judgment skewed, the oppressed accept the familiar as the inevitable and an atmosphere of false necessity prevails. By securing the consent of the oppressed to their own oppression, superiors possessing power are able to obscure its mechanisms and limit its overt exercise. Although no such system is completely effective and pockets of resistance will always exist, acquiescence on the part of the oppressed is sufficient and general enough to stymie wholesale rebellion.

Adversely Affecting the Interests of Subordinates

Another intuitive rendering of the exercise of power-over: One party exercises power over another party when the first affects the second in a manner contrary to the second party's interests.[6] This, too, is insufficient. First, superiors can exert power over subordinates in ways that not only do not set back the subordinates' interests but also intentionally advance those interests. Again, paternalistic exercises of power and interventions aimed at empowering subordinate parties are common. Second, even when one party does affect a second party in a manner that sets back that person's interests it does not follow that power-over has been exerted. For example, imagine that Leonardo is dramatically enjoying a cheeseburger as he walks along the street. He passes a stranger, Zerblonski, who is taken by how much pleasure the food is producing. Zerblonski decides to purchase a cheeseburger for herself. Unfortunately, she has extraordinary high cholesterol and severe heart disease. She has been warned to avoid all high-fat, red meat food. Zerblonski gobbles down the burger and her interests are immediately set back: she has a heart attack and is rushed to a hospital. Leonardo has unwittingly affected Zerblonski in a manner contrary to Zerblonski's interests, but he has not thereby exerted power over her. Instead, he has unknowingly and unintentionally influenced a stranger to do that which is against her own interests. Thus, to affect another person detrimentally (or beneficially) is not necessarily to exert power over her. To put the point in logical terms: to assert correctly that one party has affected a second party in a manner contrary to (or favorable to) the second party's interests is not a sufficient condition for concluding that the first party has exercised power over the second party.

However, to detail the inadequacies of traditional renderings of power should not lead us to ignore their insights. As Steven Lukes points out:

The effects of power seem clearly to bear some relation to intention and will: someone whose actions regularly subvert his intentions and wants can scarcely be called powerful. The outcome of resistance is certainly relevant where comparisons of power are at issue. Affecting behavior is certainly a centrally important form of power, though not all such affecting is power and not all power is such affecting. The cooperative and communicative aspect of empowerment certainly requires attention, as do the ways in which power maintains social systems and advances conflicting collective interests within them.[7]

Human Interests

To this point, I have used the term *interests* as if it was unproblematic and its meaning was obvious. This is far from the case. Before we continue, I must sketch different understandings of what constitutes a person's interests. The notion of a person's interests is ambiguous. Here are a few alternatives:

1. My interests may be understood as *the fulfillment of my current desires*: to fulfill my current desire to eat potato chips by providing me a large bag is to advance my interests in this sense.

2. My interests may also be understood as *the fulfillment of my long-term preferences*: to fulfill my current desire may well conflict with my long-term preferences. Thus, my current desire to eat potato chips conflicts with my long-term preferences for physical health and a trim figure. If so, by helping to fulfill my current desire you have set back my long-term preferences and thereby thwarted my interests in this sense. Thus, I may be currently interested in and have a desire for something that is not in my long-term interests to pursue.

3. My interests may be understood as *the set of preferences I would develop if I were choosing under ideal conditions*. Such an imagined state would be free from distorting influences such as external pressure, adverse circumstances, lack of information, and societal conditioning. In this hypothetical state, I would still be an individual—thus, we would not all choose the same things in the same way—but the results of

the experiment may well produce some long-term preferences that conflict with the actual long-term preferences and
current desires that I now embody and express.

4. My interests may also be understood as *what nurtures my
   objective well-being*. On this rendering, my actual or hypothetical desires and preferences may or may not facilitate
   my objective well-being. Here my choices are less important
   than what will in fact promote my well-being. This requires
   a firm definition of "well-being," one that takes into account
   my actual desires and preferences but does not confer upon
   them the status of trumps; instead, my actual desires and
   preferences gain currency only when they advance, or at least
   do not conflict with, my objective well-being, which defines
   what is in my *genuine* interests.

5. My interests may be understood as *constitutive or situated*.
   These are my interests located in a particular social setting. Perhaps, my current desires, long-term preferences,
   and hypothetical preferences are of a certain sort, but the
   social setting in which I find myself encourages different
   desires and preferences. For example, an undergraduate may
   have a current desire to remain in bed and read nothing; a
   long-term preference to read sports magazines; a preference
   under ideal conditions to read higher-level sports literature;
   an objective interest in reading the canon of literary clas-
   sics; but a situated interest to read whatever is required to
   fulfill the requirements of a certain class, obtain the college credit attached thereto, and progress toward an undergraduate degree. Accordingly, situated interests are explicitly
   focused on social settings and the roles that human beings
   assume therein. If a certain class requires reading Heidegger's
   Being and Time, an excruciating experience under the best
   of conditions, it is in an enrolled student's situated interest
   to fulfill that requirement even though he or she has no
   current desire and no long-range preference to do so. (That
   few sane people would choose to read this book while selecting under ideal conditions and that for almost all students
   reading the book will not advance their objective well-being
   I take to be stone cold truths.) The notion of constitutive
   interests, then, underscores the practical character of social

understandings—how acting habitually within established
social practices structures human relationships.

The conflict that often arises from surveying a person's immediate
desires—what the person *does* want—and comparing them to that person's
expressed long-range preferences and situated interests is exacerbated when
outsiders speculate on what that person *would* desire and prefer if selecting from an ideal vantage point. Such a hypothetical perspective will never
be realized, and invoking it invites wholesale speculation from evaluators
who may be more likely to project their own desires and preferences upon
that person than they are able to extract what the individual would in fact
choose. In that vein, summoning a person's genuine, objective interests
invites outsiders to speculate on what that person *should* desire and prefer
given a general understanding of human flourishing and well-being. This,
one might argue, only amplifies the conflict further.

One solution to this conflict is to jettison appeals to loftier renderings
of a person's interests and allow the individual to be the final judge of the
matter unfettered by external speculations and officious intermeddling. On
this view, my interests are simply what I desire and prefer, whatever subjective standards of well-being I happen to embody. Some tension would persist
between my immediate, first-order desires and my long-range, second-order
desires, but this discord is resolvable by use of individual autonomy and
is much less severe than the conflict generated by other solutions. Thus, if
my long-range preference to remain trim and physically fit does not correlate with my present desire to consume a bag of potato chips, I can judge
which interest should have priority at the moment. I may well conclude
that eating the junk food will not impair my long-range preference as long
as I do not make it a habit. Or, knowing myself better than others do, I
may judge that if I eat the chips now I will be more likely to rationalize
additional imprudent consumption in the future, thereby jeopardizing my
long-range preference for physical fitness. In either case, on this view, the
call is mine and insofar as I have accurately identified and employed my
subjective standard of well-being I have, indeed, fulfilled *my* interests.

The appealing aspects of this solution are that it simplifies matters
considerably and celebrates personal autonomy thoroughly. For you to identify what is in my interests all you must do is consult me. But simplicity
and ease of application are purchased at an immense cost. For example,
human beings do not always act in ways that facilitate their well-being even
when they understand their own subjective standards. That we sometimes
tend to undermine ourselves or even incline toward self-destructive behavior
is undeniable. Such phenomena may result from subconscious feelings of

guilt or unworthiness or fear of success or something more profound. But identifying specific causes is less important than the fact that the phenomena occur. To say in such cases that we are acting against our interests is reasonable. The general point is that our autonomous choices do not always correlate happily with our interests even when these are defined merely by compatibility with our own subjective standards.

Furthermore, our autonomous choices can be greatly affected by dominant societal ideas that shape us through socialization. Dominant ideas promulgated by societal institutions and practices often have disproportionate influence in molding the consciousness of typical citizens. Thus, whether our autonomous choices are truly "ours" is questionable at least sometimes.

Also, to preserve the distinction between foolish and prudent behavior, and that between reckless and wise choice, we must invoke a contrast between what a person actually chooses and what would truly advance that person's well-being. Thus, some appeal to a wider notion of a person's interests is necessary, a notion that goes beyond what that person actually selects. Finally, some subjective standards of well-being are simply not rationally justified. Some might be set dismally low and be unable to fulfill the needs and basic human wants of physical, emotional, and social life. A set of subjective standards might be radically at odds with justified social morality or might not embody sufficient exercise of the higher human capabilities. A set of subjective standards may also dishonor uniquely human attributes or insufficiently nurture robust self-creation.

For these reasons, the solution to conflicting notions of interests cannot be found by dismissing appeals to loftier standards of interests and replacing them by simple consultation with the subjective standards of individuals. To remain true to social reality and to retain our ability to reasonably evaluate choices and deeds, we must continue to struggle with different renderings of a person's interests and to deny that a person's interests are unitary and harmonious.

When I speak of affecting "interests" in what follows, I connote broadly at least one of the five senses of interests sketched above. When I speak of affecting "genuine interests" I mean more narrowly interests in senses (4) and/or (5) as adjusted for individual differences arising from sense (2).

Power, Passivity, and Influence

I must also note that power can be passive in that a person can enjoy some favorable outcomes and attain benefits without being responsible for triggering them. Passive power, though, must be distinguished from luck. To obtain an outcome by luck is to benefit occasionally without doing anything; thus, a farmer is lucky when the rains come at precisely the right time and in exactly the right intensity to facilitate a robust crop. The farmer exerted no influence on the weather, but simply planted his crop on his typical, annual date. Often, perhaps usually, the rains do not arrive at a propitious time or in the desired amounts. Passive power typically arises from favorable circumstances that are more systematic. An agent may lack the active power to obtain a desired outcome but get it anyway without exercising an act of will. Unlike luck, passive power involves a disposition, which is a relatively enduring capability. Thus, some people may be able to achieve a reasonable standard of living because of a strong social services network, which they did not and could not have brought about. They have the power to get certain material resources without exerting agency. These people are lucky to have been born into such a social context but once in that setting they systematically benefit in certain ways without being responsible for those outcomes: the social context confers upon them passive power to obtain material resources. They are not powerless, because they are able to obtain desired outcomes; they do not possess active power, because they are not responsible for the situation that yields those outcomes; they are not merely lucky, because the outcomes are recurrent and predictable; and they possess passive power because the beneficial outcomes are systematic. Our hypothetical beneficiaries lack the active power to obtain the favorable outcomes they enjoy but get them regularly anyway.

Intuitively, we might suspect that the amount of power an agent possesses can be measured by the resources he or she enjoys—the greater the resources, the greater the power. This intuition is erroneous. First, identifying what constitutes a resource often depends on a social context that influences the effects the item will produce if used; not even wealth is a resource as such. For example, a wealthy person may be less powerful in a meeting attended by mostly poor people. The wealthy person may be branded as ignorant of the problems endured by the less fortunate, and his or her finances may allow the others to brand the person as an elitist whose views should be ignored. Moreover, a social context often produces the outcome that people with exactly the same resource will have different amounts of power. For example, if I am the only faculty member of a five-person committee at my institution of higher learning and the two management representatives and the two professional representatives invariably vote as conflicting blocs then I, in effect, determine each outcome as the deciding vote. Each of the five committee members has the same resource but one has more power because of the social context in place.

If the other four committee members are disturbed by this over time they might band together and vote as one bloc, thereby extinguishing my power. If so, my resource is unchanged but my power has diminished radically. Where once I was the determining vote and held full power, my vote has now been rendered irrelevant and I have no effective power other than to cast my merely ceremonial opinion. In sum, resources, once identified, are necessary but not sufficient for power and thus power cannot be reduced to or measured by the amount of resources an agent possesses.

The differences between power and influence are subtle. Influence requires at least two entities; it seems awkward to say that a person, Jones, influenced herself. But Jones may have the power to do countless things on her own. Accordingly, influence is more closely related to power-over than it is to power-to. However, Jones can influence someone without exerting power over them. For example, if Jones walks by a tourist on a hot summer day wearing an exquisite outfit she may unwittingly influence the tourist to purchase a similar outfit. Jones's regal manner of wearing the clothing triggered a desire in the tourist but Jones did not exercise any power over the tourist. The tourist altered his or her own behavior and purchased a similar outfit, but not because of any power that Jones possessed over the tourist. In this case, Jones inadvertently affected the actions of a stranger by *la bella figura* Jones embodied while walking. Jones did not even try to rationally persuade the tourist to purchase any clothing. At most, this hypothetical can be viewed as an example of unintended personal persuasion: the tourist merely perceived Jones's clothing and bearing, and that induced the tourist to emulate Jones's choice of clothing. But notice that Jones did not possess a disposition that the tourist should respond in that or any way to Jones's wardrobe.

To exert power over another person, an agent must affect the outcomes or interests of subordinate parties by means of a disposition, a relatively enduring capability. For example, suppose Jones was an employer out for a summer stroll and she passed one of her employees taking an unauthorized break from work. Jones, a stern taskmaster, orders the embarrassed truant to return to the job forthwith. In this case, Jones would have exercised power over her employee. Power, then, implies a capability or disposition to affect outcomes or interests, while influence often does not involve such abilities or dispositions. The exercise of power also often involves a conflict of interests, an element typically lacking in an exercise of influence. Instead, influence often involves inducement, encouragement, or persuasion in the absence of conflicting interests between the parties involved, but even this is not always the case, as evidenced by the hypothetical involving Jones and the tourist. There, Jones influenced the tourist in the absence of inducement, encouragement, and overt persuasion.

Likewise, certain iconic dead people can exert tremendous influence over future generations even though they are unable to induce, encourage, or persuade actively: the words and lives of statesmen such as Abraham Lincoln, Martin Luther King, and George Washington may influence numerous people today and in the future. These famous people influence us without actively inducing, encouraging, or persuading. Furthermore, although their words and lives affect future generations, to conclude that these historical figures exert power over us is misguided. Lacking dispositions and capabilities, the dead can neither possess nor exercise power.

Social Power

Despite the common tendency to conceptualize power-over as dyadic—as a relationship between a superior party holding and exercising power over a subordinate party—wider social context is often critical. Wider relations constitute social power and often promote and make possible dyadic power. Moreover, in other cases social power can prevent the exercise of dyadic power. The student-teacher relationship is an example of dyadic power that is situated within and arises from a wider social context. The relationship requires, among other things, that the teacher evaluate the performances of students. One means of doing this is through the issuance of grades, which presumably places a particular student's performance in a comparative relationship with the performances of other students. Clearly, this function of grading fails if every student receives the same grade. Also, the issuance of grades is not the only means by which teachers might evaluate the performances of their students.

That teachers grade the performances of students partially constitutes the power that instructors have over their students. Because grades matter, at least to students who have an interest in graduating, going on to higher education, aspiring to certain careers, keeping parents from complaining, and the like, teachers have structural power in their enduring relationship with their students. That is, the nature of the relationship between teachers as evaluators and students as the evaluated implies that instructors have power over their students in that respect. That teachers possess power over students arises from the structure of the educational system, but whether instructors exercise that power effectively is an open question. Where power is successfully exercised, teachers need not intervene or act upon students at every discrete turn to underscore that power; instead, their recognized possession of it is enough to promote its effects. Teachers are able to induce certain behavior from students—they are able to limit or control certain choices and actions of their students—because of the structure of their ongoing relationship. Furthermore, the structure itself is in place only because of wider social relations and the actions of third parties: the issuance of a grade as such may have little effect upon a student but for the reactions of parents, prospective employers, supervising educators, and admissions directors at higher levels. If grades were only known by teachers and their students they would be experienced much differently by pupils, and the amount of power that teachers possessed over their students would decrease significantly.

Because grades do matter outside the classroom, students will read, say, poems by Emily Dickinson because they recognize their situated interest in doing so, because the material will be covered on their next exam. They will do so even though they have no immediate desire, no long-term preference, and no hypothetical preference to read the poems, and they remain unconvinced that reading the poems will nurture their objective well-being. That students study the poems is the result of the power teachers are able to exercise over them.

Of course, this power itself is constrained. Teachers who grade arbitrarily will feel the effects of their negligence from outraged parents, administrators, and students themselves. Student evaluations of their instructors are now commonly considered when teaching effectiveness is judged by administrators. Students can, in extreme cases, collectively refuse to attend the classes of teachers they perceive as especially unreasonable. Parental complaints about teachers are taken seriously, at least by administrators at institutions of higher learning. To the best of my knowledge, no student or parent has ever complained because they or their offspring received a grade of A in a course.

Also, the wider social context can exert its own pressures. For example, at my institution of higher learning, a faculty member in the department of education once explained to me why more than 75 percent of the grades her colleagues issued were As. The students in education who graduated and sought jobs needed stellar academic records, because their competitors, who also enjoyed soft grading, had such records. If graduating students from our institution were graded more harshly they would not obtain jobs and the word would filter down to high schools. That would impair future enrollments. If enrollments fell, then some faculty jobs would be jeopardized and the institution would suffer. So, unless a student was utterly irresponsible or hopelessly inept, he or she was awarded an A in virtually every education class. (Of course, the epilogue is that prospective employers soon caught on to the widespread practice and began to discount grade point average as a reliable guide to future success. They started to place greater emphasis on factors such as scores on standardized tests, which most education faculty members disdain. Delicious irony, that.) Accordingly, seemingly dyadic power relations are often structurally complex, situated in a wider context, subject to change, and loci of struggle.

Social power often arises from cultural hegemony, which is especially oppressive when the experiences, perceptions, and visions of a group of superiors become solidified as universal—when dominant groups have disproportionate ability to interpret and set the terms of social life. When these superiors project their cultural expressions as more than they are, as universal prescriptions defining human life as such, then the dominant values are perceived and experienced as appropriate, natural, and even inevitable. Subordinates internalize the dominant values and thicken their collaboration in their own oppression.

However, to conclude that a social structure systematically oppresses a group of subordinates is not automatically to posit a correlated group of superiors that intentionally and consciously exercises power over the subordinates. The effects of social practices and institutions such as education, socialization, bureaucratic management, medical treatment, the production and distribution of consumer goods, and the like need not result from the conscious conniving of a group of superiors who perceive themselves as oppressors with a purpose. While superiors and subordinates perform numerous conscious, intentional acts within an oppressive social structure, they do so in the normal course of everyday living.

In addition, to suggest that society fully coerces individuals to internalize its imperatives and ideals falsifies reality. Society constrains but also enables. Social roles partially constitute individual identities and facilitate human action. Such actions sustain and alter society. Thus, society is both the context and the result of much human activity. Social power, understood as the capability and disposition that agents possess as a result of their ongoing relationships, is embodied in social structure and is required for human agency. As always, the possession and exercise of power is subject to the ongoing negotiations and struggles of the constitutive parties. However, the ubiquity of power in social life does not imply that these negotiations and struggles are always struggles for power, even though they involve the exercise of power. To analyze social power one must examine underlying social relationships.

At this point, the concept of power-over may seem a colossal muddle. Such power may be possessed but not exercised. When exercised, power-over may or may not be exerted intentionally; it may or may not involve a relationship between two people or two groups or a social institution and the masses; it may or may not be triggered by a conflict of interests; it may or may not compel the subordinate party to do what it would not otherwise do; it may or may not be met with resistance; it may or may not elicit the consent or acquiescence of the subordinate party; and it may or may not set back the subordinate party's interests. The list could continue. One might well be tempted to conclude that the concept of power-over is either vacuous or too broad to be useful. Such a conclusion would be hasty.

Major Uses of Power-Over

The apparent problem arises from trying to conflate several different uses of power-over into one definition. Power-over can be used to oppress others or to transform them in positive directions or to treat them paternalistically. To concoct one definition of power-over that fully embodies all of these uses is misguided. A better approach is to provide a neutral definition of power-over that is compatible with the three major uses but which requires corollary concepts to distinguish the three uses from each other: *A superior party possesses power over a subordinate party when the superior has the capability (the disposition) to affect the outcomes and/or interests of the subordinate by controlling or limiting the alternative choices or actions available to the subordinate.*

This definition recognizes that the superior party may possess power over the subordinate party but not exercise that power; that when power-over is exercised, the subordinate's outcomes and/or interests may be affected negatively or positively; but that in either case exercising power-over involves controlling or restricting, in any of a variety of ways, the choices or actions available to the subordinate. In this fashion, the superior has limited the usual circumstances of agency enjoyed by the subordinate.

The use of "superior party" and "subordinate party" should not mislead us into concluding that power-over is an inherently dyadic notion. The superior party may be an individual or a group (for example, "the ruling class") or a societal institution (for example, the government or an economic system). Likewise, the subordinate party may be an individual or a specific group (for example, "the proletariat") or the body of citizens distinct from the power-holders ("the masses"). Also, the parties need not be superior and subordinate, respectively, in all respects or even in the possession of power generally. Moreover, under this definition the superior party may truncate the subordinate's available choices or actions either structurally or through distinct interventions. Enduring structural relationships embedded in society nurture power as human agents participate in them. In fact, ongoing social relations and social roles—which involve systemic, continual mutual interactions—are often necessary for the more intense and recurrent exercises of power. Also, dyadic power often arises from the actions of third parties, those who are not themselves agents in the dyad. Ongoing social and structural relations can produce a context that promotes various dyadic power combinations. Structural limitations are typically governmental, economic, or ideological and produce systematic power-over that is sometimes oppressive. Distinct interventions are typically more sporadic and overtly intentional.

An interesting question arises: Must the superior party have the capability to affect the outcomes and/or interests of the subordinate by controlling or limiting the subordinate's available choices or actions *recurrently* in order to possess power over the subordinate? That is, does the concept of power-over imply that the power holder must have the capability of *systematically* exercising his or her or its advantage? Or is it possible to have power-over in only one or in only a few discrete situations?

To possess the capability of systematically and recurrently exerting power over another party is to be able to dominate the other over relatively long stretches of time, and thereby connotes an especially virulent type of power. But I have decided not to include that element in the general definition, because I am convinced that one party can have power over another party even if the first possesses and exercises that power only once. For example, imagine that a hoodlum accosts a pedestrian on the street, brandishes a firearm, and demands that the person surrender his or her wallet or risk being killed. Given the circumstances and the weapon, to say that the hoodlum is exercising power over the pedestrian is reasonable even if the two parties never again meet: the hoodlum has affected adversely the outcome and interests of the pedestrian by limiting that person's available choices and actions by means of a threat. In that vein, a substitute teacher may exert power over his or her students, but perhaps only for the one class and one day he or she supervises and instructs them. Although the social structure in place confers on teachers recurrent power over students, this particular teacher is in a position to exercise that power only once. The same can be said of a famous person of extraordinary charisma who exercises power over a fan in their only meeting. Suppose prior to and after the session, the subordinate was immune to the personal charm of the celebrity; in such a case, to conclude that the star possessed and exercised power over the fan only once is reasonable. Accordingly, I have not included the capability of systematically and recurrently exerting power over the subordinate party in the general definition of power-over.

As stated earlier, the general definition of power-over must be supplemented by corollary definitions of the three major uses of power-over: oppression, paternalism, and empowerment. As with power-over in general, one could possess any of the three major uses of power-over without actually exercising it. Nevertheless, I will state the three corollary definitions in terms of their exercise to underscore that they are *uses* of power-over.

The first major use of power-over is oppression. *A superior party oppresses a subordinate party when the superior affects wrongfully and adversely the outcomes and/or interests of the subordinate by controlling or limiting the alternative choices or actions available to the subordinate.* This is the most commonly understood use of power-over. Here the superior party controls or limits the available choices or actions of the subordinate party and thereby affects adversely the subordinate's outcomes and/or interests through a host of possible means: force; duress; deception; personal charm; superior economic bargaining power; disseminating ideology that produces false consciousness which impairs the subordinate's ability to identify his or her genuine interests; truncating public debate to include only trivial or uncontroversial issues; through an informational or knowledge advantage; by exploiting psychological and emotional vulnerabilities; by convincing the subordinate that the judgments of the superior embody special authority; and the like. Depending upon the means implemented and the surrounding circumstances, the subordinates may resist the oppression in some cases, especially when they can still identity their genuine interests and the malevolent intentions of their oppressors; in other cases, the subordinates will consent or acquiesce or obey in anticipation, particularly when their wills and judgments have been overborne by false consciousness and structural socialization. Oppression can be dyadic or societal, and it can occur intentionally or through a social system that benefits some classes, not all of whom were agents in establishing the system, while disenfranchising other classes. Oppression can be recurrent and systematic or episodic and discrete. Importantly, oppression is not necessarily static, as possibilities for change are typically available and resistance by subordinates can be subtle. Oppression also admits of degrees in intensity and scope. Intensity pertains to the strength of the power that superiors wield, and scope refers to the number of areas and issues under their control. These vary from the most forceful and overt oppression meted out by totalitarian regimes to the milder but sometimes more effective dissemination of dominant ideologies that promote false consciousness in the masses, to the relatively milder control exerted by one individual over another in an otherwise intimate relationship. Systematic oppression involves ongoing dyadic or broader social relations in which superiors repeatedly exercise power over subordinates to the detriment of the subordinates. Finally, subordinates are rarely completely disempowered such that their status with respect to superiors is unalterable. Often, the ongoing social relations promoting and sustaining the power relation are subject to reimagination and revision.

Of course, to *exercise* power-over oppressively (or in other ways), the superior party must *possess* power over a subordinate party. Merely affecting the interests or outcomes of another person adversely is not enough to establish that oppression has occurred or that a relationship of power exists. In addition, exercising power over a subordinate party and adversely affecting the subordinate's interests are not enough to establish oppression. For example, a teacher has power over her students in some respects. Her awarding a student a low grade will, all other things being equal, adversely affect that student's interests. But the teacher has not oppressed the student, at least insofar as her evaluation was unbiased and otherwise reasonable. Thus, oppression requires a wrongful or unjustified setback of the subordinate party's interests.

Although superiors can exercise power-over in ways that promote the interests and well-being of subordinates—for example, paternalistically or transformatively—some theorists argue that the notion of "domination" is different.[8] They take domination to be the ability to limit the choices of subordinates by impeding them from living in accord with their own judgments. On this view, domination thwarts or sets back the victim's interests through coercion or confinement, by overbearing a victim's judgment to such an extent that he or she prefers to satisfy the superior instead of self, or by luring the victim into accepting the judgment of the superior as a more reliable guide than the judgment of the victim. I will not follow this usage because I see no contradiction in saying that one person dominated another, in the sense of controlled, governed, and ruled the other, for the purpose of advancing the genuine interests or objective well-being of the subordinate. For example, parents of a child with special needs may well go beyond the occasional exercise of power-over to the exertion of recurrent domination over the child but do so to promote the child's well-being. Accordingly, I do not view "domination" as inherently pejorative. I will use "oppress" or "oppression," which are inherently pejorative terms, to describe the types of behaviors that some thinkers use "domination" to connote.

The second major use of power-over is paternalism: *A superior party acts paternalistically toward a subordinate party when the superior tries to*

affect positively the outcomes and/or interests of the subordinate by control-
ling or limiting the alternative choices or actions available to the subordinate.
Paternalism is employed by superiors when subordinates either do not possess the full capabilities of identifying and acting upon their own genuine
interests because of age or impairment (for example, minors or the mentally
or physically challenged) or when subordinates have the capabilities but
lack the judgment because of psychological vulnerabilities, the presence of
conflicting interests, or weakness of will' (for example, adults who act on
immediate desires instead of long-term preferences or those who temporarily act in self-destructive or self-undermining ways because of duress or
desperate circumstances). The object of the superior's intentional use of
power-over here is to promote the objective well-being of subordinates. The
classic examples of paternalism are governmental restrictions: workers are
required to contribute to the Social Security system; motorists are required
to fasten seat belts; people are prohibited from swimming at public beaches
unless lifeguards are present; the distribution and sale of drugs deemed to
be potentially harmful are prohibited in the absence of a medical doctor's
prescription; the enforcement of certain contracts that are deemed against
public policy is prohibited; and the like. All such requirements and prohibitions are enacted to advance the genuine interests of constituents under the
assumption that left to their own devices many (most?) individuals would
not do that which would nurture their well-being in these areas. Individuals
may also act rightfully in paternalistic ways: parents supervise and force their
children to do and refrain from doing a host of actions; psychiatrists con-
fiscate dangerous objects from patients who are seriously depressed; friends
restrain intoxicated comrades from the consumption of additional alcohol
and drugs; and the like. The means used can be almost as varied as those
employed in oppression: force; rational persuasion; demands of law; personal charm; manipulation of psychological vulnerabilities; outright threat,
to name only a few.

One might argue that the purported benevolence of paternalism is a
sham because when subordinates resist the efforts of superiors but are nevertheless induced or compelled to comply their autonomy is thereby infringed.
As subordinates always have a genuine interest in their own autonomy,
paternalism is in fact oppression to some degree. This argument, however,
is unsound. First, in many cases paternalism occurs in contexts where subordinates do not possess all capabilities required to exercise full autonomy,
so no conflict between paternalism and autonomous choice embedded in
genuine interests takes place. Second, even when subordinates do possess
all capabilities required to exercise full autonomy, paternalism is sometimes

invoked justifiably when the subordinates have not identified their genuine interests or have wrongly dismissed them in deference to their immediate desires in situations where doing so foolishly invites disaster. While the scope of justified paternalism is always contestable, the bare fact that such action often conflicts with the autonomy (understood as pursuing immediate desires) of subordinates does not invalidate paternalism as such.

Subordinates will often initially resist paternalistic efforts, but often ultimately comply because of fear of reprisals, legal or otherwise, if they overtly rebel. Typically, the aspiration of superiors is that subordinates internalize the messages and values disseminated by paternalistic actions; learn to identify their genuine interests; and render future paternalism unnecessary. This, at least, is the hope of most parents, friends, and medical professions who aim at paternalism as a means to the positive transformation of subordinates. In this manner, the paternalism of superiors facilitates the empowerment of subordinates. Legal prohibitions and requirements are more enduring because they identify areas in which numerous adults with full mental and physical capabilities are likely to fail persistently to act in their own genuine interests. Paternalism is intentional and generally overt. As noted, paternalism is not static: once subordinates can identify and act upon their genuine interests, paternalism is no longer required. But, as stated, paternalistic laws of some sort will always exist in reaction to enduring human tendencies such as weakness of will; knowing genuine interests but not acting to promote them because of laziness or a conflicting immediate desire; self-destructive and self-undermining tendencies arising from alcohol or drug addiction, psychological vulnerabilities, or desperate material circumstances; and the human inclination to seek apparent pleasure in the present to the detriment of long-range preferences and genuine well-being.

The third major use of power-over is empowerment: *A superior party acts to empower a subordinate party when the superior tries to affect positively the outcomes and/or interests of the subordinate with the aim of favorably transforming the subordinate by controlling or limiting the alternative choices or actions available to the subordinate.* Empowerment is often paternalism with the direct aim of transforming the subordinate to the point where the subordinate is no longer in need of direction. The means of doing so are theoretically as varied as the other two uses of power-over but are practically limited to those that will accomplish the specific mission of empowerment. So the harsher means of exerting power-over are generally less useful here. However, this is not always the case. We can imagine parents and professionals who have captured a young adult from the clutches of a manipulative cult that has preyed upon the victim's psychological vulnerabilities.

The parents and professionals might need to use relatively stern methods of deprogramming the victim in order to nurture the goal of personal empowerment. Still, as a general rule the less restrictive and gentlest means of achieving the goal are recommended: the ends will typically be prefigured in the means used. Another example of the use of power-over as empowerment is the reeducation of a victim of false consciousness who, because of the pernicious effects of oppression, requires a more acute awareness of his or her genuine interests.

Less dramatic examples of empowerment would include parents who guide their children, whose age and lack of knowledge preclude them temporarily from identifying or pursuing their genuine interests; teachers who tend to their students in ways that restrict the subordinates' freedom in order to facilitate the time when the students can become their own best instructors and the teachers thereby have helped render themselves obsolete; coaches who administer tough love to their players for the purpose of developing and maximizing the athletic talents of their charges; and governmental efforts to ensure that workers not only can enjoy pleasant retirements by requiring contributions during their active years to pension funds such as Social Security, but also to nurture a broader, ongoing commitment from wage laborers to save a portion of their annual earnings.

Exercising power-over as empowerment may be dyadic or social and is almost always overtly intentional. Typically, less resistance is encountered when subordinates fully understand the purposes for which their freedoms are restricted. Empowerment is explicitly geared to change: superiors assume that subordinates have the potential to gain, develop, or recapture the capabilities to identify and to act to advance their genuine interests. Thus, empowerment succeeds when superiors and subordinates transcend or transform their relationships. In those cases where subordinates lack the potential to gain, develop, or recapture the capabilities to identify and to act to advance their genuine interests, exercising power-over as empowerment is futile. In such cases, enduring paternalism may be required.

The three major uses of power-over constitute neither an exhaustive nor necessary catalog. For example, often, exercising power-over involves a mixture of more than one of the uses sketched here. Moreover, my definition of the exercise of power-over as oppression could be broken down in several different uses of power differentiated by the means employed and the extent of the use. For example, some will prefer to distinguish the use of power-over by force, by dissemination of false consciousness, through domination, by personal charm, and the like. Finally, at times power-over is exercised in ways that affect the interests of subordinates neither positively nor adversely except insofar as any restriction of freedom narrows autonomous choice and action. Accordingly, my outline of the major uses of power-over is far from sacrosanct; it is only one of numerous reasonable possibilities.

For example, instead of highlighting the inequality and oppression embodied by power-over at the social level, Hannah Arendt focuses on power as a consensual notion. Agents in social groups craft agreements on how to regulate their lives: they attain their goals through cooperative arrangements.

> Power is never the property of an individual; it belongs to a group and remains in existence only so long as the group keeps together. What we say of somebody that he is "in power" we actually refer to his being empowered by a certain number of people to act in their name. . . . [Power] needs no justification, being inherent in the very existence of political communities; what it does need is legitimacy. . . . [Power] is actually the very condition enabling a group of people to think and act in terms of the means-end category.[9]

Arendt explicitly distances herself from the common connection of power with violence because she concludes that the common notion is grounded in an unpersuasive command-obedience model of power: a superior exercises power over a subordinate if and only if the superior issues commands that the subordinate obeys. Ultimately, such obedience is traced back to the fear subordinates have of the violent reactions of superiors should the underlings disobey.

On the contrary, Arendt argues that power requires the antecedent consent of those over whom it is exercised and can never truly arise from the use of violence. Even in the case of revolution, Arendt argues that power cannot be exercised through violence: "[The] superiority [of the government] lasts only as long as the power structure of the government is intact—that is, as long as commands are obeyed and the army or police forces are prepared to use their weapons. When this is no longer the case, the situation changes abruptly."[10] Thus, Arendt points out that the use of violence relinquishes its currency when the power to command obedience evaporates: the successful use of violence depends on an extant structure of power; power does not arise from violence. Accordingly, even in successful revolution the rebels emerge victorious because of their ability to secure the consent of those who possess the means of violence. Once the wielders of the means of committing violence withdraw their allegiance from the commanders in place, the power of those superiors evaporates.

That Arendt is describing what she takes to be the nature of political power is clear. Her rendering of "power" is a patently inadequate explanation of power-to and of most uses of power-over. The nature of more general social power is different, as are several uses of dyadic power. Also, Arendt assumes even in the area of political power that successful revolution flows from consent, not better military strategy or superior arms. But what if those within the established order who possess the weapons of violence are willing to use them but simply cannot wield them effectively? Although Arendt is generally correct that "in a contest of violence against violence" the established government will enjoy strong advantage, must that always be the case? We can at least imagine a robust coterie of rebels, backed by foreign allies, routing a hapless army faithful to the established government.

Moreover, Arendt ignores or downplays the role of coercive relations in preserving and deepening political power. While political authority is held disproportionally by certain individuals or groups, even by prior consent of the governed, those empowered still enjoy power over their subjects. Power relations, backed by at least the implicit threat of force if subordinates renege on their commitments, remain in play. That power was vested through mutual voluntary agreement does not imply that the resulting power relations are uncontaminated by the threat of force. Arendt obscures this by her invocation of revolution as an illustration of her view. In such contexts, the underlying social context has crumbled; a few specific reprisals are insufficient to restore order. In more normalized contexts, the implicit or explicit threat of violence can quell sporadic disobedience. Political power is neither fully consensual nor completely coercive, but a mixture.

Finally, what begins as rightful authority grounded in consent can easily expand into oppression. As certain groups have disproportionate voice in developing and maintaining social institutions and practices, and as the benefits and burdens of the resulting social life are distributed, the power to frame and disseminate culture—which is not grounded in explicit consent—may well result in some groups having power over other groups even where this was not consciously intended. Political power is most robust when superiors can induce subordinates to define themselves and their interests in terms that recognize the power of superiors as appropriate and thus as rightful authority. Political power that masks its workings in this way is not always experienced by subordinates as what it truly is—oppression. The ability to induce cooperation and acquiescence without overtly demanding it domesticates potential resistance. Political power is thereby able to shape how subordinates view their immediate desires, long-range preferences, and situated interests. Also, the exercise of political power obscures the interests of subordinates that if fulfilled would advance their objective well-being.

Still, Arendt's point, if deflated, is sound: political power can arise from the mutual agreement of a group to manage its affairs in a particular fashion that its members deem effective. Political power, then, need not flow from suspicious origins or embody oppressive intentions.

My analysis does not insist that power must be understood as a commodity or transferable substance that operates from and upon antecedently constituted human subjects.

Although rendered mostly in dyadic terms (viz., "superiors" and "subordinates"), my analysis is compatible with Michel Foucault's understanding that social power is constitutive of human subjects, functions through relationships, and operates from within and is dispersed from an intricate social web. I do not, however, believe that all dyadic power and social power is that complicated or pervasive. My agreements and disagreements with contemporary theorists of power such as Foucault, Jurgen Habermas, and feminism will emerge later in this work.

As do theories generally, theories of power compete for our allegiance. Instead of measuring the persuasiveness of a theory by comparing it to a perception of pure reality, we measure it against its competitors. The "winner" of this competition holds tentative title to the theory most warranted to believe. Several criteria adjudicate the competition: explanatory power—which theory best accounts for known phenomena and findings, and can accommodate new phenomena and discoveries; causal independence—which theory best identifies the underlying causes of known phenomena without referring to the phenomena as part of those causes; and coherency—which theory is most internally, logically, and empirically consistent. We cannot evaluate the competition without reference to an interpretive framework, but uttering this platitude does not privilege any particular interpretive framework.

I will now survey the philosophers of power in a sequence that best reveals and underscores their respective insights about the nature and exercise of power. We shall begin with two famous characters of the Platonic dialogues: the brash and threatening Thrasymachus and the noble Socrates.

II

Thrasymachus (ca. 459–c. 400 BC) and Socrates (ca. 470–c. 399 BC)

Does Might Make Right?

Power without wisdom is tyranny; wisdom without power is pointless.

—Iain Pears

Parents urging their reluctant children to attend to their academic studies more diligently and congressmen seeking an increase in monetary appropriations for education are likely to utter the adage "knowledge is power." The suggestion is that from an increase in knowledge arises greater power. The type of power (power-to, power-over, power used for what purpose) is left ambiguous.

Some of the more profound theoretical and practical questions regarding the relationship between knowledge and power, however, flow in the opposite direction: Is knowledge, in the sense of a society's compendium of established truth claims, in fact nothing more than the effects of power used oppressively? More specifically, are our most cherished moral and political principles—the normative foundation that sets the terms of social life—in fact nothing more than conventions concocted by superior parties in oppressive power relations? If so, how do and why should such principles command the allegiance of subordinate parties?

Unraveling the concepts and arguments surrounding such questions is critical for the project of distinguishing using power to oppress others and exercising power to benefit the common good. In addition, we must analyze the connection between the social discourses of truth and knowledge and the presence of power that can potentially be exercised rightly or wrongly in order to understand the origins and dynamics of power relations.

Plato (427–347 BC) confronted such questions directly through the characters of Thrasymachus and Socrates in his *Republic*. The historical Thrasymachus, a citizen of Chalcedon, was a sophist and rhetorician. But it is as a character in Plato's *Republic* that history best records his imprint.[1] As with many of the characters in Plato's dialogues, Thrasymachus's mannerisms and temperament exemplify the argument he advances. In sum, the character Thrasymachus is loud, blustery, and rhetorically bold, as is the position he urges.

The topic of the dialogue is the nature of justice. After enduring a few feeble attempts by others to define "justice," which either confuse giving an example of justice with defining that concept or misunderstand the relationship between justice and virtue, Thrasymachus bursts forth impatiently. He reasons that human beings are inherently self-interested: they act to secure their own desires. But only the strongest and most powerful can succeed. The laws of a polity specify procedural and substantive justice and only the rulers, the most powerful, craft legal systems. Acting out of self-interest, the rulers create laws that disproportionately favor their own preferences. Thus, what passes for "justice" in a polity is nothing more than a series of norms embodied in and enforced by law that advances the interests of the most powerful elements of society. So "justice" is in the interests of the strongest element in society and the exercise of power establishes what comes to be taken as much more than it is. In this sense, might (the possession and exercise of power) creates right (what comes to be taken as normatively sound behavior).

Thrasymachus then transvalues values in accord with his theory: for everyone but the ruling class what passes for "justice" is another's good (viz., the good of the ruling class); if they understood the truth, all sensible human beings who were not rulers would consider "injustice" (transgressing against norms that merely reflect the preferences of the ruling class) a virtue and "justice" (obeying norms that merely reflect the preferences of the ruling class) a vice; thus, common citizens should comply with "justice" when they must (for prudential reasons) but practice "injustice" when they are able (when they can avoid reprisals from the authorities) (R 336b–354c). In this way, according to Thrasymachus, the ruling class exercises its power to structure laws and set the terms of social discourse in service of amplifying its power over the masses.

Accordingly, Thrasymachus lays the groundwork for a host of themes surrounding power, normative validity, and human motivation that continue to animate contemporary debate:

- Normative validity is grounded in laws that are backed by coercive power.

- Such laws embody and enforce norms that the bulk of citizens come to internalize—through habit, practice, and fear of punishment—and upon which they confer undeserved (transcendent) status. Citizens thus come to take such norms as more than they in fact are.

- In reality, the most powerful elements in a society set the terms of social existence because they are able to impose their will and translate their interests into social understandings of "justice" (really a placeholder for general normative understanding).

- General normative understanding is merely conventional and rests upon conventions rigged in favor of the powerful elements in society.

- General normative understanding is not in fact transcendent, objective, or embedded in nature, but typically presents itself as being such in order to reinforce compliance. That presentation facilitates the internalization process by which common citizens unwittingly accept as their own, normative standards that in fact have no authority beyond the power of the ruling class to create and enforce them.

- Common citizens who internalize such standards and accept them as transcendent are unwitting collaborators in their own subordination. They will have difficulty identifying their own genuine interests thereafter because their reasoning and judgment will be clouded by the dominant norms they have internalized.

- Accordingly, the prevailing norms in a society are a sham: they present themselves as advancing the common good; as transcendent, objective, or embedded in nature; and as imperatives worthy of universal allegiance. In fact, they are provisional, partial, distorted conventions that arise from and advantage disproportionately the powerful elements in society while disadvantaging common citizens.

Although Thrasymachus does not highlight the connection between knowledge and power explicitly, his work as a sophist and rhetorician permits us to extrapolate and add another theme:

- The creation and acceptance of numerous claims to truth will be critical in the internalization process by which the community as a whole comes to accept as universal and objective a set of imperatives that are in fact merely contingent and conventional. Such "truths" will be produced by the same privileged elements in society that established "justice" (understood as the prevailing general normative understanding).

My reconstruction of Thrasymachus's argument smoothes out some wrinkles in his thought. For example, he does not carefully distinguish the definition of justice from the effects of justice. He claims at various junctures that "justice is in the interests of the rulers," "justice is another's good," and "justice is in the interests of the stronger." These are not equivalent expressions when taken as definitions of justice. To unravel the conceptual knot, we must understand that Thrasymachus is a sophist and he thus repudiates Socratic metaphysics, which insists that virtue is objective because it must conform to transcendent imperatives. For Thrasymachus, contra Socrates, justice and general normative validity do not correspond to actual properties of objects or human beings, but are, instead, seductive terms by which the ruling class masks its exercise of power over the masses. Accordingly, when common people comply with the imperatives comprising what is called "justice" in their society they are advancing "another's good" in that they are serving the interests of the rulers, who craft laws facilitating their own interests. In that sense, "justice is in the interest of the stronger," because widespread compliance with the laws that define justice will disproportionately advance the interests of the rulers. The effects of obeying normative imperatives that define what is understood as "justice" thereby reflect and reinforce power differentials in society. Justice and the prevailing general norms internalized within a society present themselves as more than they in fact are. They present themselves as objective imperatives or as serving the interests of everyone alike or as required presuppositions of civilization, while in fact they are nothing more than rules of conduct codified in law that benefit the ruling class that was in a position to create them.

In sum, Thrasymachus offers no definition of justice as such. Instead, he points out that what is called "justice" in a particular society reduces to compliance with normative imperatives codified into law by the ruling classes in that society. Because the effects of such compliance serve the interests of the class that crafted the laws, what is taken to be "justice" in a society is "another's good" for everyone except the rulers and thus what is taken to be "justice" is in the interests of the stronger (the rulers). An additional twist is that all this is shrouded by political propaganda: the rulers reinforce their advantage over common citizens by fraudulently presenting "justice" as more than it is, by attaching a transcendent, honorific meaning to the term that embodies claims to objectivity, rationality, and the common good. In this fashion, "justice" becomes *Justice* that commands the allegiance of everyone even though serving the interests of only a few.

By contemporary standards, Thrasymachus's understanding of the nature and effects of the exercise of power is unrefined. He fails to take into account the struggle within and possible reversal of power relations; he offers a crude description of how citizens come to internalize dominant ideas that distort their genuine interests; and his genealogy of how normative understandings arise is too neat. In addition, Thrasymachus evinces a truncated vision of human motivation, limits human interests to material aggrandizement, and equivocates on whether it is genuinely proper for the strong to take advantage of the weak in zero-sum contexts.

Socrates, however, lodges none of these charges. Instead, he denies Thrasymachus's underlying claim that "justice" is merely a set of contingent conventions. For Socrates, justice is transcendent and objective, and thus always serves the interests of those who comply with it. Justice is a virtue of the soul, whose function is to live well. Justice is both an intrinsic and instrumental good (R 352d–354c).

Although Socrates spends considerable time outlining the perfectly just state because he views the state as the "individual writ large" (R 368b–369b), the crux of his defense of the objectivity of justice focuses on the human soul. At the heart of that defense is the unstated premise that virtue is its own reward and vice is its own punishment. Performing virtuous acts facilitates an internal condition of health, balance, and harmony. Acting viciously produces an internal condition of disease, distortion, and chaos. Thus, complying with virtue is always in the interest of every moral agent regardless of how the external world responds to such action. Vicious people harm themselves because by their actions they corrupt their souls. Even if their wrongful actions are never discovered by others, and even if they appear to bring them wealth, fame, and even the reputation for virtue, their internal condition infallibly registers the effects of their deeds. The analogy here is with physical health: I can sincerely believe I am healthy when I am in fact ill and I can sincerely believe that I am ill when I am in fact healthy. On this view, both my internal state and my physical health are objective conditions about which I could be mistaken.

As for the nature of justice and virtue, Socrates is clear: these are not merely matters of convention, but are, instead, grounded in the Forms of the Good, the True, and the Beautiful. These Forms, among others, are nonmaterial, eternal, immutable entities that comprise a transcendent Reality, of which our world is merely a faint image or copy. Philosophical reasoning can guide us in attaining an imperfect understanding of the Forms while our souls are embodied, but it is only when our souls are released from our bodies at death that they can directly apprehend Absolute Truth, Beauty, and Goodness. In any event, if any ruling class acts as Thrasymachus describes, it will not have instantiated justice or a correct general understanding of normativity in its society. Instead, it would have merely subtly coerced the masses into accepting a fraudulent set of norms that remains in play only because of habit cultivated by force and conditioning. What such a society takes to be "justice" is in fact a distortion that has pernicious effects: compliance with such fraudulent norms corrupts souls. Accordingly, Socrates distinguishes norms in a *descriptive* sense—the host of customs, habits, laws, and moral practices that defines a society's ethos—from norms that pass the tests of *validity*, by reflecting the conclusions of the best philosophical arguments that capture the imperatives of the Forms of the Good, the True, and the Beautiful.

On this account, power, knowledge, normative validity, and human well-being are connected. For Socrates, worthy power is generated by the force of the best arguments produced by philosophical reasoning; virtue is knowledge in that an agent who understands virtue and the effects arising from complying with virtue will perform the requisite actions; normative validity is grounded in the foundations provide by the Forms; and human well-being is reflected in the internal condition of a person's soul, which depends upon the union of the proper exercise of power, the proper understanding reflected in genuine knowledge, and the proper undertaking of actions supported by valid norms.

Whereas for Thrasymachus human motivation is such that exercising power means effecting one's will and attaining one's self-interest (narrowly conceived in material terms of wealth, political authority, and fame) in zero-sum contexts, for Socrates exercising power is facilitating one's self-interest in terms of self-improvement that is necessarily underwritten by knowledge and the imperatives arising from valid norms. For Socrates, in principle we can all exercise power to our advantage in this sense, while Thrasymachus conceives exercising power in one's self--interest to occur in a competitive context that ensures not everyone can succeed.

Thrasymachus's account of justice exaggerates the capabilities of one class to affect its interests solely through possessing political power. Even if one class controls the coercive power of government and can identify policies and laws that advantage it disproportionately, common citizens are not merely a group of gulls who will naively accept the resulting oppression. Even if they are powerless to overtly resist their subordination, as long as they recognize the situation for what it is the prerogatives of the superior class are in jeopardy. Subordinates will resist in nuanced ways and subvert the settled order even where prudence forestalls wholesale rebellion. In order to maximize its chances for relatively enduring success, the ruling class needs common citizens to internalize the dominant values and accept them as their own. Although Thrasymachus does not explicitly address this point in his dialogue with Socrates, it may be implicit in his distinction between how "justice" presents itself—as being more than merely a set of conventions perpetrated by the rulers and as being in the interests of the common good. Such a contrivance can be secured only by a creating a knowledge base of "truths" that, among other things, masks reality and obscures common citizens from identifying their genuine interests. This, too, is no small task. Surely, a more complicated process is required whereby some of the genuine interests of common citizens (e.g., their material accumulation) are advanced by the prevailing social order. Only if the masses can viscerally experience gain of some sort can the internalization process succeed. This concession is compatible with the thesis that when considered overall the prevailing social order benefits the ruling class disproportionately and disadvantages and even exploits subordinate classes. My point is that Thrasymachus's understanding of the nature of justice, law, and normativity is much too simplistic even if we accept his cynical conclusions that the structure of the social order invariably favors the ruling class and human motivation is grounded entirely in self-interest.

Socrates's account assumes an extravagant Platonic metaphysics—the transcendent world of Forms, immortal souls, the process of transmigration, and the like—that most contemporary thinkers will resist. Moreover, whether virtue is its own reward and vice its own punishment, and whether being moral is always in the self-interest of the agent are highly contestable ideas. But stripped of these metaphysical suppositions, his point can be refashioned: justice, law, and morality must pass tests of normative validity in order to command our allegiance. They cannot merely be decrees crafted by the powerful to advance their interests to the detriment of the masses if they genuinely are to be called legitimate moral and legal imperatives. For Socrates, the power to access, or at least approximate, the valid norms underwritten by the Forms generates the only legitimate type of power-over, that arising from objective truth and knowledge that is exercised to improve human souls and in the name of the common good.

In fact, Thrasymachus must agree with Socrates in a certain respect. He, too, concludes that moral and legal imperatives that do not pass the tests of genuine normative validity should not command our allegiance beyond our fear of punishment and reprisal from those holding political power. But Thrasymachus goes farther and concludes that what I call the standards of genuine normative validity are nothing more than the effects of oppressive power relations. Thus, for Thrasymachus, might (power exercised oppressively) must make right (what comes to be taken as "justice"). Thrasymachus insists that genuine normative validity itself is a hoax because any version of it must in fact be merely conventional in one way or another.

The difficulty, then, for those of us committed to resisting Thrasymachus's dreary conclusions, will be how to structure the tests of normative validity: Are moral and legal rules and principles legitimate because they have been arrived at through actual agreements among those affected? Or must we conjure an ideal method of choice that will filter out the distorting influences of bias, prejudice, and power differentials? Or are legitimate moral and legal rules and principles not contractual at all? Instead, must they pass tests of rationality that transcend what people would agree to under actual or ideal conditions? Or do such rules and principles arise from the nature of the world and the nature of human beings? Or are they based on the commands of a Supreme Being that is all-good, all-powerful, and all-knowing? We will explore such issues further by examining the writings of the prominent philosophers that follow.

In his dialogues, Plato portrays Socrates as a tender of souls. Accepting a metaphysical dualism that understood the soul (or mind or psyche) to be different in kind from the material body, Socrates philosophized not merely to search for truth for its own sake but also to purify souls in order that they might meet their presumed destiny in the transcendent world of Forms.

For Socrates, disembodied souls once apprehended the Forms of Beauty, Truth, and Good in the other world, and earthly knowledge is fundamentally recollecting that which souls once apprehended immediately (without use of the senses). Philosophical examination, the interrogation of the elenchus, was designed to elicit from others that which lies latent within them. Thus, Socrates viewed himself as a midwife: one who adds nothing to the other but merely aids the other in discharging that which is within the other. We are all pregnant with knowledge because of the prior journeys of our souls, but bringing that knowledge to birth requires assistance.

Socrates, then, exercises power-over his interlocutors for purposes of empowerment. The use of power-over for empowerment aims at developing the higher potentials of the subordinate to the point where the agency of the superior is unnecessary. Unlike paternalism, which may continue indefinitely, empowerment seeks its own termination. Nietzsche captured this notion perfectly in his description of the teacher-student relationship:

"One repays a teacher badly if one always remains nothing but a pupil . . . I bid you lose me and find yourselves; and only *when you have all denied me* will I return to you" (EH "Preface" 4). The best teachers labor diligently to make themselves obsolete, at least pedagogically, in their students' lives: they use their own developed abilities to enhance the capabilities of their students; they hope that their students go beyond them; and only when they have done so will the former students appreciate and rediscover the contributions of their instructors.

Socrates hopes to set his listeners and interlocutors on the proper path to inner harmony and health. Socrates cannot compel the participation of those whom he interrogates. He has power over them only after they antecedently consent to taking part in a philosophical quest. As in all empowerment relationships, unequal vulnerability resides: subordinates are more susceptible to abuse than are superiors. But they also have more to gain.

However, I must not paint an overly sanguine vista of Socratic empowerment. Often, even with the purest of intentions, the superior may stumble. Having benefited from, say the mentor-protégé relationship, the mentor may subconsciously be reluctant to sever ties. Just as in many parent-child relationships, the loss of the subordinate because of the actualization of his or her higher potentials can be painful. The danger is that the maintenance, not the obsolescence, of the relationship may become the subconscious goal, especially of the superior party. The elixir of dependence can be intoxicating for both parties, and empowerment can degenerate into oppression without conscious intent.

For my purposes, the Platonic metaphysics connected to Socrates's understanding is unimportant. Instead, what is paramount is how Socrates illustrates the transformative use of power-over. His own wisdom flows from his admission of his own limits: Socrates "knows that he does not know." This paradox is easily unraveled. Socrates knows that he does not possess (except perhaps latently), or at least cannot articulate, the deep theoretical understanding that results from direct apprehension of the Forms. Whatever knowledge and wisdom he possesses arises from philosophical examination, divine guidance, and the typical sorts of knowledge-how and knowledge-that produced by everyday experiences. But Socrates grasps acutely that his knowledge falls short of the Truths eternally existing in the world of Being. Because he insists that virtue is knowledge, to know the good is to accept and to do the good, any epistemic shortcoming adversely affects the way people live their lives. The message of the Delphic oracle, that no one was wiser than Socrates or that Socrates was the wisest person (obviously, these are not equivalent messages), Socrates came to interpret as meaning that he, unlike others, knew his limitations. After interrogating in the marketplace the most prominent people of his society, Socrates found that they were either unaware of the existence of deep theoretical understanding in the world of Being, or they were oblivious to their own epistemic limitations, or they obstinately took themselves to be much more knowledgeable than they actually were.

Accordingly, Socrates's mission is to improve the lives of others, particularly those who were his students in the sense that they followed him around and participated in philosophical discussions. During the course of their relationships, Socrates typically confused, embarrassed, and even intellectually humiliated those who engaged him. But his purpose was neither sadistic nor self-serving. Socrates had power-over his fellow discussants because of his superior grasp of philosophical disputation and his exceptional skills at what we would term cross-examination. However, his aim in exercising these powers is the empowerment and transformation of others.

By coming to terms with their own limitations they enter the first stage of self-improvement. Only after embracing humility can Socrates's discussants open themselves to the skills of the philosophical midwife and give birth to what resides within them; only after accessing such knowledge can they genuinely understand virtue and lead their lives accordingly. Thus, the entire Socratic enterprise—what he described as his divine mission—is nothing other than an exercise of power over others for transformative purposes.

Critical to this quest, however, is that Socrates's discussants freely enter into their relationship with him. Too often, Socrates seems to accost prominent Athenians in the marketplace, pose profound philosophical questions to them, and in effect coerce them into a discussion because of their privileged status—if they refuse him, they lose face in the eyes of the surrounding crowd. This is not a relationship; instead, it is an encounter. Even if Socrates's aim is transformative, the other party has not freely entered into a relationship with Socrates such that the parties have attained the requisite trust and mutual understanding of the purpose of the interrogation. That at Socrates's trial his accusers mistake the purpose of Socrates's philosophical examinations—"he makes the worse argument seem the better"—is understandable. Lacking the appropriate relationship between the parties, Socrates's questioning can well be received as hostile, bullying, and gratuitously demeaning. The lesson of the story is that to exercise power transformatively, good intentions are necessary but not sufficient: a relationship of trust between the parties and a mutual understanding of the purpose of the philosophical questioning must be antecedently in place.

In any event, the Platonic characters Thrasymachus and Socrates set the stage for a wide-ranging debate about the nature, effects, distribution, and exercise of power that endures. To participate in that debate, we will now jump ahead nineteen centuries to examine the work of philosophy's most notorious apostle of power, Niccolò Machiavelli.

Niccolò Machiavelli (1469–1527)

The Ambiguity of Power

We know that no one ever seizes power with the intention of relinquishing it.

—George Orwell

Unlike Thrasymachus, Machiavelli accepts the possibility of genuine normative validity, grounded, in his view, in the moral imperatives of Christianity. Unlike Socrates, Machiavelli does not conclude that exercising power in political contexts is simply a matter of applying moral imperatives to the situations at hand. Instead, Machiavelli implicitly recognizes a conflict within moral imperatives that pass the test of genuine normative validity: political statesmen, in order to discharge their partialist obligations to their own constituents, must sometimes transgress absolute moral imperatives to wider humanity or to other constituents within their nations. As such, statesmen must dirty their hands (perform actions they recognize to be partially excused but still morally tainted) and risk their souls (jeopardize the quality of their own characters) in exercising the powers attendant to their political offices. Thus, Machiavelli places a spotlight on how political power can transform the agents who exercise it.

Although countless interpretations of Machiavelli's work haunt the literature, they converge on at least one point: the Florentine has interesting things to say about gaining, maintaining, and exercising power. The popular reading of Machiavelli emerges from his work *The Prince*, which contains, among other bromides, the following advice for potential monarchs:

Free yourself from the imperatives of conventional morality

Because of the unbridgeable chasm between how people live and how they ought to live, princes who insist on acting on moral ideals will destroy themselves. Princes who refuse to transgress conventional morality at critical times will fail because so many people lack moral rectitude. Princes must learn how to be not good, understand when to use that knowledge and when not to use it, in accord with necessity (P 15; P 18).

Recognize that the masses are concerned only with positive results

People are mystified by appearances. They judge the actions of everyone, especially those of princes, by their results. If a prince succeeds in founding, preserving, reforming, or expanding the power of the state—and thereby enhancing the well-being of its citizens—his methods will be evaluated favorably (P 18).

Use cool, dispassionate reason to assess opportunities and possibilities, and to select your methods

In the context of advising the prince on securing a grand reputation, Machiavelli warns him not to be fooled into thinking he can always choose safe options. Every choice involves risks and safeguards against one peril, which increase the probability of another danger happening. The wise prince understands the art of evaluating the seriousness and probability of the various disadvantages and in selecting the least dangerous (P 21).

Cultivate the loyalty of the masses

Machiavelli understood implicitly the difference between the coercive and directive functions of law. Law's coercive power, relentlessly invoked by Thrasymachus, is its threat of punishment: human beings, other things being equal, seek to avoid the pains and suffering of retribution for their misdeeds. But coercive power is insufficient. If the only reason citizens have for obeying law or complying with the prince's decrees is fear of punishment, then once that sword is no longer dangling over their heads they will break the law with impunity. That is, as Thrasymachus advised, they will disobey in those circumstances where the probability of getting caught is low and the benefits to them are reasonably high. Law's directive power kicks in when citizens internalize the values expressed by legal prohibitions and prescriptions: when citizens accept those values as their own and no longer perceive them as externally imposed. Machiavelli's recurrent call for strong arms and sound laws underscores the need for the prince to bring order, stability, and security to the state (P 12). A well-ordered state is the prerequisite for the socialization process that promotes the habits, traditions—the necessities—that advance the directive function of law.

Accept the fact that human beings are biologically inclined toward wrongdoing

Remember, human beings are naturally inclined toward wickedness; they will toe the righteous line only when strong-armed by necessity (P 15; P 18; P 23). Only when citizens accept for themselves that the prince's rule and his laws are appropriate, acceptable, and, yes, even necessary will the state no longer be corrupt. Animating the directive power of law includes showing the people how their self-interest is inextricably bound to the well-being of the prince; recruiting a strong army and instituting sound laws; neutralizing the ambition of the nobles; implementing disciplined education; cultivating appropriate habits and customs; enlarging the prince's reputation; and demonstrating that the system works through grand military triumphs and a sharp system of internal rewards and punishments.

Restrain your erotic and material lusts

First, the prince must train physically and be prepared mentally. Second, the prince must be disciplined and immune to the rush to luxuries. Third, the prince must attend most of all to military affairs A prince must be armed and personally command his soldiers (P 14). Fourth, the prince must refrain from abusing the women and seizing the property of his citizens and subjects (P 17; P 19). Such princely excesses invite the hatred of the masses, the one sure trigger of the prince's demise. Fifth, he must not exude *animo effeminato* (an effeminate spirit): he cannot act erratically, cowardly, indecisively, or timidly. To do so, earns the contempt of the people. The people may themselves embody *animo effeminato,* but few recognize their limitations and all expect more of their leaders. The prince, instead, must demonstrate *grandezza d'animo* (a noble or grand soul): he must reveal the greatness of his actions, and exude dignified strength, resoluteness, and endurance (P 19).

Keep your behavior in tune with the times

The prince should not stake his claim on past favorable *Fortuna. Fortuna* is a trickster and cannot remain constant. Rulers must be adaptable and conform their actions to present circumstances. Some princes, the least able, are effective only occasionally. Most princes, typical rulers, are more often successful because their temperaments are compatible with more conditions. Only the greatest princes are flexible enough to succeed in numerous situations. Only such rulers bear the military and political *virtù* (personal excellence) required for founding, reforming, preserving, or expanding a healthy state. Only they merit the enduring glory that marks the best human lives. But Machiavelli's tragic view of life whispers that men are unable to adapt to all circumstances. Their fixed character and dispositions or past successes militate that their elasticity is limited. But the situations contrived by *Fortuna* are boundless. Although boldness is preferable to timidity, it cannot redeem us from our fate: All men, if given enough time, will fail in the end (P 25).

Establish strong armies and sound laws

A prince can hire mercenary forces, align himself with auxiliary soldiers, or train his own army. Of these, the last is by far the best strategy. Mercenaries are worthless. When war is not being waged they are eager to be hired and drain a prince's finances. When war arrives, they scatter like scalded cats. They are ambitious, undisciplined, disloyal, ostentatious among allies, but cowardly among enemies (P 12). Auxiliaries are the forces belonging to another strong man, which a prince has brought in to defend his state. They are as useless as mercenaries, but more dangerous. If they lose, the prince loses. If they win, they are likely to injure the prince who hired them. Auxiliaries do have loyalties, but only to their own country and ruler, not to the prince who requested their aid. Whereas mercenaries are indifferent and lazy, auxiliaries are eager but predatory (P 13). Accordingly, a successful prince must recruit, train, and lead his own troops. As always, the prince should be self-sustaining and rely as little as possible upon outsiders (P 10).

Gain knowledge of war

A prince must be armed, but to be dangerous he must lead his own troops. He cannot lead an indolent life and retain respect. The quickest way to lose power and relinquish your state is to shy from learning and practicing the art of war. The prince must also study history. By observing and mimicking the methods of men with undeniable military *virtù*, the prince follows a long and honorable tradition: Alexander the Great imitated Achilles; Julius Caesar imitated Alexander; Scipio imitated Cyrus. He who ignores history when it comes to military matters invites disaster (P 14). The wise prince commands his troops. He acts as a general in the field. The well-ordered republic commissions a citizen. The prince's knowledge and training is not simply theoretical. Only in this way do healthy states advance their causes (P 12).

Operate within the real as it is

Machiavelli cautions the prince to rule as Machiavelli writes: focus on real problems, avoid abstractions and utopianism, and emphasize practicality

(P 15). The world of philosophers' imaginations is creative but useless for the purposes of earthly governments. Princes who delude themselves or appeal to comforting fantasies about human nature doom themselves and their homelands. History will not judge kindly dreamers or naive moralists posing as rulers.

Foster a good reputation, earn respect, but act expediently

A prince should actually embody praiseworthy qualities, not just seem to have them (P 18). But possessing so many grand characteristics is impossible (P 15). The prince must avoid being considered fickle, indecisive, cowardly—all reflections of *animo effeminato*. Exuding strength, firmness, decisiveness, and largeness of vision—the attributes of *grandezza d'animo*—is required to discourage enemies and win allies. Again, a prince who is not hated has few legitimate concerns. One such worry is from foreign enemies; the antidote is able soldiers and strong arms. If the prince can soften threats of foreign invasion he will also increase order and stability within his state. The likelihood of internal agitators forming conspiracies against the prince will decrease. The reputations of princes are amplified when the populace observes them overcoming resistance and surmounting obstacles. In general, the prince will gain esteem through grand enterprises. Impressive military victories, expansion of territory, stirring defenses of the homeland are the most obvious candidates. But internal affairs are also important. The prince must reward exceptional efforts and punish vile deeds. The people take their cue from the prince: they will emulate rewarded actions in the hope of garnering benefits and they will avoid punished deeds in order to skirt pain (P 21).

Understand the critical ends of the state

The ends of the state are the personal glory of the prince and the enhanced well-being of the citizens (P 26). Machiavelli is clear in *The Prince* and even more emphatic in *The Discourses* that these ends require territorial expansion (P 3; P 7; D II 2; D II 4; D II 6; D II 9; D II 21).

Remember: It is better to be feared than to be loved, but avoid being hated

The prince should strive to be considered merciful and not cruel. But being merciful is trickier than it may seem. Being considered cruel will not jeopardize the prince's authority if in so doing he advances the order and security of the state, and the well-being of the people (P 17). For the prince, being both feared and loved by the people is the best situation. But accomplishing both simultaneously is uncommon. If the prince cannot join these two emotions in his people, it is better to be feared than to be loved. This is the case because of human nature. People are generally ungrateful, cowardly, selfish, deceptive, greedy, and inconstant. As long as the prince serves their interests, they pledge loyalty and offer extravagant promises. They talk boldly during high times, but act timidly in adverse situations. Love is an emotion that binds people through obligation. People, who are basically wicked and self-interested, will renege on such a duty when expedient. Fear has a greater hold because it includes dread of punishment. Love, then, appeals to the better angels of our natures, making it thoroughly discretionary and unreliable. Fear addresses our consistent aversion to coercion, suffering, and physical harm, making it more reliable and predictable. Also, whether citizens fear the prince is more under his control than whether they love him. Accordingly, the fear of his subjects, again, is more predictable, reliable, and controllable than is the love of his subjects (P 17; P 18). At all costs, a prince must avoid being hated (P 17; P 19). The people will hate a prince only if the ruler confiscates their property or their women. When the prince has to kill he should be able to articulate persuasive reasons and to make a clear case. Above all, he must not seize the property of citizens: "Men forget more quickly the death of a father than the loss of a father's estate" (P 17).

Develop the qualities of the lion and the fox

The prince should take the lion and the fox as role models. The lion frightens wolves and the fox recognizes traps. Rulers who act only as lions do not fully understand the requirements of their office. The lion, as a metaphor for military might, can be tricked and neutralized by clever adversaries. The fox, as a metaphor for cunning and deception, cannot always defend itself from forceful enemies. The qualities of both beasts are needed by a successful prince (P 18; P 19).

Happily, people are easily fooled. The prince must conceal that he is playing the fox. Through cunning, deception, and by picking his spots, the prince must disguise his actual intentions. If capable, the prince will find plenty of simpletons, blinded by immediate gratifications and their own illusions, who will allow themselves to be duped. The prince must seem merciful, trustworthy, reliable, religious, truthful and the like. Such a reputation aids the art of deception. But a prince must adjust his actual behavior in accord with *Fortuna* and *necessità*. Practicing the moral virtues stringently will limit the prince's range of possible actions to his detriment. For Machiavelli, the prince must follow what virtually everyone else is already doing: talking piety, practicing expediency.

Be decisive, avoid neutrality

Machiavelli prizes autonomy and action: "It is better to act and to regret it than not to act and to regret it" (Ltr. 231: 2/25/14). Although he quotes Boccaccio in a sexual context, Machiavelli also offers a summary of his political philosophy. Women, children, and academic philosophers can dream and dawdle. Men in the political arena must act, independently and decisively.

Machiavelli disdains half-hearted measures, the kind we are tempted to apply when we are unsure of our position and options. Machiavelli offers a second guideline: Someone who causes another to become powerful undermines his own position. He would cause that rise in power by his creativity or through his strength, both of which would be distrusted by the person who has grown in power (P 3). A third guideline also related to a conquered state: a prince should make a list of all the harsh measures he must take to pacify the region, then perform all of them swiftly and only once. Repeating cruelties will make the subjects too insecure and may cultivate their hatred. Cruelties done in one fell swoop will be dwelt on less and will anger subjects less. Benefits to these same subjects should be parceled out gradually so they will be savored more. Machiavelli's fourth guideline concerns timeliness: ever allow a disorder, evil, or problem to continue in order to avoid a war. Failing to heed this advice will not evade the war, but only delay it to your disadvantage (P 3). Machiavelli anticipated the dangers of appeasement.

Machiavelli's fifth guideline of decisiveness is pivotal: avoid neutrality. A prince gains respect from unreservedly allying himself with one party in a conflict and being equally opposed to the other party in the conflict. If a prince remains neutral, the victor in the dispute will injure him and the defeated party will revel in that injury. The prince will be conquered by the former and receive no aid from the latter. The victor will not want the prince as a friend because he will be suspicious of the trustworthiness of a prince who remained neutral in time of war. The loser in the dispute will not curry the prince's friendship because the prince withheld aid when the losing party most required it (P 21).

Identify and hire trustworthy ministers

Crucial to the prince's success is the ministers he includes in his inner circle of advisers. Judging a prince by the quality of his ministers is sound. Making inept choices of ministers is a guarantee that a prince's judgment is fatally flawed. A prince must guard against ministers who are more concerned about their own interests than those of the ruler. Such men render poor counsel. The prince's interests must always be paramount. The prince must, however, secure the loyalty of his advisers by rewarding them. The prince should bestow honors, public recognition, material incentives, and the like on worthy ministers. Doing so demonstrates that the ministers benefit from their employment and that the prince recognizes exemplary service to his causes. The bond of trust thereby strengthens between the prince and the members of his inner circle (P 22).

Machiavelli underscores, yet again, the source of all loyalty, trust, and mutuality: self-interest. By tying the well-being of his ministers to his own position and largesse, the prince reinforces the link between them. He stresses that a prince must choose the right people for his inner circle.

Avoid sycophants

The prince's posse should not include flatterers, minions, yes-men, and other deplorable breeds. He must, instead, select as ministers those men who will speak the truth to power. As always, Machiavelli is concerned with protocol: excessive candor and familiarity is also ill-advised; if everyone feels entitled to speak frankly to the prince at any time, they will lose respect for their ruler. False flattery and excessive candor are both undesirable and potentially dangerous. The prince must choose wise men as ministers who will speak only the truth to and address only those subjects designated by the prince. Only his ministers have such access to the prince.

Distinguish between the art of securing and that of preserving power

A prince who artfully seizes power may have difficulty maintaining it and a prince who capably maintains power may be ineffective in obtaining it. Machiavelli argues that those who come to power through *virtù* (in this context, military and political excellence) will struggle to gain power but will easily preserve it; those who rise to power through *Fortuna* will take power easily but struggle to keep it. This is so because gaining power is quicker if circumstances and the aid of strong allies or patrons ease the way. But once attained, power cannot be maintained by luck and strong cronies. At that point, the skills of princes become pivotal. Luck and connections, without more, cannot sustain a prince (P 6; P 7).

Learn the recipe for political success

Princes should take full responsibility for popular actions and decrees, but delegate underlings to mete out unpopular policies and to perform unwel-comed actions. Where possible, princes should respect the aristocracy and avoid the hatred of the people. At times, princes who do good deeds and follow conventional morality will be hated, especially where some faction of their subjects—the people, the aristocracy, or the military—is corrupt. To hold onto power, princes are compelled not to be good. As always, the necessity flows from the wicked actions and dispositions of other people. Machiavelli's consistent message is that a ruler who insists on being good when so many around him are evil will meet a bad end (P 19). Most definitively, the prince's success is a function of the compatibility of *Fortuna* and *virtù*. Where congenial circumstances are introduced to personal excellence a beautiful union arises.

Advice such as this promotes the impression that Machiavelli is compiling the ingredients for a would-be political leader to possess and exercise power over his subjects and the international community. Of course, in order to do so effectively such a monarch must amplify his power to affect political outcomes, so that, also, is part of the Machiavellian process. The felicitous union of enhanced personal capabilities, possession of political authority, and expertise in exercising power over domestic and foreign groups create prospects for attaining an enduring glory that mollifies the inevitable victories of Father Time and the Grim Reaper.

The popular understanding of Machiavelli takes him to understand power along these lines: a monarch cannot exercise power effectively merely because he enjoys exclusive control of the means of force; coercive power alone is insufficient, he must cultivate directive power by luring the masses into internalizing the values that sustain the ambitions of the prince; this is accomplished by convincing the masses to identify the ruler's interests with their own; this identification requires playing upon the masses' proclivities for accepting appearances, for judging deeds only by their outcomes, and for acting from habit and tradition; strong arms and sound laws nurture the order, stability, and security to the state that are prerequisites for the socialization process that underwrites the monarch's aim. The prince must avoid being hated by common citizens, but he need not be loved—fear is a more reliable emotion. Thus, he must avoid the infliction of gratuitous violence to property and persons, which animates vengeful feelings.

On the international level, the prince must take care in appointing ministers, he must be resolute, and he must develop the qualities of the lion and the fox. In all situations, he must grasp reality firmly and judge circumstances accurately. The prince must not indulge utopian fantasies or deny reality because doing so gratifies his ego. The exercise of power, domestically and internationally, often requires understanding the requirements of conventional morality, but placing them aside in deference to political necessity.

Accordingly, on the popular interpretation of Machiavelli, he writes in order to compile what he has learned about the possession and successful exercise of political power. His innovation resides in the specific pieces of advice he renders; in his subtle portrayal of how Thrasymachus was mistaken; and in his conceptualization of power.

Whereas Thrasymachus concluded that what people take to be "justice" (and normative understanding generally) is nothing more than the interests of the rulers codified into law, Machiavelli accepts that morality (and normative understanding generally) is more than this but demonstrates when and how it must be dismissed by a ruler if he is to exercise power effectively. For Thrasymachus, as long as a ruler understands his own interests, embodied in material terms, then no conflict exists between wielding power and doing "justice"—might makes right in that sense. For Machiavelli, the most serious situations for a ruler arise from conflicts between the exercise of power and the imperatives of morality. To know when and how to cast aside the imperatives of morality is paramount if a ruler is to exercise power successfully.

On the popular interpretation, Machiavelli's conceptualization of power underscores the need to supplement coercive force with directive force. Machiavelli appreciates that coercive force alone is a thin reed upon which to rest one's claim to power. Thus, he prefigures Marxist understandings of the roles ideology and socialization assume in reflecting and sustaining power regimes. In addition, he locates and takes into account critical elements of human motivation, biological inclination, and mass psychology that can either fuel or obstruct the internalization process required to energize the directive force of law. Accordingly on the popular interpretation, Machiavelli is the philosopher of power par excellence who advises potential rulers on how to brandish power effectively through force, fraud, and manipulation.

By 1559, all of Machiavelli's works were condemned by the Roman Catholic Church and placed on its index of prohibited books. Extolling force and fraud, praising evil methods of statecraft, applauding murder, ignoring or minimizing love and friendship, elevating cynicism to an art form, debasing religion, glorifying autocrats, advising endless treachery and scheming, and manipulation of appearances, Machiavelli was viewed as an instrument of the Dark Side and "Machiavellian" became a shorthand invective for duplicity and thuggery. For centuries, the dominant picture of Machiavelli was that of a dangerous man who divided the world into con men and gulls, political gangsters and marks. Machiavelli's alleged obsession with the conquest, preservation, and expansion of political power at the expense of moral and spiritual values was unanimously disparaged by clergy of all denominations, dramatists, poets, monarchs, and other righteous thinkers. This interpretation retains vitality today in the popular conception of Machiavelli and in the ongoing use of "Machiavellian" to connote political and personal opportunism and expediency.

While much can be said in favor of the popular interpretation of Machiavelli, centuries of readers have advanced alternate understandings of his writing. These understandings have arisen from placing the *Prince* in context with Machiavelli's other works such as the *Discourses, The Art of War, The Florentine Histories*, as well as his private correspondence with friends and diplomats. I will sketch a few of these alternate understandings with an eye toward how they affect our perceptions of Machiavelli's conceptualization of power.[1]

Machiavelli as Patriot

One such alternate understanding takes the *Prince* to be a nationalistic call to arms. On this account, Machiavelli is a fervent Italian patriot who aspires to unveil a blueprint for Italian unification. On this view, *The Prince* is precisely what it presents itself to be: a manual for princely success. But that success is qualified. The new ruler should use his power to reform a corrupt, weak state as preparation for the emergence or return of a healthy, expansionist republic. The manipulative, conniving, forceful measures of the prince—exercising the subtle wiles of the fox and the frightening domination of the lion—are the prerequisites for the vigorous republic Machiavelli mythologizes in *The Discourses*. Moreover, the prince's overarching goal is to make himself, or at least render the scope of his authority, obsolete. *The Prince*, then, is the beginning but not the end of Machiavelli's heroic account of political triumph.

According to the Machiavelli-as-patriot interpretation, *The Prince* is a manual for unification in an unsettled context. Once the monarch attains national unity, promotes the common good, and nurtures a strong national character, his power should be dispersed. Once the conditions required for a sound republic are in the place, the advice of *The Discourses*, which celebrates republicanism, should prevail.

In Machiavelli's judgment, the five loose-knit regions of Italy were in a dire predicament in the early sixteenth century. They could either remain separate and provide easy targets for invading barbarians or they could follow the leadership of a strong man, rise above factional bickering, and unite for the greater good: either continued victimization or unification. In *The Prince*, Machiavelli argues that the regionalized people of Italy were generally corrupt—they lacked civic *virtù*—so the monarch would sometimes be forced to use fraud and coercion to unify the nation, invigorate citizens, and fend off external aggressors. Sounds peculiar, does it not? The cure for corruptness is fraud and coercion? What Machiavelli meant was that the prince, while governing, should not always abide by the standards of conventional private morality. If certain inherently evil practices had to be used, that should be thought of as "evil well-used" because they flow from necessity: external forces, antecedent events, and compelling circumstances. Necessity will often compel the ruler to commit deeds that are correctly judged immoral when performed outside the political arena: miserliness, cruelty, deceit, and promise breaking are often politically preferable to liberality, mercy, honesty, and promise keeping. The purpose, though, of the prince's strategies is unequivocal: he maximizes his prospects of earning enduring glory by imposing order and security, and beginning the reformation of his corrupt citizens and subjects.

Machiavelli was convinced that only an absolute monarch can transform a corrupt society. In his judgment, civic *virtù* in Italy had disintegrated and this made a popular republic impossible. *Virtù* could only be spawned through proper laws, training, and education. The corrupt, fragmented state cannot rehabilitate itself. Instead, an omnipotent lawgiver must mold it by crafting a pure social foundation based on strong arms and sound laws. The strong, unified state prevents foreign intrusions, and eventually helps citizens rise above selfish individualism, establishes communal bonds, increases the material and spiritual quality of life, and cultivates personal and national *virtù*.

The implications for Machiavelli's conceptualization of power are clear. The prince does not exercise power over his subjects and international competitors merely for purposes of self-aggrandizement; the prince is not an oppressor. Instead, he often exercises power harshly, but paternalistically and transformatively, over his subjects to facilitate the common good and to improve the collective character of the masses. As does the good teacher of students, the prince aspires to make his political agency and the monarchy itself obsolete once the masses have been spiritually transformed. Accordingly, on this account, the greatest of princes must amplify his political power and reign over his nation by exercising power paternalistically and transformatively, while sometimes oppressing foreigners and obstreperous domestic opponents.

Machiavelli as Ironist

Another interpretation of the *Prince* concludes that readers should not take the work at face value. This interpretation has a long history and takes ingenious twists and turns. The claim is that Machiavelli was a foe of tyranny and his purpose could not have been to instruct power mongers, but to unmask their pretensions, reveal their way of operating, and teach the multitude of their evil machinations. Machiavelli was, under this view, an investigative reporter bent on exposing the ways of tyranny in order to neutralize their efficacy. By mocking the fashions of autocracy, under cover of refining them, Machiavelli was able to exemplify duplicity for salutary purposes. Thus, what Machiavelli is really doing is holding a mirror to prevalent princely actions of his day. He is describing but not endorsing the practices he chronicles in that book. His genuine purpose is to expose the machinations of the powerful in order to diffuse the effectiveness of the methods employed in service of oppression. On this account, Machiavelli is wielding his own power as a writer and observer of politics transformatively: he hopes to reveal how monarchs use force and fraud, and how they nurture the directive dimension of law through socialization, in order to destroy their oppressive power. If correct, we should not read Machiavelli literally, but, instead, understand the *Prince* not as an instruction booklet for princes, but as a subversive manual for citizens and subjects.

Machiavelli as Realist

Some interpret Machiavelli as a realist, one whose writing is purely descriptive. True, he draws conclusions of what a prince should do given the conditions of the world and of politics, but such prescriptions are prudential and strategic, not moral. Machiavelli's methods are the means of his time, indeed all times, and the only ones offering hope for political success. Political leaders sometimes lie, connive, threaten, plot, coerce in order to attain their ends and advance the interests of their polity. What is the source of the scandal? Whereas Plato hoped to change the world through his utopian vision, Machiavelli aspires to succeed politically in the world as it is. Machiavelli is not *championing* the autonomy of politics from morals nor is he delighted that the world is as it is. Instead, the successful statesman will learn how to gain the competitive edge in a world not of his making. His constituents deserve nothing less.

Machiavelli is also convinced that the world cannot be changed, because of inherent defects in human nature, the zero-sum nature of international affairs, and the natural scarcity of desired resources, but this, too, is a description of reality. Strong men will press forward to establish, preserve, and extend their power. Machiavelli does not confer moral blessings on these circumstances and events. He does not, as did Thrasymachus, conclude that might makes right and that what is taken as conventional morality consisted of guidelines in the interests of the strongest in society. Instead, for Machiavelli effective use of force and fraud translate to political success, which is beyond moral assessment.

On this account, Machiavelli is writing a book of advice for would-be rulers, but one that separates politics from morality. Political power cannot be exercised paternalistically or transformatively over subjects or international parties because the context in which it operates is fixed, is inherently of a zero-sum nature, and suffers from an enduring scarcity of resources. Because political power on this account must be independent of moral evaluation, it should be assessed only by considerations of prudence, effectiveness, and national success. Accordingly, political power is inherently coercive and exercised oppressively to advance the interests of small groups domestically and to advance the interests of one's own city or nation internationally. On this view, Machiavelli does not confer a moral imprimatur on the methods he discusses but, instead, isolates political power from moral assessment.

Machiavelli as Roman Moralist

This interpretation concludes that Machiavelli does not separate politics from morality as such, only from a certain version of Christian morality. Machiavelli weds politics to a pagan morality that places state interests above all religion and honors only those religions that render the masses loyal and governable. The *Prince* describes a clash of two value systems: a pagan (Roman) ethic and the conventional, Christian morality. Instead of conceiving Machiavelli as positing two autonomous guiding-action realms, the moral and the political, this view sees the conflict in Machiavelli as waged between two competing versions of morality. Machiavelli, then, is not advocating the separation of politics from ethics, but only the marriage of politics to a morality different from the conventional, Christian version.

The pagan or Roman morality embodies goals as ultimate and legitimate that differ from those celebrated by Christianity. Christianity treasures faith, hope, charity, love, mercy, adoration of God, forgiveness of transgressions by enemies, selflessness, compassion for others, redemption of the soul, suspicion of worldly goods, and focus on earning a blissful afterlife. This, for Machiavelli, is an ethic for private people seeking transcendent salvation. Roman religion stressed the establishment, preservation, and expansion of a well-ordered social whole. This required men of character: "inner moral strength, magnanimity, vigor, vitality, generosity, loyalty, above all public spirit, civic sense, dedication to the security, power, glory, expansion of the *patria*."[2] Through glittering displays, bloody sacrifices, sound laws, and carefully defined education, the Romans sanctified pagan virtues: "Power, magnificence, pride, austerity, pursuit of glory, vigor, discipline . . . this is what makes states great."[3] This, for Machiavelli, is an ethic for leaders in public roles striving for personal (worldly) glory and the founding, reforming, or preservation of a healthy, expansionist polity. Such social ends, Machiavelli insists, are natural and prudent for men to pursue.

To wholeheartedly welcome Christian morality is to consign oneself to political fecklessness. For Machiavelli, the importance of Rome as an example largely flows from the extent and duration of its power; that Rome could have influenced so many people for so long a time makes it the supreme case of collective civic *virtù*. Through his study of ancient Rome, Machiavelli found support for his instinctive personal values: passion for competition, zest for honor, yearning for community, and distrust of other states. The Romans recognized no difference between moral excellence and reputation; praise was what every citizen most desired; to place personal honor above the interests of the entire community was considered barbaric; citizens were educated to harness their ambition in service to the common good, although in their relations with other states and *stranieri* (strangers), no such limitations constricted their competitive instincts.

Accordingly, on this account the exercise of political power is amenable to normative assessment but only in accord with Roman morality. That morality carefully circumscribed its concern to the citizens of its nation. Thus, political power would be exercised domestically—sometimes oppressively, occasionally paternalistically, and at times transformatively—in order to secure the aims of the nation and shape the characters of citizens. Exercising political power internationally would be a study in domination and oppression. In both arenas, success would be measured by the Roman aspirations and values sketched above. Evaluation by religious (Christian) values would be considered superfluous, naive, or a category mistake (inappropriately applying criteria that are relevant to *other* human enterprises but that are irrelevant to *this* enterprise).

Machiavelli as Political Subversive

This innovative interpretation holds that Machiavelli is not subversive in the sense of trying to animate the masses to a deeper understanding of politics that will energize their rebellion or subtle resistance to entrenched oppressive power. Instead, Machiavelli strives to misdirect the rulers and would-be monarchs who would read his work. Rather than providing a savvy handbook for the oppressive exercise of power, Machiavelli is using his power as a writer to seduce princes into exercising authority in ways that will maximize their prospects for failure. What could be more Machiavellian!

For example, Machiavelli insists that human beings act from habit and their fixed characters. At times, when *Fortuna* allows, temporary success is attainable. But *Fortuna* is not fixed, and circumstances will arise where the inflexibility of human beings must signal their downfall (P 25). Machiavelli's well-known call to adaptability and shifting with the times is undermined by his firm conviction that our actions flow from our immutable characters and fixed dispositions. If true, then *The Prince* is, at best, a chronicle of transitory glory. We all must fail in the end. Accordingly, we should not take seriously the mainstream perception that *The Prince* is a manual on princely success.

Moreover, Machiavelli presents *virtù* as an animating force in his depiction of military and political success. Yet, he applies the notion of *virtù* so haphazardly that it is worthless as a conceptual tool. For example, Machiavelli exalts Borgia as a man of *virtù*, but takes Agathocles of Sicily to task for actions that are indistinguishable (P 7; P 8). If one of his two main engines for glory is flawed at its core, how can the *Prince* be taken seriously as a handbook on government?

Also, Machiavelli vacillates between seeing *Fortuna* as a controlling force that mocks human aspirations and efforts, and insisting that some human beings—those embodying *virtù*—have the capabilities of managing *Fortuna* effectively (P 7; P 13; P 25). The fragility of Machiavelli's most cherished conceptual linchpins—*virtù* and *Fortuna*—is taken not just as a malady of logic but as revealing a cryptic message: The Medici must fail but Machiavelli can gain.

In that same vein, Machiavelli advances a bleak picture of human nature in the *Prince*, insisting, among other things, that men are untrustworthy. But he then argues that what a successful prince needs most is a trusted *consigliere* (P 22; P 23). How can this be squared? Can a prince truly rely on clever, independent advisers bent on advancing their own interests? The prince may control the powers of the lion, but intimate advisers make the prince vulnerable to the connivings of the fox. On this account, the only consistent thread in *The Prince* is Machiavelli's dogged commitment to using for his own ends those to whom he offers his services ostensibly as a mere instrument.

Machiavelli offers success to the prince who follows his advice, yet the conclusions of his arguments implicitly demonstrate that failure must result. In the early part of the work, careful readers detect three paramount obstacles the Medici must confront: they are new princes; they rule a former republic; and they attained power through foreign armies and *Fortuna* (P 3; P 6). But like all *gabbiani* (gulls), the Medici, Machiavelli suspects, will believe only what comforts them. The tacit message—the stone cold truth—will fly by their trusting eyes. Thus, on this account, Machiavelli intended to undermine the Medici by rendering advice that, if followed, would dissolve their power and hasten the restoration of the Florentine republic. The *Prince* exemplifies the deception that it advises. It appears to embolden a prince with methods and manners for success, but if followed, the prescriptions of *The Prince* accelerate the prince's demise. The work itself is political *action,* not political *theory.*

In sum, a major target of this interpretation is the herd of contemporary scholarly *gabbiani* who take Machiavelli at his surface level, those who interpret the *Prince* as rendering his best advice on how a ruler with absolute power can reform a corrupt state and cast the foundation for an expansionist republic. Such readers defang Machiavelli by making him less Machiavellian and more congenial to modern methods. Unfortunately, contemporary gulls deny Machiavelli the guile of the fox and, lacking that quality themselves, stumble into the trap the Florentine set for the Medici.

Accordingly, on this interpretation, Machiavelli is exercising his power as a writer in order to undermine extant oppressive power relations. The *Prince* demonstrates how those in subordinate positions are never powerless or without resources to reverse or unsettle asymmetrical power relations. Taking the rule of the Medici to be oppressive, Machiavelli exercises his unique resource as a writer to seduce the Medici into employing tactics that would be counterproductive to their aims. If this is the case, Machiavelli compiles a textbook of duplicity intended to overturn the monarchy by luring the rulers into exercising their power against themselves. On this account, Machiavelli cleverly advances the recipe for a bloodless revolution that turns oppressive power against itself.

Assessing the various interpretations of Machiavelli would go well beyond the contours of this work. Obviously, not all of these accounts can be accurate as most of them conflict, despite some overlapping agreement.

However, I have evaluated these interpretations and others in detail elsewhere.[4]

My favored interpretation is a refined version of Machiavelli as patriot, the outline of which is as follows: (1) Machiavelli accepts absolute principles of conventional morality—principles that are absolute not in the sense that they cannot be legitimately overridden, but absolute in the sense that violations of these principles retain an element of wrongness even if partially excused; (2) Machiavelli keenly appreciates the particular duties of public office—the extra responsibilities, the imperative to advance the interests of constituents over those of foreigners, and the need to advance the collective interest embodied by the state; (3) A tension thereby exists *within* conventional morality between impersonal, impartial prescriptions that apply to all moral agents and particular, partial imperatives that accompany political office; and (4) Machiavelli underscores the necessities of international affairs—the intrusions of *Fortuna,* the zero-sum nature of the contest, the deficiencies of human nature, and the natural scarcity of resources.

The life of a political leader is lived in tension among the four competing vectors sketched in the previous paragraph. It is not as if such a leader merely casts off the cloak of conventional morality when he enters his office or job quarters, and adorns himself in the liberating dress of a Roman pagan. Such action would increase the likelihood of his degenerating into a tyrant or an official who uses cruel measures when they are not required. The competing moral and political vectors pressing down upon a Machiavellian ruler are deep, dark, and dense. Their conflicting demands cannot be simultaneously fulfilled.

If he is correct, statesmen must dirty their hands while discharging their duties. That Machiavelli was one of the first major political thinkers to describe the problem of dirty hands is well recognized.[5] The paradox of dirty hands seemingly rests on two convictions: categorical moral prohibitions are sometimes appropriately transgressed or overridden in political and everyday contexts; and a good person will feel and be guilty from having broken those prohibitions, while a politician embodying the excellences of his office will understand the necessity of sometimes doing so. Military and political leaders, acting on our behalf and in our name, sometimes act in ways that are incontestably condemned by the imperatives of impersonal morality, but under certain circumstances such acts prevent great harms or achieve great goods for limited constituencies to whom these agents owe special duties.

Political leaders are at the helms of states that embody a monopoly on the legitimate use of violence and coercive means; they operate in a competitive context with numerous unscrupulous agents; they have special responsibilities to their limited constituencies that sometimes require them to infringe on the interests of humanity in general; they must sometimes appear to be what they are not in order to retain their authority; and their decisions involve higher stakes than those of private citizens. Thus, unlike private citizens, statesmen confront dirty hands situations systematically.

At the international level, statesmen confront moral paradoxes generated by conflicts between the imperatives of impersonal morality understood from the impartial perspective of an Ideal Observer and the partialist obligations they bear to their national constituents. This is a conflict *within* morality and not, as often supposed, a conflict between two different types of morality (Christian versus pagan) or between two different normative domains (moral versus political). Moreover, as Machiavelli never tires of pointing out, statesmen will sometimes need to use violence or dissimulation in foreign affairs given the nature of the world. Even if he is incorrect in thinking that the world is wholly and inevitably a ruthless forum for zero-sum competition, Machiavelli accurately cautions statesmen that they must embody the power of the lion in order to frighten the numerous political wolves extant among them and the cunning of the fox in order to recognize and evade the traps and machinations of their peers.

At the domestic level, statesmen will often face moral paradoxes generated by conflicts between their duty to promote the common good and their obligation to honor the interests of individual citizens. In democratic and republican forms of government, they will be required to facilitate deals and broker compromises directed at accommodating diverse interest groups. The decisions of statesmen involve more people and more critical issues than the decisions of private citizens. Often, those decisions are enforced through coercive state power. In general, different groups of constituents will lodge conflicting, severe demands on statesmen. Typically operating under conditions of epistemological uncertainty and normative disagreement, statesmen must often arrive at monumental decisions while struggling with incompatible or incommensurable values.

Dirty hands contexts in politics are driven by agents who exercise their power to use evil well, but who do not conclude that their deeds arose from wrong choices or from situations in which the reasons supporting alternate actions were equal. Instead, agents who retain their souls will recognize their deeds involved violations of paramount principles of impersonal morality recognized by themselves and their constituents. Also, the victims of such deeds will conclude that they have been wronged by those violations. To risk but not lose their souls, statesmen must retain their reluctance to dirty their hands even where doing so is necessary for the national good. They must acknowledge the moral remainder, the cost, of their necessary actions. Otherwise, such leaders will too easily dirty their hands when doing so is not necessary, thereby losing their souls and jeopardizing the common good of their nations. Machiavellian statesmen must learn how not to be good, but still retain all the goodness permitted by their institutional roles. Again, they must risk but not lose their souls. The nature of the world and the structure of the moral conflicts they must confront prevent them from attaining Plato's ideal of the perfectly balanced soul, but permit them to retain their humanity. Or so we must hope.

Thus, statesmen must be ardent patriots who love their nations more than their souls (Ltr. 331: 4/16/27; Ltr. 224: 12/10/13; Ltr. 270: 5/17/21; FH III 7; AW I 7). The morally wrongful remainders that accompany evil well-used imply that statesmen risk their souls in the service of their countries. *To risk one's soul is to jeopardize one's character, to potentially transform oneself unworthily.* Statesmen must not lose their souls because if they do they will obscure the distinction between evil well- and ill-used and thereby enter into evil too willingly; they will invariably become tyrants instead of stewards of the common good. Nor can they truculently adhere to the imperatives of impersonal morality and retain their clean hands, because in so doing they will renege on the duties of their office and fail as patriots. Statesmen who risk but retain their souls will garner the highest award available to human beings: deserved, enduring glory that confers a measure of immortality upon the greatest among us (P 7; P 8, P 14; P 24; P 26; D I 10). Such a person will have softened the triumph of the Grim Reaper to the extent possible for finite beings.

We can explain many of the actions and much of the mindset of an ideal Machiavellian ruler from the standpoint of power. A Machiavellian ruler, of course, must possess an abundance of power-to, which arises from his *virtù*. Machiavellian rulers must also wield power-over. Often, and especially in dirty hands contexts, a Machiavellian ruler must oppress a foreign enemy or a segment of his own constituents in service of the greater good of his nation. A Machiavellian ruler often acts paternalistically toward his constituents, especially in the early stages of his rule when the people lack the civic *virtù* required for full political participation. A Machiavellian ruler also aims at the transformation and empowerment of his constituents, either as the prelude to the transition from a principality to a republic or the transition from the early to mature stages of a republic. As always, nurturing the civic *virtù* of constituents is critical to the advancement of national interests. When interpreters focus too heavily on the use of power-over as oppression or even define Machiavellian power in those terms they generate much confusion as to the Florentine's normative message.

In sum, statesmen who risk but do not lose their souls acknowledge several guidelines: they must often privilege their partialist duties to advance the interests of their constituents over their obligations to support the general interests of humanity; they must sometimes choose to promote the common good of their constituents at the cost of infringing upon the interests of individuals who are also constituents; and they should not advantage members of their own family or their friends at the expense of other constituents. But such guidelines do not soften the burden of discharging the duties of statesmen; instead, they underscore the inevitability of dirtying one's hands and straining one's soul while holding high political office. In this manner, statesmen take the burden of evil upon themselves to secure the common good for constituents.

Defending thoroughly my interpretation of Machiavelli would also go well beyond the contours of this work. However, I have done so in detail elsewhere.[6]

Given the numerous plausible interpretations of his work, Machiavelli should be taken to be *the* classical philosopher of power. Not because the popular interpretation of *The Prince* is definitive, but because when filtered through centuries of interpretive scholarship, we can reasonably view Machiavelli as having exemplified, both through his writing style and the content of his works, virtually every nuance of power considered important by contemporary thinkers: the three major ways power-over can be exercised (oppressively, paternalistically, transformatively); the development of power-to in countless dimensions; the uses that power-to can be put in service of power-over; the relationship between power-over and normative validity; and the possibilities for reversals of extant power relations. Perhaps paraphrasing what Alfred North Whitehead said about the relation between the European philosophical tradition and Plato is the best way to conclude this section: "The safest general characterization of the Western philosophical tradition on the nature of power is that it consists of a series of footnotes to Machiavelli."

Perhaps the most imaginative footnotes on Machiavellian power were compiled in the nineteenth century by Friedrich Nietzsche, who insisted that "the world is the will to power and nothing else" (BGE 36).

IV

Friedrich Nietzsche (1844–1900)

The Will to Power

The quality of the will to power is, precisely, growth. Achievement is its cancellation. To be, the will to power must increase with each fulfillment, making the fulfillment only a step to a further one. The vaster the power gained, the vaster the appetite for more.

—Ursula K. Le Guin

Is it possible that the quest for more power is the fundamental drive of human existence? Is it possible that accumulating power is not merely the obsession of a few, overly ambitious strivers psychologically compensating for their deep-seated feelings of inadequacy, but is, instead, the subconscious motivation of all human action? If so, would this suggest that Thrasymachus lodged a telling point after all: the struggle for power is at the core of all human conventions, including our renderings of justice, morality, political association, and conclusions that come to be taken as established truths?

Friedrich Nietzsche considered all such questions and argued that power relations are the engine of social life. Nietzsche places personal power and its transformative effects at the forefront of his analysis. As a result, he famously invoked the will to power as a cornerstone of his perfectionist philosophy. But unraveling precisely what Nietzsche meant by "the will to power" and understanding exactly the implications of embracing that slogan have been ongoing subjects of scholarly debate.

In general, the bulk of scholars agree on the broad contours of the notion: the will to power, taken as the fundamental drive of all living things, is the impulse to dominate one's environment and extend one's influence. In human beings, the will to power sometimes manifests itself as brute force, but more frequently requires creativity, boldness, and innovation.

Accordingly, domination over others is not the essence of the will to power, although the aspiration for such control could be a first-order desire that animates the will to power. More essentially, the will to power connotes a process, which has growth, expansion, and accumulation at its core. The will to power can neither seek nor achieve final serenity or a fixed state of affairs. Beyond these broad strokes, scholarly controversy reigns.

The Will to Power

Nietzsche argues that growth, expansion, and accumulation are the core functions of human life, and the avidity with which we pursue those activities that define and develop our power is a paramount measure of our worth. For Nietzsche, a shorter life that exudes a noble will to power is far more valuable than a longer life that aims only at self-preservation. Thus, he replaces the will to live, as defined by the zeal for self-preservation, with the will to grow, expand, and accumulate (Z II, "On Self-Overcoming"; WP 1067).

But what, exactly, is the will to power? The literature contains numerous interpretations.[1] Assessing the respective merits of each version is beyond the scope of this work. Instead, I will describe my preferred view. At times, Nietzsche suggests that the will to power is not only the fundamental but the *only* drive of life. He expresses this view most forcefully in his *Nachlass*: "*This world is the will to power—and nothing besides!* And you yourselves are also this will to power—and nothing besides!" (WP 1067; see also, Z I, "On the Thousand and One Goals"; Z II, "On Self-Overcoming"; Z II, "On Redemption"; BGE 13, 36, 259; GS 349; GM II 12). As such, one might be tempted to conclude that for Nietzsche human beings can strive only for power; that power is the sole motivating force in the world; and power is thus the only goal that can be and is desired. On this reading, Nietzsche would open himself to the charge that he mistakenly reduces the complexity of human psychology and life to only one overly broad concept and that concept thereby lacks determinate meaning. To translate all human action into one grand motivation is misguided on its face. Is it not plausible to believe that human beings are sometimes motivated by impulses other than the desire to grow and extend their influence? Must other possible motivations such as the pursuit of pleasure or happiness or intimacy be reducible always to an extension of power? The problem with this common but unpersuasive rendering of Nietzsche's view is that by making the will to power encompass virtually everything, the will to power means almost nothing.

A more convincing interpretation is that the will to power is not the only drive or motivating force animating human life. Instead, the will to power is (1) a second-order drive to have and fulfill first-order desires and (2) to confront resistance and (3) to overcome resistance in fulfilling first-order desires. When resistance is overcome and a first-order desire is fulfilled, the will to power is initially satisfied but soon frustrated because it lacks a first-order desire and resistance to its fulfillment. Thus, the will to power requires ongoing first-order desires and resistance to their fulfillment. These first-order desires—for example, to compete in sports, master a musical instrument, gain knowledge, attain social status, drink in order to quench thirst, eat in order to relieve hunger, and the like—do not *arise* from the will to power. That is, the will to power itself does not determine *which* particular first-order desires we will pursue. Drives and impulses other than the will to power must provide the first-order desires that animate the will to power's activity. Thus, the will to power cannot be the only drive or impulse embodied by human beings (TI "What I Owe to the Ancients," 3; GM III 18; HAH I 142; EH, "Why I am a Destiny," 4). The desire for power alone cannot by itself provide the necessary determinate first-order desires. Our first-order desires, then, are critical in that they are the specific expressions and aims that animate the will to power's general need to grow, expand, and accumulate.[2]

Understood in this fashion, Nietzsche is committed to a thin essentialism, which given his views on perspectivism (roughly, that our worldviews and value claims are interpretations flowing from particular, partial vantage points, none of which are ultimately authoritative) and the world of Becoming (a world of ongoing change), he cannot hold dogmatically. That is, the wide variety of first-order desires embodied and pursued by different human beings prevents Nietzsche's will to power from fossilizing into a thick, universal essentialism that would rest uneasily with his general epistemological and antimetaphysical views. Moreover, even the thin essentialism suggested by the will to power as a general second-order desire cannot be interpreted as a fixed, metaphysical fact. Instead, the will to power is Nietzsche's perspectival interpretation and thereby profoundly presupposes certain psychological and normative values. Accordingly, the will to power is Nietzsche's best interpretation of human motivation and activity at the time he wrote, but cannot be consistently taken as a timeless discovery immune from revision.

Nietzsche argues that the will to power is not fulfilled unless it confronts struggle, resistance, and opposition (GM I 13; GS 363). Pursuing power, in the sense of increasing influence and strength, requires intentionally and actually finding obstacles to overcome. Indeed, the will to power is a will to the precise activity of ongoing struggle with and overcoming obstacles. Because suffering and pain attend the experience of such struggle, a robust will to power must desire suffering (BGE 225, 228). The resulting paradox is that the fulfillment of the will to power—the overcoming of resistance—results in dissatisfaction as the struggle has (temporarily) concluded. The will to power requires obstacles to the satisfaction of its specific first-order desires because beyond specific desires, the will to power has a more fundamental desire to struggle with and overcome obstacles. In sum, the will to power deeply desires resistance to the satisfaction of its own specific first-order desires.

Accordingly, the will to power implies the impossibility of final serenity. The satisfaction of one specific, first-order desire brings both fulfillment, a feeling of increased strength and influence, and dissatisfaction, as resistance has been overcome and is no longer present. Only endless striving and continual conquests fuel a robust will to power. Nietzsche, then, embraces the criterion of power: exertion, struggle, and suffering are at the core of overcoming obstacles; and human beings experience and truly feel their power only by energetically engaging in this process. Understood as a desire to desire, the will to power cannot be permanently satisfied; its essential nature is relentless activity. In essence, the will to power reflects an internal world of Becoming embodied by human beings. The process—the striving to confront and overcome resistance in service of fulfilling first-order desires—constitutes and strengthens the will to power. As a microcosm of the world of Becoming, the will to power can never find a final resting point or realize permanent fulfillment; ongoing activity defines its nature. If human beings could fulfill all first-order desires and could not generate new ones, then the will to power would wither away. For Nietzsche, final fulfillment is antithetical to human life because insatiability as embodied by the will to power constitutes our fundamental instinct (GS 310; WP 125, 689, 1067).

But what is the point of the endless striving that defines the will to power? Do human beings grow, accumulate, and expand only for the sake of doing so? Can progress be made in ways that parry the objection that Nietzsche's celebration of ongoing activity reflects yet another depressing invocation of Sisyphus's pointless, eternal journey?

Understood as a second-order desire to have ongoing first-order desires and overcome resistances and obstacles in fulfilling them, the will to power loses some of its initial linguistic panache. At first blush, the expression "will to power" connotes a relentless drive to dominate other people and control one's environment. We imagine the world in terms of Hobbes's state of nature: a brutal, inevitable zero-sum contest—*bellum omnium contra omnes* ("a war of all against all"). Some of Nietzsche's more hyperbolic pronouncements support such an interpretation. But a closer reading suggests that the core meaning of the will to power is personal strength and development, a type of self-transcendence (in contrast to self-realization) that involves self-mastery and self-overcoming (Z I, "On the Thousand and One Goals"; Z II, "On Self-Overcoming"; D 348). This understanding permits us to describe why and how Nietzsche's will to power is not merely endless, pointless striving. Exercising a robust will to power should result in discernible progress. We are not merely covering the same gloomy path in the same dreary way continually.

As such, Nietzsche's underlying invocation is power-to, not power over others. The first wall of resistance confronted by the will to power is internal: we must master the dwarf within us that seeks comfort, a life of indolence, the accumulation of pleasures obtained passively, and that is inclined toward seeking external validation through conformity with the dominant ideas. Those willing and able to assume the Nietzschean project must, then, assert power over their own tendencies to underachieve, defined as failing to maximize their higher capabilities. Doing so is the first step toward strengthening the will to power by increasing our capabilities, actualizing our higher potentials, and risking confrontation with ever-increasing challenges.

This is not to say that Nietzsche's will to power precludes domination and oppression. Much depends on one's first-order desires which do not arise from the will to power itself. Seeking to increase one's power-to might well include maximizing one's power over others through oppression. Although I am firmly convinced that oppression betrays an unworthy underlying psychology that conflicts with Nietzsche's highest value of *amor fati* (love of fate and of life), on my view his notion of the will to power does not of itself dictate the first-order desires that animate human action.

Perfectionism

Nietzsche locates personal progress in terms of self-overcoming and self-development. His is a perfectionist ideal. Under philosophical doctrines categorized as "perfectionism," nurturing and refining the properties constitutive of human nature define the good life. Human beings should strive to maximize their higher potentials. But perfectionism need not and should not presuppose that *attaining* perfection in this regard is possible. Thus, Nietzsche is not a perfectionist in the sense that he believes that human nature is perfectible or that the majority of human beings will maximize their higher potentials or that there is one final goal to which all human beings should aspire, or even that human beings can attain a final goal or constitute a finished product; but he is a perfectionist in a more modest sense.

Nietzsche's perfectionism is individualistic and aristocratic. As such, he does not intend that his normative message be embraced by everyone. In fact, he speaks only to the few who have the potential to understand fully the tragic nature of life yet affirm life in all its dimensions.

The crucial ingredients that define higher human beings, for Nietzsche, are the capability of enduring great suffering and turning it to practical advantage; the impulse to exert high energy and enthusiasm into projects requiring uncommon creativity; and full participation in the ongoing process of personal construction, deconstruction, reimagination, and re-creation. For the greatest among us, our paramount artistic project is crafting a grand self.

The ongoing process of construction, deconstruction, reimagination, and re-creation marks the progress of those brandishing a robust will to power. To prepare to even approximate a higher human type, we must pass through "three metamorphoses" of discipline, defiance, and creation. The spirit, like a camel, flees into the desert to bear enormous burdens (the process of social construction); the spirit, like a lion, must transform itself into a master, a conqueror who releases its own freedom by destroying traditional prohibitions (the process of deconstruction of and liberation from the past); but the lion cannot create new values, so the spirit must transform itself into a child, whose playful innocence, ability to forget, and capability for creative games signals the spirit's willing its own will (the processes of reimagination and re-creation) (Z I, "On the Three Metamorphoses"). This describes the full process of Nietzschean becoming—recurrent personal construction, deconstruction, reimagination, and re-creation—the virtues of the grand striver who embodies a staunch will to power.

But no project, however successful, can complete the self once and forever. Our lives, instructs Nietzsche, are processes that end only with death or from that moment when we lose the basic human capabilities required for self-making. Until then, we should view ourselves as elegant artists whose greatest creations are the selves we continue to refine. Thus, growth, expansion, and accumulation—the increased power we realize as the will to power engages us with life—animate Nietzsche's perfectionist ideal. Unlike Sisyphus, who was condemned to endure a tedious, everlasting task, human beings fueled by the will to power can realize increased strength, process values, and undeniable progress in their quest toward self-perfection.

Thus, the will to power underscores Nietzsche's appreciation of personal construction, deconstruction, reimagination, and re-creation. He is clear that "all great things bring about their own destruction through an act of self-overcoming; thus the law of life will have it, the law of the necessity of 'self-overcoming' in the nature of life" (GM III 27; see also Z I,"On the Way of the Creator"; Z II, "Upon the Blessed Isle"; Z III, On Old and New Tablets").

Unsurprisingly, not all manifestations of the will to power have equal value for Nietzsche. Life-affirming power flows from psychological abundance. Having forged a unity out of multiple, often conflicting, drives, the healthy will to power has the clear direction of self-overcoming. Moderation arises from joy in restraint, it transforms suffering and hardship into creative opportunities, it sublimates and spiritualizes cruel impulses into cultural advantages, and it finds joy in confronting the ambiguity of the world of Becoming.

The robustness of various wills to power can be evaluated based on the significance of the obstacles they are willing to confront and overcome, and the suffering they are willing to endure in the process. The stronger the will to power a person embodies, the greater resistance he or she is able to overcome. First-order desires can also be evaluated on a host of dimensions, including the role they play in maximally affirming life ("*amor fati*"), the opportunities they offer to exhibit creativity, the resistance they may encounter, and the ways they help craft a worthy self.

Nietzsche extols overcoming resistance and obstacles because he privileges power that transcends or at least undermines current contexts. His celebration of the three metamorphoses implies that the most capable individuals—those who are most powerful—aspire to go beyond received opinion, dominant ideas, and the social understandings in place. Thus, they must expect and, indeed, their robust wills to power demand strong opposition that they must overcome.

But from a non-Nietzschean perspective resistance as such is not necessary to increase power if we are content to reach accommodations with our present environment. That is, a person's power might well increase if resistance to his or her goals is minimized if that power aims at growing within its present context. Here context-preservation or gaining the capability to affect outcomes within the received order assumes pride of place. This is decidedly not a Nietzschean ideal, but it does reflect the counsel of a long line of classical thinkers who concluded that accepting and conforming to extant social reality was a paramount ingredient for attaining a good human life. In contrast, Nietzsche prizes the increased strength of the will to power itself as it confronts and masters resistance. He places little or no value on increasing one's power to attain ends or affect outcomes by working within and adapting to dominant social practices and institutions. As always, increasing the strength of the will to power itself is paramount.

Happiness and the Last Man

Nietzsche reserves special contempt for that "most despicable" human type he calls the "last man." The last man shrivels before the thought that the cosmos lacks inherent value and meaning. In their search for security, contentment, and minimal exertion last men lead shallow lives of timid conformity and superficial happiness. They take solace in a narrow egalitarianism that severs them from the highest human possibilities: intense love, grand creation, deep longing, passionate exertion, and adventure in pursuit of excellence.

> "We have invented happiness," say the last men, and they blink. They have left the regions where it was hard to live, for one needs warmth. One still loves one's neighbor and rubs against him, for one needs warmth. Becoming sick and harboring suspicion are sinful to them: one proceeds carefully. A fool, whoever still stumbles over stones or human beings! A little poison now and then: that makes for agreeable dreams. And much poison in the end, for an agreeable death. One still works, for work is a form of entertainment. But one is careful lest the entertainment be too harrowing. One no longer becomes poor or rich: both require too much exertion. Who still wants to rule? Who obey? Both require too much exertion . . . everybody wants the same, everybody is the same. . . . " We have invented happiness," say the last men, and they blink. (Z I, "Zarathustra's Prologue," 5)

The highest ambitions of last men are comfort and security. They are the extreme case of the herd mentality: habit, custom, indolence, self-preservation, and muted will to power prevail. Last men embody none of the inner tensions and conflicts that spur transformative action: they take no risks, lack convictions, avoid experimentation, and seek only bland survival. They invent "happiness" as the brutish accumulation of pleasure and avoidance of suffering. They "blink" to hide themselves from reality. They ingest "poison" now and then in the form of religious indoctrination focused on a supposedly blissful afterlife. Last men lack the vigor and exalted will to power that can view this world as it is, yet maximally affirm it.

Like cockroaches after a nuclear explosion, last men live the longest. Nietzsche understands that higher human types are more fragile, more likely to squander their abundant passions in acts of self-overcoming than last men, who are concerned narrowly with personal and species survival. Expanding one's influence and discharging one's strength often jeopardize self-preservation. For Nietzsche, the quality, intensity, and authenticity of a life are higher values than its duration.

We must be clear: the last man has a will to power. But his first-order desires are unworthy as they aspire to nothing more than complacency, conformity, feeble exertions, and bland happiness. His will to power cannot overcome strong resistance and therefore pursues undemanding goals. Lacking strength, ambition, and self-mastery, the last man barely grows, expands, and accumulates. Put colloquially: the last man is soft, both mentally and physically. Last men engage only in trivial pursuits. Because they risk little their personal growth is minimal.

Understanding the relationship of the will to power to happiness is crucial. In the literature, happiness is portrayed in different ways, the more predominant of which are a maximum satisfaction of desires; the accumulation of a great balance of pleasures over pains; or the attainment of a particular internal condition such as serenity. For Nietzsche, all such renderings fail to connect happiness to value and are thereby flawed (Z, "Zarathustra's Prologue," 3; Z IV, "On the Higher Man"; Z III, "On Virtue that Makes Small," 2; AC 1; D 60). Satisfying our first-order desires engenders no honor where our desires themselves are unworthy or grounded in trivial pursuits or where they arise from delusions and are thus unconnected to reality.[3] The satisfaction of such desires contributes virtually nothing to self-transcendence and to the ongoing project of crafting a worthy self. Likewise, the pursuit of pleasure can take place in contexts, such as those enjoyed by the last man, that facilitate only conformity, complacency, and personal weakness. In that vein, Nietzsche derides British utilitarianism: "Man does not strive for pleasure; only the Englishman does" (TI, "Maxims and Arrows," 12). For Nietzsche, pleasure is, at best, an accompaniment to the attainment of our ends; it is not itself a proper goal. Finally, attaining fixed, inner peace denies basic human nature, which Nietzsche takes to be based on the eternal striving of the will to power and the ongoing rhythms of the three metamorphoses. At bottom, human beings embody conflicting impulses and multiple drives that resist final serenity and fixed contentment.

Nietzsche does not deny that those who satisfy effete desires or pursue pleasure or yearn for inner peace can attain their versions of happiness—for example, he concedes that the last man can be happy—but he refuses to conclude that achieving these types of happiness is valuable.

Nietzsche offers an alternative view of *worthwhile* happiness—happiness connected to value:

> What is good? Everything that heightens the feeling of power in man, the will to power, power itself. What is bad? Everything that is born of weakness. What is happiness? The feeling that power is growing, that resistance is overcome. Not contentedness but more power: not peace but war; not [moral] virtue but fitness. (AC 2)

The predominant notions of happiness are mistaken in that they aspire to eliminate or minimize resistance and suffering, both of which are required for increased power and strength, which are in turn required for higher human beings to make progress toward the perfectionist ideal (AC 2; BGE 212, 228; GM III 17; WP 155). As noted previously, the will to power does not and cannot will the overcoming of all resistance or the attainment of a fixed, final serenity. An enduring contentment in which nothing remains to be desired would, at best, generate suffocating boredom and, at worst, prefigure the last gasps of the will to power. For Nietzsche, the ongoing desire to engage in challenging activity defines a robust will to power. The difficulty of satisfying a first-order desire adds to its value. Accordingly, overcoming grave obstacles and defeating stiff resistances are critical to "the feeling that power is growing." More power, greater proficiency, and accelerated self-revision are the hallmarks of Nietzschean happiness. As such, worthwhile happiness is not the attainment of a particular state or enduring condition; instead, it is experienced and deepened in the exercise of the will to power. Thus, suffering greatly in the course of confronting and overcoming major obstacles and resistances is critical to worthwhile happiness. Nietzschean happiness is not a particular state or condition to be achieved, but an ongoing activity distinguished by increased power that is accompanied by the feeling that power is increasing. In this manner, the feelings of happiness are connected to value because they arise from the continual activity of a salutary will to power.

Value and Individualism

The measure of value is power, understood as expressing and transforming ourselves, extending our influence, dominating our environment, and progressing toward the perfectionist ideal. In contrast, conscious subjective states such as pleasure, contentment, internal peace, and the like are not valuable as such. At best, they may accompany or follow an increase in power, which remains the genuine value. Power, then, is the linchpin of Nietzsche's project to transvalue or reevaluate prevalent notions of value (GM III 27; WP 69n39, 391, 674).

> A happiness which man has not hitherto known—a God's happiness, full of power and love, full of tears and laughter, a happiness which, like the sun in the evening, continually gives of its inexhaustible riches and empties into the sea—and like the sun, too, feels itself richest when even the poorest fisherman rows with golden oars! This divine feeling might then be called—humanity! (GS 337)

In contrast to the last man and others who timidly pursue pleasure and happiness wherever and however they may be found, Nietzsche offers a sketch of the process that higher human types might undergo and a host of general attributes they might embody:

1. *Rejoicing in Contingency and Ambiguity*: the ability to marginalize but not eliminate negative and destructive impulses within oneself, and to transfigure them into joyous affirmation of all aspects of life; to understand and celebrate the radical contingency, finitude, and fragility of ourselves, our institutions and the cosmos itself; to regard life itself as fully and merely natural, as embodying no inherent or transcendent meaning and value;

2. *Nurturing a Pure Spirit and Appreciation of Process*: to harbor little or no resentment toward others or toward the human condition; to confront the world in immediacy and with a sense of vital connection; to refuse to avert our gaze from a tragic worldview and, instead, to find value not in eventual happiness, as conceived by academic philosophers, but in the activities and processes themselves;

3. *Pursuing the Impossible Dream of Perfection*: to refuse to sup-
plicate oneself before great people of the past but, instead,
to accept their implicit challenge to go beyond them; to give
style to our character by transforming our conflicting internal passions into a disciplined yet dynamic unity; to facilitate high culture by sustaining a favorable environment for
the rise of great individuals; to strive for excellence through
self-overcoming that honors the recurrent flux of the cosmos
by refusing to accept a "finished" self as constitutive of personal identity; and to recognize the Sisyphus-like dimension
to human existence: release from the tasks described is found
only in death. Given the human condition, high energy is
more important than a final, fixed goal. The mantra of "challenge, struggle, overcoming, and growth," animating and
transfiguring perpetual internal conflict, replaces prayers for
redemption to supernatural powers. Part of our life struggle
is to confront and overcome the last man within each of us,
to hold our internal "dwarf" at bay.

Philippa Foot captures well Nietzsche's contrast between the last man
and higher human types:

And he saw as decadent the type of [last man] encouraged
by Christian teaching, describing him as an accommodating,
industrious, gregarious individual who was mediocre and dull.
Against this portrait he set that of a stronger "higher" type of
individual, bold, independent, and ready to say "yes" to life.
Such a man would not be much concerned about suffering,
whether his own or that of others. Among his equals he would
behave with restraint; to the weak he might be dangerous, but
if he harmed them it would be rather from disregard than from
malice. The weak man, however, is afraid of suffering for himself
and preoccupied with the misfortunes of others. He tries to build
a safe life which shall not require too much exertion. . . . He
preaches the morality of compassion, though filled with secret
ill will toward others.[4]

Clearly, Nietzsche's new image of human beings is not projected for
or achievable by all. It is an explicitly aristocratic ideal that is pitched only
to the few capable of approximating it. Greatness and genius are fragile and

vulnerable: they bring about their own destruction but arise stronger than ever. In the end, however, the only way to evaluate Nietzsche's new image of human beings is to live it (UM, "Schopenhauer as Educator," 8). In the end, the reward for Nietzsche's most successful grand strivers and glorious creators is a touch of immortality: "To create things on which time tests its teeth in vain; in form, in *substance,* to strive for a little immortality—I have never yet been modest enough to demand less of myself" (TI, "Skirmishes of an Untimely Man," 51).

Power in Context

Nietzsche's specific genealogical account invokes the images of master and slave moralities. The master morality defines "good" in terms of men's character, not their actions. Under this view, "good" equates to worldly success: achieving one's goals of conquest, fame, wealth, and adventure; and embodying pride, strength, passion, and guiltless joy. Nietzsche relishes the master morality's limit-breaking activities and robust nobility. Moreover, the master morality prefigures some of Nietzsche's broad themes: the need to transcend present contexts and create values out of the abundance of one's life and strengths; the desire to creatively use passion; the joyful affirmation of this world; the manifestation of self-possession; the lack of repressed hostility; and the production and honoring of higher human types.

The master morality, which for Nietzsche symbolizes the Greeks of the Homeric age, did not perceive itself as unconditional or universal. This morality did not prescribe how others (nonmasters) should conduct their lives, and understood explicitly that its evaluations pertained only to a certain type of human being. In that vein, masters sought friends and adversaries only from members of their own rank. Nietzsche approves of recognizing the rank order of human types and of applying different evaluations appropriate to the various types of human beings.

The master morality was dominant and ruled over slaves. These slaves, however, developed their own version of morality. Slave morality reflected and sustained what was beneficial for the masses or herd of human beings. The slave morality's notion of "good" applied to the actions and intentions of human beings, instead of their dispositions and characters. Because the herd is inherently mediocre its values celebrate sympathy, kindness, and general benevolence: virtues that serve the weak and aspire to widespread equality. The values of masters—such as power, self-assertion, and world success—are retranslated in slave morality as vices. While the masters were essentially indifferent to slaves, viewing them as different human types, slaves bear *ressentiment*—a sense of hostility directed at that which one identifies as the cause of one's frustration—toward the masters. In effect, the slaves subconsciously blame the masters for the frustration that overwhelms them.

Prior to the slave revolt in morality, which led to the end of the domination of master morality, the "bad conscience" emerged. When human beings become enthralled with society, civilization, and peace, their instincts are not discharged externally, but are instead internalized. This process culminates in self-hate and self-destruction (GM II, 16, 17–19). The bad conscience, although at first blush the facilitator of repression and internal turmoil, can be used creatively by the excellent few to control, sublimate, and integrate their multiple drives.

In contrast to masters who act on their emotions and then forget their past grievances against others, slaves repress their hostile feelings because of their fears, which stem from their relative powerlessness. For Nietzsche, forgetting exhibits strength because it opens the way to self-overcoming and re-creation (GM II, 1). *Ressentiment* is bottled-up hatred, bitterness, and aggression caused by repressing one's hostile feelings. Although masters are the source of the slaves' hostile feelings, slaves are afraid to confront their superiors. Accordingly, the slaves' intense humiliation and hostility are internalized. These hostile feelings, however, are eventually expressed in cunning fashion: they produce the slave morality whose cleverest trick is the revaluation of master morality.

> The slave revolt in morality begins when *ressentiment* itself becomes creative and gives birth to values: the *ressentiment* of natures that are denied the true reaction, that of deeds, and compensate themselves with an imaginary revenge. While every noble morality develops from a triumphant affirmation of itself, slave morality from the outset says No to . . . what is "different" . . . and *this* No is its creative deed. This inversion of the value-positing eye—this need to direct one's view outward instead of back to oneself—is of the essence of *ressentiment*. (GM I, 10)

Accordingly, the pursuit of sex, power, overt aggression, and conquest become refashioned as immoralities, while chastity, humility, obedience, and meekness become the cornerstones of "morality." Slave morality also extols the unconditionality and universality of its own perspective and attempts to undermine the character advantages and superiority of masters by labeling them "evil." These strategies are indispensable to the success of the slave revolt: unless slaves could universalize their values their leveling efforts would be unsuccessful and slaves would still be vulnerable to the greater powers of masters.

Slave morality, then, is fundamentally reactive and fueled by fear and hostility. To solidify its powers of revaluation, slave morality appealed to a transcendent world ruled by a supernatural being. Thus, the triumph of equality, deprecation of this world, and celebration of fixed values in the West were begun by the Jews and refined by Christianity (BGE 195; GM I, 7 and 8).

> Christianity has been the most calamitous kind of arrogance yet. Men, not high and hard enough to have any right to try to form man as artists; men, not strong and farsighted enough to let the foreground law of thousandfold failure and ruin prevail, though it cost them sublime self-conquest; men, not noble enough to see the abysmally different order of rank . . . between man and man—such men have so far held sway over the fate of Europe, with their "equal before God," until finally a smaller, almost ridiculous type, a herd animal . . . has been bred. (BGE 62)

Invoking the imperatives of a supreme being solidified several themes of slave morality: the equality of all humans despite their obvious factual differences; the vision of this world as an inferior copy of a transcendent world; the assurance that a final judgment of all human actions will constitute perfect justice; and the full meaning and consequences of the terms *guilt, personal responsibility and moral autonomy,* and *good and evil.*

A series of dualisms underwrite these themes of slave morality. The herd privileged the soul over the body; reason (carefully circumscribed by religious authority) over the passions; and the transcendent world over this world. In this fashion, according to Nietzsche, the slaves' *ressentiment* culminates in revenge: the revaluation of the masters' judgments. Thus, slaves reduce the importance of robustly living this life, for "the meek will inherit the earth"; they minimize the pursuit of worldly success, for "it is easier for a camel to pass through the eye of a needle than for a rich man to enter heaven"; they elevate pity and sympathy, sentiments permitting herd members to wallow in their weakness, to virtues; and they deny currency to factual human differences in deference to the virtues of modesty, deference, and humility. In this insidious manner, and especially through the connivance of the priestly class and its invocation of a supposedly omnipotent God, people of excellence become, unwittingly, collaborators in undermining the social conditions under which they had flourished.

For Nietzsche, the slave morality, particularly its glorification of pity and sympathy, encourages a life of minimal exertion and avoidance of risk. Nietzsche judges moralities, cultures, and people in part by the way they confront suffering and the tragic dimensions of life. The robust life requires self-mastery through confronting obstacles, overcoming suffering, and affirming tragedies. Greatness and excellence require creative confrontation with suffering and pain: surmounting obstacles is the core of the will to power.

Instead of reveling in the adventure that is life, however, the slave morality aspires to eliminate pain and to nurture limited vulnerability and few demands: the "good" person is merely one who assiduously avoids proscribed actions. Worse, the celebration of pity and sympathy stem from weakness and timidity: "Pity . . . is a weakness, like every losing of oneself through a harmful affect. It increases the amount of suffering in the world. . . . Supposing it was dominant even for a single day, mankind would immediately perish of it" (D 134). The noble human being may well help the unfortunate, but not as expression of pity. Instead, the noble man, who is invariably severe with himself in terms of expectations and the bearing of burdens, acts from his "excess of power" and is proud that "he is not made for pity" (BGE 260).

Nietzsche identifies three dubious metaphysical assumptions about human beings that underwrite slave morality: that human beings embody a free will that permits independent moral choice; that human motives and intentions for action can be discerned and evaluated comparatively; and that human beings are morally equal. These three assumptions lead to further conclusions about the institutions of morality: individuals are responsible for their actions; they deserve to be either rewarded for good actions or punished for evil actions; and the application of moral principles must be universal.

Nietzsche resists the three metaphysical assumptions and the conclusions they generate. First, he denies the notion of free will as a wrongful reification of cause and effect, as mistaking conventional fictions for metaphysical explanations, as positing an underlying substance called "will," which can be free or determined (TI, "The Four Great Errors," 7; BGE 17, 21 and 213; D 148; WP 484). For Nietzsche, just as there are no things-in-themselves, there are no substantial selves. We are merely our passions, past experiences, drives, instincts, and other dispositions, which language seduces us into attributing to the individual subject. Each human being embodies similar basic drives, whose intensity varies from person to person.

Second, Nietzsche questions our ability to discern and evaluate motives and intentions for acting. He is convinced that human intentions are merely signs or symptoms that require further interpretation. Much that lies psychologically beneath conscious intentions and motives is crucial to understanding human action (BGE 32; GS 335; D 119, 129; WP 291, 294, 492).

Third, Nietzsche holds adamantly that values serve particular interests at particular times, that humans have strikingly different interests, and that universalizing moral judgments of the slave mentality under such circumstances itself promotes the interests of the herd. The slave morality takes itself to be more than it is. In its pretenses to unconditionality and universality, the slave morality camouflages how it privileges the interests of the masses and marginalizes the interests of potential noble human beings (BGE 221, 43).

Finally, the three metaphysical assumptions about human beings that support slave morality betray a misunderstanding of the complexity of the world of Becoming. These assumptions posit a dualistic world of good/evil, altruism/egoism, love/hate, and so on, which wrongly denies the interdependences between the posited elements. Oppositional dualisms trouble Nietzsche primarily because they renege on life's complexity. They fail to appreciate the interdependences of our motives and the genealogy of our practices: how morality flows from immorality, selflessness emerges from selfishness, truth blossoms from illusion, and good from evil. For Nietzsche everything valuable once depended on a seemingly opposed value (GS 19, 21, 121; BGE 2, 229; GM I, 8).

Furthermore, Nietzsche resists the conviction that certain actions or beliefs are *inherently* good or bad. Context and perspective are required for evaluation. Thus, human beings endow drives, activities, and beliefs with value according to the group interests that emerge victorious in social power struggles. Human beings have always done this, although the will to objectification has often led them for strategic reasons to present their values as transcendent.

Despite his occasional disclaimers to having preferences as between the two moralities, that Nietzsche prefers master morality to slave morality is clear. In his view, the slave morality embodies numerous deficiencies. First, its origins are unworthy: *ressentiment* of the superiority of nobles and vengeful commitment to reorder values. Second, it embraces suspicious metaphysical assumptions: belief in a supreme being, the fixed duality of good and evil, and the existence of a transcendent world. Third, it produces harmful consequences: it nurtures a pernicious egalitarianism, devalues our world in deference to the world beyond, privileges social conformity, and suffocates human creativity. Fourth, its content is unworthy: it celebrates pity, limits human possibilities, and champions submission to external authority. Finally, it is grounded in dubious second-order beliefs: the advocates of slave morality are steeped in universalism, dogmatism, and absolutism. For Nietzsche, the worst aspect of slave morality is its failure to restrict its convictions and imperatives to members of the herd. By extending its reach to everyone, slave morality contaminates social life and deflates numerous glorious expressions of the will to power.

But, as usual, simple statements such as this one are too crude to capture Nietzsche's full evaluation. Nietzsche accepts slave morality as appropriate for the herd. He is upset only by the slave morality's pretensions to dogmatism and universalism, which deny the rank order among human beings and undermine social conditions necessary for excellence. Thus, it is not the existence or even the substance of slave morality that triggers Nietzsche's concern, only the scope of its application and its metaphysical underpinnings. Moreover, the master morality consists of unrefined, unsublimated passions that too often lead to brutality instead of higher culture. We cannot and should not return to the simple Homeric warrior ethic. Finally, Nietzsche recognizes that the slave morality introduces a cleverness, cunning, and mendacity to human beings that was lacking in the crude master morality (GM I, 6, 10).

Nietzsche's main aim is, as always, the undermining of dogmatism. By showing how social practices emerge from power struggles, he unsettles the conviction that our practices and values are embedded in the rationality of nature. Recognizing the perspectival character of values and practices also promotes our reimagining and re-creating them. In order to remain loyal to his broad themes, Nietzsche cannot claim his genealogical accounts are pure, dispassionate descriptions. His own aristocratic commitments, psychological understandings, and personal interests intrude freely, as they must. As do all explanatory accounts, Nietzsche's presents itself as accurate history while masking its own mythological and psychological origins. This is mainly the result of the limitations of our language and categories of logic. Nietzsche cannot claim that he escapes his context; instead, he nourishes the subversive seeds contained therein. Given his commitments to his broad themes, he cannot claim that his genealogical account is the only available interpretation of the "data" or that it emerges from an impartial vantage point. His account must be self-consciously partial and a product of his own will to power.

A critic may well wonder on what ground Nietzsche can claim superiority for his account given that he offers an admittedly biased genealogy of the origins of dominant morality, an account that he hopes will resuscitate aristocratic fervor.

Nietzsche knows that he cannot undermine dogmatism directly, by meeting it on its own logical grounds and by using its own criteria of acceptable philosophical argument. Those grounds and criteria presuppose dogmatism so any attempt to employ them directly to undermine dogmatism will ultimately reinstate the "necessity" of dogmatism. That is precisely how charges of self-referential paradox (roughly, "your view undermines itself by its own presuppositions") gain their currency. Instead, Nietzsche must chip away at dogmatism indirectly: through self-consciously partial genealogical accounts, by demonstrating dogmatism's unprovable presuppositions, by appealing to different pictures of life, by dancing to a different rhythm.

What Nietzsche does is show the poverty of the fact-value distinction. As corollaries of perspectives and power relationships, values cannot inhabit a logical category separate from facts. If Nietzsche's genealogical account is successful it will not establish a new, fixed understanding of the origins of our dominant values, but will, instead, stimulate the creative interpretive and practical activities of others. Once again, genealogy returns to and substantiates the power of Nietzsche's broad themes.

Still, critics might insist, What about Thrasymachus? He anticipated Nietzsche's position on the relations between value and power, but provided a much different account of the origins of conventional morality. Thrasymachus claimed that our notions of justice were established by the strongest in the society, by those able to exert their will because of their social position and overall power. They set the terms of existence because they had the might to do so and, after time, those terms became codified in concepts of "justice" and "right." Nietzsche advances a different view: "justice" is in the interests of the weakest elements in society, the herd. Here we have two different "genealogies" of morality advanced by two figures who agree broadly on the connections between value and power.

Perhaps, however, Nietzsche and Thrasymachus are less different than first imagined. For Nietzsche, the highest human types are also the most fragile. They are strongest in the sense of physical, mental, and spiritual creativity, but it does not follow that they are more likely than the herd to be preserved. On the contrary, they are more likely to perish in explosive self-annihilations (TI, "Skirmishes in a War with the Age," 44).

So which is truly stronger, the herd or the nobility? The answer must be typically Nietzschean: there is no stronger as such, only a stronger in relation to specified criteria. In regard to creative genius and cultural excellence the noble class is stronger; in regard to numbers and survival instincts the herd is stronger. Moreover, if Nietzsche is correct, the herd supplements its strength by invoking supernatural authority and the promise of eternal happiness—if you toe the herd's line! Thus, it is reasonable to see some convergence between Nietzsche and Thrasymachus: "justice" is in the interests of the strongest. But what Nietzsche and Thrasymachus take to be the criterion of "strongest" differs. From a Nietzschean perspective, Thrasymachus failed to understand how those with social power—at least in the ages of democracy, socialism, communism, and the major religions—have already been deeply infected with herd mentality. Alternately, one can read Thrasymachus as tolling Homeric themes, as recalling a time when leaders set the terms of existence in accord with master morality because they ruled prior to the ages of our mainstream religions and politics. Under either interpretation, Nietzsche and Thrasymachus have much in common. At least, no necessary contradiction exists between their two genealogical accounts of conventional morality.

In that vein, we can invoke another character in a Platonic dialogue, Callicles in the *Gorgias* (480a–522e). Callicles is a tough, aspiring politician—a man of action much like the historical Pericles. He argues that morality is merely a matter of social convention, not the felicitous correspondence of reason to the imperatives of nature. He insists that the truth of nature is that the stronger, physically and mentally, profits, while the weaker suffers. But the weaker, understood collectively, invent morality to constrain the stronger. They invent words and notions such as "dishonorable" and "unjust" to shame the stronger into submission. While nature rewards the more powerful, conventional morality benefits the weaker. Callicles's account precedes Nietzsche's by more than twenty-one centuries. We can assume that Nietzsche was familiar with Plato's work; thus, to conclude that Nietzsche was influenced by the *Gorgias* is reasonable. This conclusion effaces the originality of Nietzsche's account of morality, but also underscores my earlier point regarding the lack of a necessary contradiction between the understandings of Nietzsche and Thrasymachus. In the *Gorgias*, Socrates responds that if weak men band together they are collectively stronger than a few powerful men, making the collectivity the superior force. Accordingly, what we accept as the criterion of the stronger is crucial in these debates.

For my current purposes, the significance of Nietzsche's rendition of the master and slave moralities is its implications for our understanding of power. Nietzsche highlights how power relations are not fixed; how resistance to oppression can arise from subconscious forces and seething resentments; how subordinates can manufacture an omnipotent deity in service of their transformation of values; and how superiors can succumb to false consciousness and serve as unwitting collaborators in their own loss of privilege.

The Power of Slave Morality

Even if Nietzsche's explanation of the rise of the slave morality fails as a historical account, it profoundly illustrates Nietzsche's understanding of power. Nietzsche highlights how the masses were able to reverse their own oppression by luring the nobles into reimagining and re-making their own self-image. The nobles, in effect, became unwitting collaborators in their own disenfranchisement: the former oppressors became the oppressed. Nietzsche does not claim that this transformation arose from the conscious efforts of the masses. He does not suggest that the masses congregated, crafted a strategy, and then slyly executed their plan. Instead, the subconscious *ressentiment* of the masses generated the process through which the nobles endured a reversal of fortune. As such, hitherto repressed hostility leavened by the projections of the masses' needs sparked the transvaluation of values that changed the course of the Western world: subconscious forces were the vanguard of social change. The masses inwardly seethed at their own impotence in the face of the power of nobles and they deeply yearned for a connection to enduring value, a rational and just world, and an ultimate culmination to their lives. The mythology of Judeo-Christian religion allowed the masses to discharge their resentments and fulfill their deepest psychological cravings. But why did the nobles internalize values that undermined their privilege and pride of place? In Nietzsche's account, they succumbed to greater power. For who underwrote the values of the masses? An all-powerful, all-knowing, all-benevolent supreme being, who was too powerful to be overcome and too aware to be deceived. The values of the masses triumphed only because they were presumably enforced by the highest power. By comparison, the earthly prerogatives of the nobles would seem puny and ultimately meaningless.

On Nietzsche's account, once the slave morality is firmly in place human beings must conceive themselves as creations that must serve the purposes and obey the imperatives of their creator, God. The human function or *telos* is understood as compliance with the preordained purpose of the creator. Although for Nietzsche all evaluation is perspectival, the slave morality masks its partiality with a thick coating of presumed objectivity. The nobles accept the universality of the judgments and conclusions of the slave morality because these evaluations presumably flow from an impartial, powerful commander: God. The vantage point of the supreme being trumps all perspectival, merely human interpretations. In this fashion, through the creation of an ideology that is backed by ultimate power and encourages the nobles to perceive and experience themselves in a radically new way, the slave morality oppresses those who were formerly dominant. New values, then, serve as a means of reversing power differentials as that function is obscured by appeals to objectivity and universality.

In effect, Nietzsche's account concludes that the nobles become mystified by false consciousness: they can no longer identify their genuine interests; having been mesmerized by appeals to objectivity, universality, and divine power, they are unaware of the actual process by which they have internalized a new set of values; and the interests and preferences they embody collaborate to deepen their own subjugation. As such, Nietzsche conjures a classic example of oppression through ideological supremacy and socialization that promotes the compliance of subordinate classes. The slave morality secures the acquiescence of the nobles who limit their own choices and actions in deference to the presumably impartial, objective, universal imperatives issued by the supreme being.

Notice that crude, overt, brute force plays no role in this process. Nietzsche parallels Marx in arguing that the most invidious power is that which can conceal its own workings. Under certain circumstances, human beings can promote ideologies that have the effect of seducing other human beings into using their own minds to collude unwittingly in their own subordination. Knowledge is power in several senses, one of which is that when certain doctrines and dogmas become solidified as "truth" the structures and institutions they support may come to be perceived as natural, appropriate, and perhaps even inevitable. The chains of false necessity are most difficult to sever when subordinate classes have internalized the values that function to oppress them. Nietzsche goes beyond Marx in that his account of the slave morality portrays ideology as constitutive of oppression, as a fundamental means of establishing oppressive relations. As we shall see, Marx invoked ideology and false consciousness as methods that deepened and reinforced oppression that was already in place because of the needs of an economic system. In addition, Nietzsche describes the triumph of slave morality as a reversal of power relations between the masses and the nobles. Accordingly, Nietzsche anticipates Gramsci in his conviction that the formation of an ideology that opposes the existing set of dominant relations can be a means of rebellion and an instrument of social change.

Furthermore, Nietzsche follows Machiavelli in emphasizing the connection between exercising power and personal transformation. Like the Florentine, Nietzsche understands acutely that the manner in which human beings embody power and how they use it affect not only events and personal relations in the world but also the agents themselves. In that vein, both Machiavelli and Nietzsche anticipate Foucault in suggesting that power partially constitutes human subjects.

In sum, even if we suspect that he overstates his interpretations and amplifies his evidence, Nietzsche demonstrates that there may well be a sense in which the pursuit of power, which is not automatically oppressive, is at the core of human existence. Furthermore, he provides an illustration of why and how power relations are dynamic and admit of reversals. Even if we contest on historical grounds his saga of the conflict between master and slave moralities, and his uncompromising rejection of everything egalitarian, we should recognize Nietzsche's insights on the fluidity of power relations and the prerequisites for resistance and transformation.

Prior to illustrating the connections among Nietzsche, Marx, and Gramsci regarding power, we will be well served by examining the most unusual take on power relations in the history of philosophy. The Stoics cultivated a version of power-to such that they were able to not only resist oppression, but make it irrelevant to their lives. Stoics dismissed oppression by removing themselves from the power superiors thought they wielded over them. By championing the power of the human will, the Stoics aspired to extinguish the conventional understanding of oppressive power relations.

PART TWO

V

Stoicism

Overcoming Oppression through Attitude

Power resides only where men believe it resides. . . . A shadow on the wall, yet shadows can kill. And ofttimes a very small man can cast a very large shadow.

—George R. R. Martin

Intuitively, many suspect, as did Thrasymachus, that (1) only a few powerful people truly set the terms of social life, that (2) the masses are doomed to be subordinates in oppressive power relations, and that (3) even if reversals of such relations are possible they require the mobilization of considerable resources, the presence of facilitating external conditions, and a significant amount of good fortune. In addition, most philosophers, however much they may disagree about numerous aspects of power, unite in concluding that (4) the effects of power exercised oppressively upon subordinates and superiors are necessarily palpable and transformative.

The Stoics denied all these intuitions with the exception of the first. But even if relatively few people have disproportionate control in crafting the terms of social life, Stoics were convinced that individuals—all of us—have the innate resources to make ourselves invulnerable to external oppression. For Stoics, if the proper dispositions are nurtured, the human will is strong enough to construct a citadel of the self that resists wrongful exercises of power. In this manner, those people taken to be subordinates in oppressive power relations can unilaterally dissolve their chains.

Founded by Zeno of Citium (336–264 BC), Stoicism's most famous early disciples were Cleanthes of Assos (331–232 BC) and Chrysippus of Soli (280–207 BC). The most impressive and influential later Stoic philosophers included Lucius Annaeus Seneca (4 BC–AD 65), Musonius Rufus (30–100), Epictetus (55–135), and Marcus Aurelius (121–180).

Background Views

Stoics were monotheists and adhered to natural law, a universal code of morality. Everything happens as it must happen, according to fate. The world-soul or Zeus or Nature directs everything for the best. Happiness flows from reasonableness, from understanding the natural law, and from judging and acting compatibly with natural law. Although external events are fated, our attitudes toward and judgments about those events are in our control. Unlike Platonists, who believed that our world is a shadowy imitation of a higher reality, Stoics were materialists. Only bodies exist; but time, void, place, and the meanings of utterances subsist (exist as abstractions). Some entities, then, may not exist, but still be something. For Stoics, Platonic Forms or Universals, though, neither exist nor subsist; they are mere imaginings.

Stoics maintain that genuine freedom is realized neither in commanding nor in being commanded. Instead, freedom is grounded in a self-sufficiency that aspires to render the self invulnerable to external events. Such freedom can be won through refashioning the will, carefully distinguishing what is and what is not fully under one's control, and disciplining one's attitudes and judgments. By acquiring the power to seize freedom, Stoics gain power over themselves and ensure that others cannot effectively exercise power over them.

Basic Stoic beliefs included the following: the gods exist and act providentially; the human soul is divine and immortal; the human will can earn freedom; the proper path to the good life is to follow nature; the universe is governed by natural law; the virtuous and the rational are united; the virtuous person is self-sufficient and happy; and moral duty requires human beings to live honorably. Most interesting is the view that human beings are not antecedently free, but the Stoic sage wins freedom by aligning his desires with natural law in accordance with Zeus's overall plan. Fate, then, is a continuous series of causes flowing from that plan and embodied in natural law. Stoics assumed that innate human tendencies—our natural dispositions—should be retained in any adequate rendering of human wisdom. They looked to the tendencies already present in newborn babies as strong evidence of what is innate in us. This approach is now known as the cradle argument: the fundamental drive of all living creatures is self-love, which is reflected in the tendency of babies to desire what supports health and to reject what does not. That which flows from nature and produces consequences in accord with nature is worthy.

> The first duty is to preserve one's self in one's natural condition; the second is to retain those things which are in accordance with nature and to repel those which are not; the third is choice conditioned by duty, once the principle of choice and rejection has been discovered; and the fourth is choice which is constant and in accordance with nature, at which final stage the good, properly so called, emerges and is understood in its true nature.[1]

But in their writings, Stoics conflate two different notions of "natural": what is natural in terms of our biology (what we are naturally inclined to do) and what is natural in terms of what will facilitate our fulfillment (how our natures are best nurtured—what is natural normatively). Unfortunately, the two notions do not always converge. For example, we are not naturally inclined by biology to adopt Stoicism. Learning and practicing that doctrine require proper instruction and the cultivation of appropriate habits. Thus, adopting Stoicism is unnatural from a biological standpoint. But practicing Stoicism is presumably what best fulfills human nature. Thus, adopting Stoicism is natural in the normative sense of that term. From this observation, a critical question emerges: Why are human beings not biologically inclined to embrace the way of life that will best promote their well-being? Why does nature plague human beings with two sets of conflicting desires: our biological inclinations and our normative pursuit of personal well-being?

Part of the answer to such questions is somewhat mysterious. Because Zeus is not omnipotent, this is the best possible world in only a limited sense. Obviously, dangers and difficulties abound: natural disasters, pain and suffering, and human fragility and mortality. The world is ordered and functions only as well as Zeus's powers extend. Thus, the more frequently spoken Stoic bromide is that external events of themselves are neither inherently good nor bad. Our attitudes and judgments about those events, though, are good or bad depending on whether they exercise reason well or poorly. If we judge that an external event is bad—when it is in fact indifferent to our flourishing—then the judgment, not the event, is bad. If we judge that an external event is irrelevant—when it is in fact irrelevant to our flourishing—then the judgment is good. Zeus has done the best he can for everyone given the structures available to him. Human beings are limited in their direct power to affect external events; we are responsible only for consequences flowing from our own judgments, attitudes, choices, and actions. What is outside our control need not and should not adversely influence our values or well-being. By crafting the human good narrowly—to concern only the inner condition of individuals—Stoics finesse the problem of evil.

A Stoic might rely on this doctrine and argue that Zeus was simply unable to align perfectly our biological inclinations with what promotes our genuine well-being. Yet we have within our control possibilities for softening any dissonance between our innate and normative inclinations—namely, our proper use of reason and free will.

The Stoics defined happiness as inner peace. Their recipe for attaining happiness included minimizing desire, controlling our own judgments and attitudes, and acting in accord with natural law. Stoics explained how and why following this recipe makes us happy by analyzing human desire and our relationship to the world. To judge external events as good is as misguided as judging them bad. Such judgments are erroneous because for Stoics all external events are indifferent: only moral virtue is good. Moreover, such judgments cultivate improper emotions.

Stoics took happiness to be freedom from passion and the realization of inner peace. We should be indifferent to joy and grief, and flexible when facing life's changes. Virtue and right attitude are enough for happiness. By living according to nature, elevating reason over the passions, nurturing good habits, freeing ourselves from the desire to change the unalterable, and being indifferent to pleasure and pain, we can achieve the inner peace that defines happiness.

Preferences and Goods

To understand the Stoical life, we must distinguish between three categories of events and things: preferred indifferents, nonpreferred indifferents, and goods.

A *preferred indifferent* is an event or thing that human beings naturally and rationally desire from a biological standpoint; we prefer such events and things to their opposites (nonpreferred indifferents); but neither result—whether we attain a preferred indifferent or its opposite—promotes our goodness and happiness. In short, to prefer certain events and things to their opposites is biologically natural but either normatively neutral or normatively unnatural (if attaining the preferred indifferent thwarts our pursuit of the human good).

A *nonpreferred indifferent* is an event or thing that human beings naturally and rationally do not desire from a biological standpoint; we do not prefer such events and things to their opposites (preferred indifferents); but being beset by nonpreferred indifferents need not set back our goodness and happiness.

The human good is that which is by nature perfect; what is useful is in accord with the good; value is our estimation of the good. In short, following Plato and Socrates, Stoics understand the human good as defined by our inner conditions. Regardless of external events and the balance of preferred and nonpreferred indifferents a person accumulates, that person can attain the healthy, harmonious, virtuous, inner core that defines the human good.

For example, Stoics divided preferred indifferents into three categories: per se (for example, acceptable physical appearance), instrumental (for example, material goods), and both (for example, health). Again, although it is biologically natural and rational to prefer such things to their opposites, both results are irrelevant to human goodness and happiness. Stoics recognize that human beings prefer one scenario, say, a warm lunch with a loved one, over another, the brutal murder of that loved one. They would deny that one scenario is better than the other in terms of the observer's good. They would understand that we would prefer, say, a gourmet Italian dinner to hunger. They would deny that the Italian dinner is better than hunger. Nothing is inherently good or evil other than moral virtue defined in the strict Stoic fashion. Human beings label events good or evil. Eliminate the labels and we remove much needless anxiety and suffering. Stoics can thereby account for our preferences—we are not *antecedently* indifferent to numerous events—but retain their view that outcomes are inherently neutral. By focusing on the inherent neutrality of events, Stoics aspire to mute our reactions to and judgments of them.

The human good, our fulfillment or happiness, depends entirely on virtue. The virtuous person is happy and fulfilled regardless of circumstance and fortune. Thus, the citadel of the self is invulnerable. Once we understand that the good life is fully under our control, regardless of our station and the outrages of others, we are liberated. Our judgments, attitudes, choices, actions, and affective responses are internal to us and under our control. They can be evaluated with the coherent pattern that defines our biographical lives. They are good or bad insofar as they facilitate or impair, respectively, our fulfillment as human beings. So-called external goods—health, material goods, fame, glory, and the like—are in truth neither good nor bad; they are indifferent in that they do not affect our prospects for attaining the human good. Human beings will, of course, prefer good health, material resources, high reputation, and the well-being of family and friends over their opposites. But attaining these preferences is not completely under our control—luck and the responses of others are critical elements to success.

Thus, realizing my preferences is not part of my good, which consists of my character, beliefs, and actions. If I am a teacher, for example, I will want my students to learn and prosper. This motivation should spur me to do everything in my control to nurture those goals. But whether my students learn and prosper is not fully under my control and not, strictly speaking, part of my good. That I do all in my power to nurture those goals is under my control and is part of my good. In sum, pursuing robust health, material well-being, favorable reputation, and the like is appropriate for human beings, but achieving those goals is not truly good for us and failing in our quest is not genuinely bad for us.

Unfortunately, human beings typically assume that attaining external goods is not merely a goal appropriate to pursue, but that realizing that goal is part of our good. Accordingly, we bemoan and mourn ill health, financial loss, diminished reputation, and the like because we wrongly conclude that our good has been set back. From a Stoic perspective, our false judgment makes us unwitting collaborators in needless misery. We also invite and cheer robust health, financial gain, favorable reputation, and the like because we wrongly conclude that our good has been amplified. From a Stoic perspective, this false judgment distorts our vision and distracts us from what truly constitutes our good. Ultimately, our false beliefs generate emotional distress; correct epistemology is the remedy for better living. Stoics advise us to pursue our preferences as long as we do so with the understanding that our success in achieving external goods is not part of our genuine good and our failure to amass external goods is not a genuine setback.

What is crucial, then, from a Stoic perspective is distinguishing things within our control from things beyond our control. Our judgments, attitudes, and evaluations are the only things solely under our control. By controlling these, we can attain right will and virtue. The usual litany of desirables—love, honor, wealth, good health, worldly success, avoiding mal-treatment from others, the well-being of friends and relatives, congenial family life, personal freedom—depend too much on external circumstances beyond our control, including the actions of others. Once we accept the slings, arrows, and seductions of life without rebellion or discontent, we are in control of our lives and happiness is attainable.

Epictetus succinctly and precisely captured the crucial Stoic distinction between those things totally within our control and all else:

> Some things are under our control, while others are not under our
> control. Under our control are conception, choice, desire, aversion,
> and in a word, everything that is our own doing; not under our

control are our body, our property, reputation, office and, in a word, everything that is not our own doing. Furthermore, the things under our control are by nature free, unhindered, and unimpeded; while the things not under our control are weak, servile, subject to hindrance, and not our own . . . if it has to do with some one of the things not under your control, have ready to hand the answer, "It is nothing to me." (EN 1)

Accordingly, for Stoics, increasing our power to affect outcomes requires that we focus on only one type of result: disciplining those matters fully under our control—our judgments, attitudes, beliefs, and evaluations about events. To do so, we must treat both attaining preferred indifferents and incurring nonpreferred indifferents as irrelevant to our good. Stoics also advise us that if we find ourselves as subordinates in oppressive power relations we have the power to soften and even eliminate the lash of wrongful domination. Finally, Stoics would counsel that we must avoid becoming oppressors ourselves. The only appropriate uses of power-over are paternalistic and transformative, uses that facilitate the subordinate's conversion to the Stoic regimen.

Emotions

The Stoics advance a cognitive theory of the emotions. For the Stoics, emotional responses are not merely unreflective instincts or drives; they are judgments. Accordingly, human beings are responsible for their emotions because emotions are voluntary actions. Although our emotional responses are not under our conscious control at every specific instant, they flow from our beliefs and our evaluations of those beliefs. Even when we feel we are carried off by, say, anger or jealously to act against our self-interest, our emotional response follows from cognitive commitments: our rational assent to the truth of certain beliefs and to an evaluation that reacting angrily is appropriate to the situation. As such, our emotions are within our control because our cognitive commitments are within our control.

Human beings trying to actualize their best potentials should eliminate most, if not all, emotional responses. Our emotional responses are rational in a *descriptive* sense: they originate cognitively in our beliefs and judgments. But our emotional responses are not rational in a *normative* sense: they depend on wrong attributions of value to events outside our control; and they mistakenly assume certain events and the realization of external goals are part of the human good. The Stoics insist that what is grounded in false beliefs should not be part of a wise person's life plan. Hence, those aspiring to the best human life should eliminate emotional responses as much as possible. The Stoic condemnation of emotions, then, is grounded on the connection between sound epistemology and the human good. If our strong emotions and feelings originate from correct judgments about value, such reactions are valid. If I react strongly to, say, my accurate realization that I had not responded appropriately to an event that was completely within my control, my strong feelings are warranted. Although the initial strong feelings can serve a corrective function, we should also recognize that persistent self-flagellation and lingering self-recrimination typically serve no healthy purpose.

Physical calamities cannot impair our souls unless we wrongly assent to some beliefs about them. Epistemological errors corrode our judgments, some of which solidify into wrongful emotions. For Stoics, forming judgments involves perception, evaluation, and understanding. Impressions, whether sense perceptions caused by observations or products of reasoning flowing from the mind, imprint themselves on the soul. We turn the impression into a proposition and then we either accept or reject the proposition. For example, we look in a certain direction and gain sense perceptions. We turn the sense perceptions into the proposition that "there is a dog relieving itself against a tree." We then either accept or reject the proposition depending on, in this case, how convinced we are that there truly is a dog relieving itself against a tree. Sometimes the propositions we form may contain a value judgment such as "that a dog is relieving itself against a tree is a good (or bad) event."

The impressions we get, the sense perceptions, are beyond our control. They imprint themselves on us. However, whether we accept or reject the propositions accompanying those impressions is within our control. Even Stoics may fall prey to "first movements"—being overwhelmed by the force of a first impression. If someone suddenly cracks me over the head with a club, I garner immediate impressions of pain. Instantaneously, I form the propositions, "I have been smacked upside the head; my head hurts; and this event is awful, unwarranted, unjust, and, in general, not conducive to my good." (In truth, at least in my case, the propositions would be richly spiced with expletives and embraced with overflowing anger.) I will not, though, at this point have wrongly concluded, from a Stoic perspective, that incurring a physical injury is a bad event. I have succumbed only to a first movement, which is not a judgment but only an immediate reaction.

I have not yet assented to the proposition that the physical injury is bad for me. I still have time to reconsider and affirm Stoic wisdom that only corrosions of my soul are genuinely evil and physical injury is merely a nonpreferred indifferent.

Accordingly, Stoics dismiss my spontaneous reaction to a first movement as essentially involuntary and even natural. For, aside from the Marquis de Sade and his fellow travelers, who enjoys being struck across the head? The proposition I formed consisted of both the sense perception (sensations of pain) forced upon me and the involuntary initial value judgment. But my final assent to or rejection of the value judgment marks me as a Stoic. For Stoics, external events are neither good nor evil. When I assent to a proposition containing in part a value judgment describing an external event, I stumble into epistemological error. In this manner, my emotional response to giving assent—"I am angry at the injustice of this evil assault"—is wrong, based on a mistaken judgment, and fully under my control.[2]

The cognitive and normative connections between beliefs and passions are straightforward: if I believe (1) that an event has occurred or is occurring; (2) that the event is bad or evil; and (3) that responding to it passionately is appropriate; then my emotions will flow. My emotions should cease when any of the three links is no longer accepted. Suppose I believe that Jones had spread lies about me. I also believe that my favorable reputation has been well earned and is part of my good. I further believe that anger is an appropriate response to an undeserved wrong. In all probability, I will become angry. The intensity of my anger will be greatly influenced by how bad I believe the event to be and how appropriate I think an emotional response would be. Over time, as my beliefs cease to be fresh, my anger will typically, although not automatically, subside. (The adage that "revenge is a dish best served cold" disputes what is typical.)

But imagine that I immediately learn that the event never happened: Jones has said nothing about me. My anger will stop, although I will experience residual ill feelings and agitation. If someone asks, "Are you angry at Jones?" my answer must be "No." Or imagine that Jones *has* spread lies about me, but I am an accomplished Stoic. I would prefer that Jones not lie about me, but I believe that the event of Jones spreading lies about me is neither part of my good nor a detriment. I also believe that anger is an inappropriate response to that which is neither good nor bad for me. In all probability, I will not become angry.

From a Stoic vantage point, grief, for example, is "unhealthy, unmanly, unnatural and unnecessary; no one owes it to anyone, least of all to the gods; it accomplishes nothing, interferes with our doing what we should, and does nothing for the departed; it is absurd to care for the dead more than oneself; and in general, it contradicts Stoic values."[3]

Against the Stoics, one might object that the emotions are better viewed as the products of judgments or a complex judgment, not a simple judgment itself. If a loved one dies, I might judge that that event is bad and that grief is an appropriate response to such a bad event. As time passes, I may still judge that the event was bad, but my grief will subside in part because I no longer judge continued grieving to be an appropriate response to a distant event.

Stoics might respond that my assent to or rejection of an impression, which triggers emotions such as anger and grief, reflects the inner disposition of my mind, which is not identical to the inner disposition of your mind. The impression in and of itself is not enough to compel my assent or rejection. Our actions are ours in the sense that they flow from the internal condition of our minds. Yes, the state of our minds is greatly influenced by genetics, socialization, peer pressure, and the like, but those factors do not compel my dispositions to form as they do. Inner agency influences complex fated events and external causes.

As does any position that accepts a strong version of fate, Stoics certainly have a problem with free will. What we take the scope and meaning of "fate" to be is crucial. However, if the distinctions between causation and compulsion, internal and external causes, and simple and complex events bear currency, Stoics may be in no worse position than contemporary advocates of soft determinism. In any event, regardless of the fragility of their theory, Stoics surely believed that human beings were responsible for their actions and merited praise and blame in response to the quality of their deeds. If their theory cannot accommodate that conviction, modern Stoics need only adjust or dispense with their notion of fate. The Stoics' moral programs and normative categories do not depend on accepting their traditional version of fate. The tie-in to fate only solidifies a person's acceptance of everyday events because they are supposedly decreed by Zeus: loyalty to god requires acceptance of external happenings. Fate, then, is invoked to motivate human beings to embrace the inevitable. But this reinforcement is not genuinely required for the Stoic moral regimen.

The Stoic sage is an ideal: infallible, powerful, strong, free, happy, and masterful. Sages will replace desire with selection and fear with disselection: "Selection is the belief that some future thing is a [preferred] indifferent of such a sort that we should reach out for it. Disselection [rejection] is the belief that some future thing is a [nonpreferred] indifferent of such a sort that we should avoid it."[4] The purging of emotion is the complex result of cognitive understanding, spiritual exercises, and the cultivation of proper habits. For Stoics, emotions flow from erroneous judgments and veridical judgments require more than grasping doctrine or poring over texts. A true sage, though, would reach the stage where he is no longer fighting emotional impulses; through proper education and training he would no longer experience wrongful emotions: "Sages are aware of their own virtue and feel joy at it; they can direct their efforts towards maintaining their virtue in the future, and thus exercise volitions; and they can take steps to avoid becoming vicious in the future, which means being cautious."[5]

Stoic Power

At first blush, the Stoics seem poor candidates for the title of philosophers of power. Their lifestyle is designed to minimize wants, strictly define needs, and meticulously discipline inner lives. They neither brandish nor celebrate a will to power. They reject the image of Nietzsche's grand striver; instead, Stoics seek the good life through limiting desires and identifying well-being with careful attention to and control of only those things fully under their control.

But Stoics are probably the best teachers of the relationship between subordination and yearning. Theirs is a negative power in that they are able to not only resist oppression, but make it irrelevant to their lives. As such, a successful Stoic would not *experience* subordination in the way most victims would. More precisely, by refusing to recognize suffering or subordination as an infringement of their good, Stoics remove themselves from the power superiors might think they have over them. Moreover, Stoics do this without falling prey to false consciousness. They would argue that they can identify their genuine interests—defined by their attitudes, judgments, choices, and ensuing actions—and that they cannot truly be harmed by those who inflict suffering, material deprivations, and even death upon them. Stoics also use what they take to be their genuine interests to inform their current desires and long-term preferences. Accordingly, successful Stoics do not embody a conflict among the different senses of interests commonly invoked. To be harmed one must endure a thwarting or setback to one's interests. By defining their genuine interests narrowly, Stoics apparently nurture the power to undermine what the rest of the world would perceive as the power over them possessed by superiors. Finally, Stoics parry the capability of others to control or limit their choices and action. Other people and events such as natural disasters cannot restrict a Stoic's choices or deeds because a genuine Stoic is concerned only with those choices and deeds that are fully under his or her control: one's own attitudes, judgments, and evaluations. Stoic power, then, arises from making the self a citadel against external assault. The invulnerable self neither experiences the actions of presumed superiors (those whom non-Stoics would view as having power over Stoics) as harmful nor does it conclude that its choices or actions have been circumscribed by those actions and events.

To Thrasymachus, Stoics say that whether the ruling class sets forth laws and normative understandings whose content advances the material interests only of the members of that class is irrelevant to a Stoic's personal good (and to the good of the members of the ruling class). To Socrates, Stoics say thanks for setting us on the right course by highlighting the importance of a person's internal condition; the unimportance of material aggrandizement; the adage that "no evil can befall a good person, either living or dead"; and the connection between sound epistemology and moral virtue. But not even Socratic asceticism goes far enough for the Stoics. To Machiavelli, Stoics say the pursuit of enduring glory through military and political success is counterproductive because it wrongly elevates the pursuit of such preferred indifferents to the highest great human good. As a result, that Machiavelli's ideal statesman at best is a highly vulnerable person who must jeopardize his soul and at worst is a practical impossibility does not surprise. To Nietzsche, Stoics say that the grand striver, robustly exercising his will to power, is a person of ongoing dissatisfaction who can never attain the harmonious, healthy internal condition that defines and reflects the human good. For Stoics, Nietzsche's higher human types are overly vulnerable to misfortune and to the vicissitudes of external events over which they lack significant control. To make oneself so dependent on reactions and conditions in the world is to misidentify genuine power, which Stoics locate in self-sufficiency, and, instead, to chase an ersatz version of power relentlessly and futilely.

Even if we reject Stoicism as fanatical or radically ascetic, the moral of this story is clear: the importance subordinates assign to the presumed power over them held by superiors is often crucial to the experience and existence of oppression. The lack of power is often a function of desire: we strive to fulfill our yearnings for apparent goods, and our inability to obtain those goods deepens our sense of powerlessness; when other human beings intercede to stymie our ability to obtain these goods or the social structure will not permit our yearnings to be realized, we interpret our failures as arising from the power that others have over us. By transforming our desires we can detach ourselves from the experience of powerlessness and disaggregate the power that others formerly held over us. Stoics aspire to full independence from external interveners and social structures. As such, they evade numerous vectors of power. They also distance themselves from the ongoing disappointments arising from unfulfilled desires. Accordingly, to the extent that subordinates can reasonably disregard power in the absence of false consciousness, they can negate its effects and presence. Of course, the limitation of this moral is the modifier "reasonably." Most readers will conclude that Stoicism pushes the philosophical envelop well beyond that point. For example, to claim that significant physical or material deprivation (up to and including death) is not really harm strains the imagination. Still, the larger point remains: human beings often have the power to neutralize the authority that others presume to have over them by adjusting their desires and by prioritizing their genuine interests.

Limitations of Stoicism

The broader critique of Stoicism is by now a cliché. While Stoicism can bring consolation to those struggling under harsh conditions, its expectations are too low for general use. The expansive richness and creativity of human experience are sacrificed on the altar of accommodation. Although it does not insist on passivity, Stoicism inclines in that direction.

Can we, should we, be indifferent to poverty, disease, natural disasters, suffering, and evil in the universe? Imagine going home today for lunch. Under the first scenario, you are met by a loved one, engage in a wonderful social interaction (fill in your own details, make them as wonderful as you can), and return to work with maximum fulfillment. Under the second scenario, you discover your loved one has been brutally murdered (fill in your own details, make them as gruesome and upsetting as you can). How can a person be emotionally unaffected by these two scenarios? If someone were indifferent to the horrifying slaying of a loved one, would we not stigmatize that person as psychologically impaired? To be indifferent under such circumstances is to relinquish what we value most.

Stoics would agree that we would prefer the wonderful scenario to the gruesome murder, but insist that the satisfaction of our preferences does not define our good. Why, though, would we prefer one scenario over another? The simplest answer: because we take the preferred scenario to be better or to be good, because we *value* one scenario over another. Stoics have a heavy burden that goes unaddressed: to account for *why* we prefer X over

Y without referring to our values. Some preferences have their genesis in mere personal tastes or whims. Other preferences exist only because a value judgment, a labeling, has occurred. The Stoic bow to common sense, which acknowledges that we do prefer some events over others, is purchased at a stiff price: A spectacularly unpersuasive view of the relationship between preferences and goods. We prefer the loving lunch to the brutal murder because we judge, accurately, that the loving lunch is a good while the brutal murder is monumental evil.

Stoics, though, have a response. They are not *antecedently* indifferent to the two scenarios: Stoics prefer a loving lunch to a brutal murder. However, they are *posteriorily* indifferent to what in fact occurs: once the brutal murder takes place they do not regard it as an evil or even relevant to their good. In that vein, the sage prefers a tasty meal to starvation. But, unlike the non-sage, he is neither pleased after consuming a meal nor is he disappointed if no food is available. Regardless of the outcome of his preferences he feels the same: a sense of indifference because he understands that whether he eats or not is irrelevant to his human good. Only the condition of his soul, his virtue, constitutes his good and that is not influenced by his diet.

But why would the sage prefer a scrumptious dinner to starvation if he did not, in some sense, recognize the value of eating? Does not even the sage, deep down, admit that nourishment is good and starvation is bad? Not exactly. The sage, says the Stoic, is merely following nature. To prefer starvation to nourishment or disease to health or injury to physical well-being is unnatural. But following nature is a Stoic creed. Does that not concede that preferred indifferents, as the natural way, are part of the human good? Invoking the distinction between the *biologically* natural and the *normatively* natural may help. As a matter of fact, as a function of their biology, human beings will prefer some states of affairs, such as health, to their opposites, such as disease. But from the normatively natural perspective the satisfaction of those preferences is irrelevant to the human good. Our well-being as rational, virtuous beings is unaffected by preferred indifferents. Accordingly, we should treat the outcomes of pursuing our preferences with indifference. The only value indifferents have is that of selecting or disselecting them in accord with our biological, or descriptively natural, preferences. Stoics must insist that we have reasons to pursue preferred indifferents but those reasons do not include the fact that preferred indifferents are good things. Stoics would concede that two widely disparate types of value exist: the value of attaining preferred indifferents and the value of attaining virtue. Only the second type of value is linked to human good and is conducive to human fulfillment.

A life of virtue exactly consists in a life in which agents exercise their rationality in the pursuit of indifferents. It is exactly by choosing wisely and avoiding bravely, by selecting temperately and distributing justly, that a life which in some sense is taken up with and given over to indifferents can nevertheless at the same time be a life directed towards the end of virtue.[6]

Although I have spoken only of preferred (for example, health) and nonpreferred (for example, disease) indifferents, a third category of utterly neutral indifferents exists (for example, whether I have an odd or an even number of nostril hairs). Stoics argue that pursuing preferred indifferents too avidly runs risks of conferring too much value upon them, of courting frustration when we fail to attain them, and of unwittingly nurturing strong emotions. But critics will be unsatisfied because the marriage of preferred indifferents to strong effort—which Stoics claim is still permissible—virtually ensures the destruction of genuinely Stoic aspirations. Fervently desiring certain externalities but refusing to be disappointed when we fail to attain them courts a type of schizophrenia. Although Stoics can, technically speaking, strive vigorously to attain preferred indifferents, their doing so jeopardizes their refusal to view these externalities as genuine goods. They seem to be claiming that preferred indifferents are worth choosing and pursuing, but also that whether we succeed in our efforts to obtain them does not matter. If so, then why choose and pursue such externalities? Other than celebrating moral virtue, Stoic theory seems to provide no genuine guidance on what to choose and what to reject.

How, then, are wisdom and virtue connected to things that really do not matter? The outcomes of our strivings for preferred indifferents are irrelevant to our good, say the Stoics. Why, then, are the strivings themselves of any consequence? Is it not better to spend our time and efforts on the cognitive understanding, spiritual exercises, and cultivation of proper habits that lead to the purging of wrongful emotions than to squander our concern on the pursuit of indifferents?

One might argue, as Aristotle did, that a measure of good health and material goods are preconditions of leading the virtuous life or of living at all. To attain the good of virtue one must be alive and capable of undergoing the prescribed Stoic regimen; that requires some concern for health, food, drink, and the like, not just as preferred indifferents but as requirements for the good life; what is a requirement for the good life is at least derivatively or instrumentally good; thus, the reason virtue is connected to exercising rationality in the pursuit of indifferents is that attaining some so-called indifferents is required for virtue to blossom. However, this line of reasoning is not available to Stoics.

Suppose Jane slashes Joe with a finely honed stiletto. Louise, a medical doctor, cares for the wound. According to Stoicism, neither action advances or frustrates Joe's good. Jane inflicts a nonpreferred indifferent, physical injury, upon Joe; Louise confers a preferred indifferent, restoration of health. From the standpoint of the human good, the two actions are equally irrelevant. Circumscribing the human good to only the internal dispositions of the soul toward moral virtue and then defining moral virtue only in terms of distinguishing what is fully under our control from everything else shrinks the moral universe.

Stoics can experience and cultivate genuine emotions, but their proper scope is limited and uninspiring. Feeling joy in awareness of one's own virtue is legitimate because the judgment that underlies the emotion is rational and sound: I have attained virtue; that is the only true good; my internal condition is harmonious; joy is an appropriate response to a good, internal event. However, such joy may be appropriate only for the sage, should such a paradigm exist. The rest of us are imperfect fools and madmen. (Is it appropriate to feel joy when one makes moral progress? Or would joy hinder continued moral growth?) If a person loses her moral virtue, if she backslides, some emotion—caution? wishing for redemption?—might be appropriate because a genuine good is in jeopardy. Still, for a Stoic what is done is done. Maybe regret and remorse are misplaced as they are emotions directed to the past. An emotion that looks to the future with resolve and rehabilitation, though, might well be permitted.

Still, the Stoics were wrong. Grieving, sorrow, and suffering are not vices. Human beings are by nature valuing creatures. We cannot be stonily indifferent and retain our humanity. To value something is to make it an object of concern. We cannot coherently value everything. We partially construct who we are through what we value. If we remain indifferent to the loss of what we value, we call into question the intensity of our commitment, we hedge our bet. Because our evaluations, convictions, and actions define our lives, we cannot be indifferent to our defeats, disappointments, and losses. We stake our being on and experience life most directly through our values. Grief, sorrow, and suffering are appropriate responses to the tragedies of life. The Stoics were correct in thinking that sorrow and suffering are too often exaggerated, that they can impinge on a worthwhile life, that we can obsess inappropriately on our losses. However, to remain indifferent to everything not fully under our control is unwarranted. We should not cry over spilled milk. We should cry over spilled blood.

Outlooks, such as Stoicism, that appeal to fate have trouble accounting for robust action. If I aspire to change the world I am focusing on things outside my control and trying to alter fate. I have judged the status quo deficient and taken steps to change it. If that aspiration and the results attendant to my actions are themselves fated then my judgments about external events—how I evaluated the state of the world prior to my actions—are not under my control. I was fated to a negative view of the world and the motivation to try to change it. Rendering my freedom and control over my own judgments and actions, the pervasive direction of the World-Soul, and vigorous social action compatible is no simple choice.

Even if we eliminate the presence of the World-Soul and natural law, are my judgments and attitudes about events totally within my control? They are probably more in my control than most social and natural conditions in the world. But many influences, my socialization in a broad sense, contribute to my outlook. That my conscious judgments and evaluations arise fully from my freedom is far from obvious.

The presence of natural laws that are both descriptive and prescriptive complicates matters. Following the natural law, which binds all human beings in all places at all times, is reasonable, proper, and enhances prospects for happiness. According to Stoicism, such laws are antecedently external to those things within our control, but we should not be indifferent to them. We should understand and abide by them because they are good. Although outside our control, they provide the ground for our action. If so, then "good" and "evil" are more than labels that human beings wrongly attach to events. Events and actions that violate the prescriptions of natural law are evil as such. To regard such events and actions indifferently would itself not be in accord with natural law. Again, we see that fundamental Stoical doctrines do not coalesce easily.

Nietzsche ridiculed the Stoics' advice to "live according to nature" as either mendacious or self-deceptive. Nature not only fails to send human beings unambiguous messages, nature is utterly indifferent to the human condition. Instead, philosophers look to nature and project their own images and psychological yearnings upon it. They then use the supposed message from nature to justify their own projections in a classically vacuous, circular exercise.

> "According to nature" you want to *live*? O you noble Stoics, what deceptive words these are! Imagine a being like nature, wasteful beyond measure, indifferent beyond measure, without purposes and consideration, without mercy and justice, fertile and desolate

and uncertain at the same time; imagine indifference itself as a power—how *could* you live according to this indifference? Living—is that not precisely wanting to be other than this nature? Is not living—estimating, preferring, being unjust, being limited, wanting to be different? . . . Your pride wants to impose your morality, your ideal, on nature . . . you demand that she be nature "according to the Stoa," and you would like all existence to exist only after your own image—as an immense external glorification and generalization of Stoicism. . . . [Philosophy] always creates the world in its own image; it cannot do otherwise. (BGE 9)

Anticipating Rousseau, Stoics believed that human beings were naturally disposed to virtue and that we stray because of shoddy external socialization and epistemological errors. Yet they also insist that adopting Stoicism requires serious reflection and training. The Stoical life, then, will not develop on its own from our inherent natures. Perhaps we are also naturally inclined toward epistemological errors—succumbing too easily to first movements—or, as an empirical matter, almost all of us are spawned in social contexts uncongenial to Stoic living. In any event, the malleability of appeals to nature remains striking. Most important, even if immunizing our psychology such that we make ourselves invulnerable to external events is possible it can be attained only at an unacceptable cost: by relinquishing our connections to much of what we esteem, value, and love. As our loves and what we value partially constitute who we are and what is best about us, molding ourselves into psychologically invulnerable creatures is less an exercise of wisdom and more a descent into dehumanization.

Stoicism's kernel of insight—do not dwell on misfortune, put suffering behind you, do not become intoxicated with unimportant pursuits or frivolous desires—is obscured by its demand that nothing else matters that much. Consequently, the Stoic doctrine that only states of mind are good or bad leads to a too easy acceptance of social, political, and economic inequalities and wrongs. Dismissing matters in these domains as merely preferred indifferents trivializes human misery caused by poverty and defers too facilely to physical deprivations generated by tyrannies. The notion that human beings can be happy—in the sense of being fulfilled by attaining their human *telos*—while being tortured reduces Stoic doctrine to absurdity. Only if we are being tortured for a higher cause that defines our life's mission—witness the martyr, hero, or saint—can such a view be plausible. Does complying with Stoic doctrine itself constitute such a project? Is a project that teaches us to place value only on our internal states of mind sufficiently noble to fit that bill?

Moreover, Stoicism's view of preferred indifferents calls into question our settled convictions about charitable deeds. Stoicism can be unappealingly insular and egoistic. For example, Epictetus when advising a person who was concerned about his slave's virtue, sputtered: "It is better for your servant to become vicious than for you to become unhappy" (EN 12). After all, the virtue of other people may well be, at most, a preferred indifferent. Whether others are vicious or not should not affect my well-being. As for charitable contributions, the consequences are unclear. On one hand, I might be generous with my material possessions because I view them as indifferents. On the other hand, I might see charitable contributions as irrelevant and possibly a hindrance to the genuine good of the disenfranchised. Perhaps recognizing health, food, and clothing as preferred indifferents would tip the scale in favor of donating to those in material need. Oddly, my willingness to donate or not to donate is motivated by my Stoic conviction that the money or things I donate are not genuine goods. So in either case the phenomenon of charitable contributions is radically altered from contemporary understandings.

We typically consider feeding the hungry, clothing the poor, providing shelter for the homeless, and the like paradigm cases of morally praiseworthy actions. Indeed, such actions are extolled in the sacred texts of religions and endorsed equally by secular humanists. However, under Epictetus's philosophy, philanthropists have performed no significant service for the downtrodden. Donors have only satisfied the yearning for preferred indifferents, while providing no automatic benefit for the goodness of the souls of disenfranchised people. Would it have been better to have slipped starving people a treatise on Stoicism so they might learn that their well-being lies not in food but in proper judgment? Perhaps a Stoic lecture on why the content of their character, not a satisfied belly or a clothed body, is the key to happiness? If time was a factor, maybe a few kernels of Stoic wisdom: no harm can befall a starving, destitute, impoverished person unless he is an unwitting collaborator; the only evil is in misjudgments, not in physical deprivations; the yearning for preferred indifferents, including food, clothing, and shelter, is the root of all evil; difficult circumstances should be viewed as a test of character; the more one has, the more one has to lose; if a circumstance is genuinely unbearable, suicide is always a wise option? Indeed, perhaps our imaginary philanthropists, by providing the basic necessities of survival, have reinforced the yearning of the destitute for preferred indifferents and unwittingly added to their long-term misery. Would it have been better to console them by reading Stoic chapter and verse on the true sources of good and evil as they starved to death?

The Stoics wisely advise us that we are too often unwitting collabora-tors in producing needless suffering because we obsess over an unalterable past and matters that are beyond our control. But their overall prescriptions for the good human life are minimal and uninspiring. Still, Stoicism embod-ies lessons about power: human beings can increase their power by attending to those matters fully (or mostly?) under their control; subordinates have more personal power to soften or reverse oppressive power relations than is commonly believed; human beings aspiring to the good should never be oppressors nor complaint collaborators in their own oppression; and supe-riors should use power over subordinates only in service of empowerment or paternalism.

When most people first think of power relations they imagine two parties, an oppressor and a subordinate. We tend to assume, incorrectly, that wrongful domination is the paradigm exercise of power and that dyadic (two-party) relations are critical to that paradigm. No thinker, other than perhaps Nietzsche, has dissected the dynamic of dyadic relationships of pow-er with greater psychological and philosophical insight than Georg Hegel.

Georg W. F. Hegel (1770–1831)

The Dynamic of Dyadic Relationships of Power

> Someone that you have deprived of everything is no longer in your power.
> He is once again entirely free.
>
> —Aleksandr Solzhenitsyn

Recall that my operational definition of power-over used oppressively is that a superior party oppresses a subordinate party when the superior affects wrongfully and adversely the outcomes and/or interests of the subordinate by controlling or limiting the alternative choices or actions available to the subordinate. This definition, understandably, does not address the transformative effects that the exercise of oppression has upon superiors and subordinates.

Thrasymachus seems to conclude that oppression has the effect of amplifying the material resources of superiors, which they perceive as heightening their good, while further disenfranchising subordinates, who accept the regime as appropriate because they have internalized the normative understandings (for example, of "justice") flowing from the power exercised by superiors. Thrasymachus does not assess the ongoing changes in the internal condition of the agents of power relations.

Because they identify the human good so closely with the internal condition of the human soul, Socrates and the Stoics thoroughly examine how the exercise of power affects the relevant agents. Put simply: subordinates who understand the human good will not be adversely affected by oppression, while superiors will be deluded into thinking that their tyrannical power enhances their good although in fact they are the most impoverished people because their souls are vicious and thereby thoroughly unhealthy.

Machiavelli does not explicitly examine the connection between the internal conditions of agents in power relations, but he contributes to the discussion by leaving clues as to the effects upon statesmen of being required by the duties of their offices to use evil well and dirty their hands in service to their constituents and in pursuit of enduring, deserved glory. In addition, when statesmen are effective in exercising power oppressively, paternalistically, and transformatively, as appropriate, the masses of citizens will benefit and develop civic excellence.

Placing high value on a robust will to power as definitive of human greatness, Nietzsche stresses the role that confronting and overcoming obstacles to the fulfillment of first-order desires plays in enlarging the human spirit. Nietzsche's genealogical account of the power struggle between master and slave moralities, even if historically suspect, casts much light on the dynamics of power relations.

Nietzsche's German precursor, Hegel, however, delves deepest into the psychology of dyadic power relations, the effects of oppression on superiors and subordinates, and the ways in which surprises within and reversals of such relations can occur. Hegel described a relationship of power sometimes translated as master-slave or lordship-bondage. For the sake of terminological consistency, I'll use superior-subordinate. For Hegel, human self-consciousness differs from animal consciousness because of ego and desire. Hegel's account of the lordship-bondage relationship might be interpreted as a historical explanation of a condition found in society or as a description of certain factors about human self-consciousness that persist in all societies. I prefer a broad reading that goes beyond a contingent dyadic relationship and, instead, centers on the conditions of developing and maintaining self-consciousness within any social context and that can be extended and applied to a host of power struggles involving complex social relations.

In fairness to Hegel, however, we must note that he advanced his account for a narrower purpose: "The fight for recognition pushed to the extreme here indicated can only occur in the natural state, where men exist only as single, separate individuals; but it is absent in civil society and the State because here the recognition for which the combatants fought already exists."[1] Despite this disclaimer, I will argue that Hegel's analysis reveals paramount features of power struggles generally.

Here is a rough reconstruction of Hegel's analysis of the lordship-bondage relationship:

Stage One: The Incipient Ego

Here a human being is a consciously thinking subject whose object of consciousness is only itself. The incipient ego confronts natural objects and must decide whether to overcome or ignore these objects in accord with survival needs and its fundamental requirement of self-development.

Stage Two: Desire and Elementary Self-Consciousness

A human being recognizes a rudimentary self-consciousness that equates to basic desire. At this stage, such a human being is little more than an animal because self-consciousness cannot develop concretely without encountering another self-consciousness of the same kind.

Stage Three: Beyond Animals

A human being develops the desire to go beyond nature and liberate himself from nature's control. In negating the objects of nature, through consumption and use, human beings remain only at a bestial level of desires. Human consciousness cannot obliterate the external world, and self-consciousness soon realizes that it must seek its development through an encounter with another self-consciousness of the same kind. Human consciousness must confront another of its kind, one that can be negated without being abolished. However, conceiving itself as entirely self-sufficient, human consciousness regards any encounter or relation to another entity as a threat to its own independence. The initial paradox is that human beings aspire for complete independence but the development of full self-consciousness depends upon recognition earned only from another self-consciousness.

Stage Four: Desire for Recognition

A human being explicitly realizes the desire that distances the human from the bestial: a desire for a recognition that cannot be gleaned from interactions with the natural objects of the external world or with nonhuman animals. Only a self-consciousness of the same kind can recognize and acknowledge the nature and actions of the human self-consciousness. But such recognition is not automatically forthcoming. The process of recognition between two self-conscious human beings must be negotiated. For Hegel, human self-consciousness establishes and demonstrates its freedom and self-identity by overcoming the conflict between itself and another human self-consciousness. In this manner, it forms a self-conception about what it takes itself to be, a self-conception that allows it to attain and express its value. Recognition, then, is the process by which self-consciousness is both recognized and becomes aware of itself as recognized. On this account, the initial paradox deepens: human self-consciousness aspires to be constituted entirely by its own independent activity. That is, human self-consciousness exercises a fundamental drive to be what it is by depending on nothing other than its own activity. But the subject depends on external reality to reflect back to him what he is. This requires a competing subject that can be negated but must remain. Recognizing another is a necessary condition for all recognition, including self-recognition. But oscillating between the fundamentally conflicting yearnings for independence and recognition, which suggests dependency in some sense, constitutes a peril for the human condition.

Stage Five: The Initial Encounter

Upon confronting another self-consciousness of the same kind, a human being comes to understand that the other, unlike the external objects of nature, cannot be negated (destroyed or consumed) or overcome simply. The other self-consciousness is not merely a passive entity upon which to act and execute one's designs. Self-consciousness aspires to perceive itself as being recognized as valuable by another entity that it accepts as valuable, at least to some degree. At this point, some confusion pervades: a self-consciousness understands its own self, but is unclear as to the status of the other self-consciousness and the nature of its own relationship to the other. Self-consciousness desires the complete negation of every assertion of self-sufficiency other than its own. No other entity should be able to impose constraints on its will and beliefs. The demands of independence resonate.

Stage Six: Stalemate and Confusion

Each self-consciousness retains the confusion described above, but also (1) retains the desire for recognition, (2) but understands that it must recognize the other self-consciousness as similar to itself to at least some extent (e.g., admitting that the other is not merely passive, but self-acting), and (3) retains its earlier discovery that it cannot negate all of nature. Each self-consciousness must go beyond nature to develop itself; gain recognition from another self-consciousness of its own kind; and negate the opposing self-consciousness in some way and in some sense. Only another self-conscious subject of its kind will do because only such an entity can negate itself—only such a subject can recognize another of its kind as having value and as embodying beliefs and desires that could forge constraints on it. Thus, each self-consciousness must strive to prove its superior status by confronting another self-consciousness that it takes itself to be both above and independent of. The independent and exalted status of each is, ironically, dependent on the other. That the other is essential to the realization of each self-consciousness' conception of itself demonstrates that the initial desire to be entirely self-sufficient was not sustainable. A fulfilled subject must depend to some extent and in some way upon another external entity to prove its self-sufficiency.

Stage Seven: Life-and-Death Struggle

The recognition each accords the other is unequal in that each seeks to be viewed by the other as the only absolute subject. Each seeks to force the other to negate itself by recognizing its counterpart as superior and able to impose constraints on it. Each self-consciousness struggles for freedom, understood as attaining its own independence as a developed entity (the external state of affairs criterion) and proving to itself that it is an independent being through a confrontation with the other that involves grave risks (the internal criterion). Thus, the life-and-death struggle arises between two self-consciousnesses. Each subject seeks a one-sided recognition from the other and is willing to risk death in service of that quest. In so doing, each party demonstrates that their full maturation as self-conscious beings is more valuable than continued existence as a dimly developed subject of experience.

Thus, in life-and-death struggle two consciousnesses strive to affirm themselves by confronting each other. Each consciousness is threatened so deeply by the existence of the other that each seeks to destroy the other through explicit physical force. Here no enduring relationship is formed because a victor will emerge from the zero-sum context in play, usually sooner rather than later. The destruction of one consciousness implies that the victor can no longer gain recognition from it. Physical force in such contexts, then, cannot sustain relationships.

Stage Eight: The Possibilities and Their Results

Five possibilities are in play: (1) both potential antagonists withdraw from combat; (2) both engage in struggle, but neither survives; (3) both engage in struggle, but only one survives; (4) both engage in struggle, but no clear victor emerges from combat; (5) both engage in struggle, both survive and a clear victor emerges.

In the first case, neither party develops its self-consciousness. Thus, the two parties regress to stage seven: neither establishes nor proves its independence, nor wins its freedom, nor gains the recognition that it sought.

In the second case, both fail to attain their goals because they perish prior to developing self-consciousness.

In the third case, the victorious party achieves only some of the aims of the struggle: the other has been negated (slain); independence has been established; but recognition is not attained because the other self-consciousness is dead. Thus, the objective proof of freedom has evaporated. There is nothing left with sufficient status to substantiate the value that self-consciousness takes itself to possess. The victorious party must seek another life-and-death struggle.

In the fourth case, both engage in struggle but no clear victor emerges. Thus, neither subject gains the recognition that it sought. Both parties revert to their condition prior to their combat. They must renew their own hostilities or find another combatant with whom to engage in order to attain their ends.

In the fifth case, the losing party yields rather than die at the hands of the victor. The victor attains all the ends that animated the combat: the victor has negated the other self-consciousness in a certain way and in a certain sense; has transcended nature in pursuit of self-development; and gains recognition from the vanquished foe. In this manner, the lordship-bondage relationship begins.

Stage Nine: The Lordship-Bondage Relationship

The subordinate surrenders independence, freedom, and full self-consciousness in order to preserve his or her life. The superior enjoys an initial triumph as he maintains and deepens his independence, while using the subordinate to mediate the superior's relationship with nature. The superior underscores that the external objects of nature are inessential in that only the subordinate now deals with them directly: the subordinate transforms the external objects of nature to make them suitable for the superior's consumption or use. The superior has also proven to himself that he is a self-consciousness that exists for itself alone. Finally, the superior regards the subordinate as inferior, as a mere instrument to be used for the superior's purposes. In effect, by virtue of being victorious in the life-and-death struggle, the superior benefits from the labors of the subordinate, who acts as the superior's instrument in the struggle with nature. The superior's independence seems secure as the subordinate recognizes and bears witness to the superior's will and desires as authoritative. The consciousness of the subordinate at this stage is utterly dependent upon the consciousness of the superior: "Its essence is life or existence for another."[2] By surrendering in the life-and-death struggle, the subordinate has not attained the recognition required to attain the value of full self-consciousness.

Superior-subordinate relationships promote ongoing, mutual, but unequal recognition: superiors could destroy subordinates but superiors do not exercise that power. However, because superiors retain that power subordinates have reason to obey the directives of superiors out of fear. The implicit threat of a superior's destroying a subordinate engenders the subordinate's obedience. Moreover, the ongoing, systemic nature of the relationship renders it oppressive. Unlike episodic occurrences of power, here the enduring possibility of the exercise of power largely constitutes the ongoing relationship. The choices and actions of subordinates are structurally constrained such that superiors need not make any explicit threats. Subordinates act no differently than if a threat had been made because of the unchanging social structure in place.[3] The superior reaps benefits from the subordinate's continuing obedience to the superior's demands.

But Hegel makes a more subtle point. To conclude that the superior causes the behavior of the subordinate is too simple. Instead, it is the relationship between the two parties that is the material cause of the behavior of both superior and subordinate, while the efficient cause is the particular manner in which the two parties act out that relationship. For Hegel, the superior also acts from constraints embodied by the relationship and the subordinate also has casual agency in shaping the results of confrontations with the superior. The abilities of subordinates to affect outcomes flow from the distribution of social powers within their relationship with superiors. The relationship itself constitutes a continuing negotiation grounded in the respective powers of the parties. Thus, the encounters between the parties are not episodic and contingent, but arise from the ongoing, structural feature of their social lives. The relationship of superior and subordinate is one of mutual dependence.

Stage Ten: Unequal Recognition

The subordinate is initially fearful of the superior because of the power the superior holds over him or her. The subordinate obeys the superior and even anticipates the superior's desires. At this stage, both parties recognize the superior as independent and dominant, while the subordinate is dependent and obsequious. The subordinate relinquishes the quest to establish independence and, as the loser of the struggle with the superior, understands that he cannot realize the aims that animated participation in the contest. The subordinate has failed and is reduced to a desirous being oscillating among stages two through four. The subordinate reverts to struggling with the external objects of nature as an unessential, dependent being. Worse, the labors of the subordinate are no longer his or her own, but arise from the commands of the superior. The subordinate is alienated from his work and derives no satisfaction from his externally controlled labors.

Stage Eleven: The Reversal

However, the superior's satisfaction derived from this relationship is only temporary. The superior is unaware that a chasm will soon emerge that represents the distance between what the superior thought his triumph over the subordinate would earn him and the results that actually arise. By requiring the subordinate to mediate his relationship with the external objects of nature, the superior no longer confronts the resistance that previously energized his creativity and strengthened his will. The initial advantage in bravery, decisiveness, and recognition enjoyed by the superior will soon pass. In like fashion, the freedom that the superior won will soon be called into question.

To transform the asymmetrical power relationship, subordinates must first realize that their cooperation is required by the superiors if the latter are to continue to enjoy a power differential. Once subordinates understand that they are capable of limiting and impairing the interests of superiors, the opportunities for transformation increase. Power relations are almost never completely one-sided, but are, instead, typically asymmetrical. A superior has more power in the relationship than a subordinate, who is not thereby powerless.

Time passes and the relationship is transformed. The superior becomes dependent on the subordinate and the products of the subordinate's labors. The subordinate develops self-consciousness through labor, even if alienated in important ways from it. The subordinate confronts resistance from the external objects of nature and begins to experience independence in his struggles with those objects as he strives to transform them.

Moreover, the subordinate is the unwitting engine of the transformation of his relationship with the superior because of his fear of the superior. Because his or her life is constantly threatened, the subordinate is alienated from life completely and has only work to express self-consciousness: "Through work, however, the bondsman becomes conscious of what he truly is."[4] The fear of death nurtures the subordinate's capability for absolute negation, which will prove necessary for self-sufficient subjectivity. The prospect of death liberates the subordinate from the narrow particularities of his life and his parochial vision of the self. The subordinate, through labor, both creates and is created. The subordinate is an active agent whose independence is won through the transforming effects of creative labor: the subordinate asserts his or her being by shaping the external objects of nature. In shaping and altering the objects of nature, the subordinate fashions and molds the topography of the self: objects are created and the subordinate gains consciousness of also creating the self.

The subordinate glimpses independence by asserting authority over the objects of nature, which become dependent upon the subordinate: "Through this rediscovery of himself by himself, the bondsman realizes that it is precisely in his work wherein he seemed to have only an alienated existence that he acquires a mind of his own."[5] Moreover, the subordinate has "constantly before his eyes, in the [superior], a concrete picture of what it is to be a sovereign subject, where one's own will and point of view carry authority for other subjects . . . his relationship to the [superior] provides him with a living exemplar of sovereignty that, however incomplete, will function as a guiding ideal in his future spiritual development . . . his interaction with the [superior] transforms him, without his knowledge, in ways that will enable him to realize a more complete form of self-sufficiency than the [superior] is capable of."[6]

In confronting resistance and in fashioning the external objects of nature, the subordinate masters, to a degree, the natural world. He imposes his pattern upon the environment, which begins to reflect him through his creations. In so doing, the subordinate is creator and is created. The subordinate's enslavement by the superior established conditions under which the subordinate could win what he could not achieve in the life-and-death struggle.

The superior, meanwhile, desires, uses and consumes the products of the subordinate's labors, products that are unconnected to the superior's own efforts and labors. While the subordinate exercises his agency and begins to conceive of himself through labor as more independent, the superior grows ever more dependent on the subordinate to satisfy his consumptive desires and fails to develop his agency and higher human capabilities. The superior cannot be certain of the truth of his freedom for three reasons: first, because the superior recognizes this truth only through the presumably unequal, inessential, dependent subordinate; second, because the recognition is coerced, not voluntary; and third, because the life crafted by the superior ultimately undermines his own agency and arrests his full development.

In short, the recognition first sought and apparently won by the superior in the life-and-death struggle has proved illusory. The superior cannot see himself reflected in the subordinate and is, instead, surrounded by a world that he depends upon but which cannot fulfill his most profound psychological needs.

Stage Twelve: The Power of Labor

Through labor and obedience to the superior, the subordinate develops the capability for self-discipline required for genuine sovereignty, a capability that the superior never fully develops. The subordinate learns to abrogate his own desires for the interests of purposes perceived to be greater. The transformative power of labor also changes the subordinate's attitude toward the superior. Earlier, both parties understand the superior's independence as external yet essential to the subordinate. When the subordinate becomes self-existent through labor, the self-existence and independence of the superior remains external but no longer essential to the subordinate. The subordinate has overcome complete alienation, and his fear of the superior softens. The subordinate no longer views the external world as hostile and foreign to him, but instead as a domain in which his subjectivity can flourish. The subordinate's fear of death softens as he heightens his subjectivity through labor. Meanwhile, the superior becomes lethargic and passive. Lacking a creative outlet and exercising agency limited to issuing orders, the superior's lack of participation in creative labor undermines his personal development.

Accordingly, the subordinate enjoys a healthier relationship to the external world of nature than does the superior. While the subordinate creates and transforms, the superior only consumes and uses. Thus, the subordinate, unlike the superior, does not merely negate but instead fashions the objects of nature in ways that testify to the subordinate's subjectivity. In this manner, the superior no longer experiences himself as fully self-sufficient and as someone able to craft his own design upon the world. Instead, the superior is able only to consume and use the objects created and transformed by the subordinate. Moreover, the superior derives ever-decreasing satisfaction from the muted recognition the superior gleans from the subordinate. Recognition from those regarded as mere things and instruments bears little currency for self-making. The subordinate becomes increasingly indifferent to the superior's designs and less susceptible to the superior's threats. The subordinate attains independent self-consciousness by overcoming the fear of death through the transformative power of labor.

Stage Thirteen: The Climax

The superior becomes oddly dependent on the subordinate and the subordinate's labors. The superior is not prepared to revert to the life of labor as depicted in the earlier stages of this narrative and therefore cannot eliminate the subordinate without replacing him. The superior must, on some level, now recognize the subordinate as a self-existing being upon whose labors the superior relies. The superior, then, suffers from having crafted a noncreative life, from dissatisfaction with recognition arising from a being presumed inferior, and from perceiving on some level that he is increasingly dependent on the labors of the subordinate.

Accordingly, all that was won in the life-and-death struggle is now in jeopardy. Most strikingly, for Hegel, genuine self-sufficiency requires rejecting the claim to absolute sovereignty as individuals and instead realizing freedom through identification in the collective will. Of course, this is Hegel's narrative of the development of the Absolute through history and the agency of human beings—a topic beyond the scope of my present inquiry.

Hegelian Power

At first blush, most of us probably assume that oppressive dyadic power relations disproportionately benefit the superior power at the expense of the subordinate party; that the subordinate party begins with a weak sense of agency that becomes even feebler; that the superior party begins with a strong sense of agency that amplifies over time; that the superior party enjoys the fruits of his oppression unambiguously, at least insofar as he harbors no guilt over his wrongdoing; and that the subordinate party is almost always unable to transform the relationship and thus suffers a crisis of personal identity. Hegel argues that such a picture is overly simplistic and untrue to human life.

Hegel strikingly prefigures some critical aspects of the philosophies of Nietzsche and Marx. His stress on the primacy of confronting resistance, avoiding indolence, and imposing order on the world is at the heart of Nietzsche's understanding of self-creation through increasing the strength of one's Will to Power; while Hegel's celebration of the transformative effects of creative labor resounds in Marx's account of human fulfillment.

The lessons of Hegel's narrative for the phenomenology of power are clear and extensive. First, within an oppressive relationship are the seeds of transformation and even reversal: relations of power-over are neither static nor one-sided. Second, exercising power over others oppressively can frustrate the superior party's personal development and fulfillment, which can trigger the transformation or reversal of the power relationship. In Hegel's tale, the superior does not seek mutual, equal recognition in his quest for complete self-consciousness because he erroneously believed that he had gained what he had sought in his victorious life-and-death struggle with the subordinate. This error proves fatal to the attainment of the superior's quest. Third, when superiors fail to develop and exercise their higher human capabilities outside of power relationships—for example, by failing to engage in robust, creative labor—they become overly dependent on subordinates for their sense of identity and self-worth. Fourth, human beings are dependent upon one another to gain a salutary sense of identity, but overly emphasizing one's presumed status as a master or superior unwisely heightens the master's dependence on subordinates: the master becomes a slave to his own oppressive power relationship. He relies too extensively on his subordinates for assertion and recognition. Fifth, through the exercise of creative labor, subordinates can gain self-reliance and a form of independence (even under alienating conditions?). Sixth, human beings do not win freedom and self-worth by oppressing others of their kind. Most important, Hegel's paramount message is that human flourishing requires mutually validating, equal self-consciousnesses that preclude structures of oppression. Only union and solidarity with another of one's kind can generate full consciousness of freedom and full, salutary self-consciousness. Although Hegel's narrative is explicitly dyadic, his lessons can be extended to wider social relations. Hierarchical inequality arises from violence and coercion, and must be overcome. Social institutions must embody wider notions of communal freedom and justice. We must transcend the forced inequalities of superiors and subordinates and construct affirmative, mutually sustaining social relationships: "Only in such a manner is true freedom realized, for since this consists in my identity with the other, I am truly free only when the other is also free and is recognized by me as free . . . it is only when the [subordinate] becomes free that the [superior], too, becomes completely free."[7]

Accordingly, the most important message of the lordship-bondsman narrative is that human flourishing and genuine freedom require both asserting the self and affording recognition, in its fullest sense, to others. As illustrated earlier, these paradoxical requirements of human development implicate both an insistence on a measure of independence and an acceptance of a healthy dose of dependence. During and after the life-and-death struggle, the superior refused to accept his dependence on the subordinate and sought only one-sided recognition. The results of refusing to acknowledge and live within the paradox of independence-dependence proved disastrous for the superior. The only alternate to living within this paradox is the oppression of some by others. Hegel teaches that the pernicious use of power-over often generates unwelcome surprises for the supposed superior party.

In Hegel's account of the superior-subordinate relationship, the superior's power over the subordinate rests on the superior's mutually acknowledged ability to destroy the subordinate. As such, fear is the motivation that keeps the subordinate in line. But a more reliable foundation of oppression would result if superiors could entice subordinates to internalize the values that nurture the superiors' privileges. As Thrasymachus first taught, if superiors can convince subordinates that those values are appropriate, natural, and even inevitable, then the authority of superiors will be firmer and more sustainable. The motivation of fear is softened when the ability of a superior to destroy a subordinate weakens. But a motivation of obedience grounded in internalized values—those that partially constitute a subordinate's sense of identity—persists even when a superior is aged and feeble. The power of false consciousness is that it wins the acquiescence of subordinates in the absence of fear: the underlings cooperate in their own oppression even when the ability of superiors to destroy them disappears. Thus, on the level of society, the most oppressive tyrants enjoy their privilege of place only as long as their brute force to destroy those who dissent cannot reasonably be challenged. Theirs is a reign grounded in fear. But a regime that can control the masses through ideological supremacy can alter the self-image of human beings in ways that ensure continued rule in the absence of threats, implicit or explicit. False consciousness, then, marries resignation and acquiescence: subordinates resign themselves to the appropriateness of the social order in place because they learn to view it as unavoidable even if they are uncomfortable with its effects on them; and subordinates acquiesce to the structures that legitimate their oppression when they internalize the dominant values of that social order.

Karl Marx and Antonio Gramsci, scions of Thrasymachus but with normative moorings, are the masters at explaining, analyzing, and offering solutions to the ideological process by which ruling elites secure the acquiescence of the oppressed to their continued victimization. To these exterminators of ideological illusion we must now turn.

VII

Karl Marx (1818–1883) and Antonio Gramsci (1891–1937)

Securing the Acquiescence of the Oppressed

> Power revealed is power sacrificed. The truly powerful exert their influence in ways unseen, unfelt. Some would say that a thing visible is a thing vulnerable.
>
> —Guillermo Del Toro

Karl Marx leveled several criticisms about Hegel's work, particularly its focus on abstract thought and absolute knowledge. As a result, according to Marx, Hegel's narrative of developing self-consciousness provides only a mental picture of human self-realization: "Hegel makes man the man of self-consciousness instead of making self-consciousness the self-consciousness of man, of real man, i.e., of man living also in a real, objective world and determined by that world."[1]

In addition, Marx notes that Hegel's lord-bondsman account situates the development of self-consciousness in an alienated context: "[Hegel] grasps labour as the essence of man . . . he sees only the positive, not the negative side of labour. Labour is man's coming-to-be for himself within alienation, or as alienated man. The only labour which Hegel knows and recognizes is abstract mental labour."[2] In short, Marx scolds Hegel for overlooking the fact that the bondsman's self-creation remains a form of alienation because of the context in which it was forged. As always, for Marx, only through unalienated labor can human beings attain the fulfillment of their creative natures.

However, as we would expect, he cheered Hegel's understanding of the transformative effects of labor:

The outstanding achievement of Hegel's *Phenomenology* and
of its final outcome, the dialectic of negativity as the moving
and generating principle, is thus first that Hegel conceives the
self-creation of man as a process, conceives objectification as loss
of the object, as alienation and as transcendence of alienation:
that he thus grasps the essence of labour and comprehends
objective man—true, because real man—as the outcome of
man's own labour.[3]

For Marx, Hegel's narrative, despite being overly abstract, remains
instructive because it underscores the importance of labor in the process of
robust self-creation; demonstrates that the lord-capitalist becomes alienated
from nature and ultimately himself because of his lack of creative labor;
reveals how the lord-capitalist, although seemingly free initially, becomes
dependent upon both the labor of bondsman-worker and social conditions
over which he loses control; and illuminates how human beings attain freedom only by transcending their alienation. Of course, Marx downplays
much of Hegel's psychological appeals to desires, recognition, and fear of
death; instead, Marx's more social analysis bangs the drum loudly for the
primacy of labor. In addition, Marx stresses the need for unalienated labor
as the springboard for self-realization and freedom. For Marx, transcending alienation must include altering the objective, external social world in
specifically prescribed ways.

   In his own account of the dynamics of social power, Marx, expanding
extravagantly on the suggestions of Thrasymachus, provides the clearest, most
direct account of how the acquiescence of the oppressed can be secured, thus
rendering them unwitting collaborators in their own oppression.

Human Nature

Many people embrace a thick theory of human nature, one that describes
who we are by referring to a set of fixed attributes. For example, to portray
human nature as inherently self-interested or perhaps even selfish, or as
inherently altruistic is not uncommon. If we are inherently self-interested
then the role of society may be to moderate our inclinations in order to
establish workable interpersonal relations and promote civilization. If we are
inherently altruistic then the role of society may be to not overwhelm our
inclinations by inviting invidious interpersonal comparisons and heartless
competition. In any case, a thick theory of human nature argues that we

are defined biologically by a particular set of persistent characteristics that limit possibilities for political associations.

Abrogating all thick theories of human nature, Marx argues that human possibilities are historically created, largely by the needs and demands of economic systems. Although human beings are limited by their biological makeup, their natures can embody an indefinite variety of forms: our human nature is elastic and moldable. Accordingly, Marx embraces a thin theory of human nature. The only unalterable aspect of human nature is our need to create and to produce. In his view, the greatest human need, beyond those factors required for biological survival, is for creative labor that is freely chosen and thereby inherently stimulating. Marx's highest value is the fulfillment of what he calls our "species-being."[4]

The enemy of creative labor is alienated work. In general, to be alienated is to be hostilely estranged, to be antagonistically disconnected from others, the environment, and even one's self. To be alienated, then, is to be opposed to or distant from our proper relationship to others, the environment, or our selves. The alienated person is unfulfilled and may be unaware of the causes of the dissatisfaction. In Marx's view, the history of the world has been the continuing narrative of the alienation of human beings from their productive nature.

For example, classical Marxism argues that under capitalism workers become alienated in at least four ways. First, they are alienated from their employers, the capitalist owners who dictate the terms of workers' production. Second, Marxism warns that workers in the capitalist system, competing for economic crumbs tumbling off the owners' tables, will soon be alienated from each other. Workers will view each other as competitors in a zero-sum capitalist game. My victory, better wages and working conditions arising from a promotion, can come only at your expense. Third, workers become alienated from their labor. Lacking control over what they produce, how they produce it, and what happens to what they produce, workers experience labor as burdensome. They work only because they must satisfy their survival needs. They dread yet another day at the factory, while looking forward only to holidays and weekends. Fourth, workers become alienated from themselves, from their highest aspirations and grandest potentials. They, instead, are tethered to a capitalist yoke, sunk in everydayness, as their lives are sets of dreary routines punctuated by a few, low level diversions.

Again, Marx insists that human nature is plastic and formed primarily by the needs of economic structures that reign in turn but are doomed to evaporate in time. The only ineradicable human yearning is our lust for unalienated labor during which we fulfill our species-being.[5] For Marx, genuine self-realization is not grounded in material consumption. Instead, human fulfillment requires the full, free actualization and externalization of our higher creative capabilities. We need to actualize our higher creative potentials and refine further our actualized capabilities. To externalize our higher creative capabilities our talents must become observable to the public. Unlike alienated work, unalienated labor becomes more enjoyable and fulfilling with repetition.

For Marxists, our species-being—our individual and collective human fulfillment—centers on productive activity that is free, social, challenging, stimulating, and transformative. We need to develop our highest creative potentials, choose our own productive paths, engage other people in the process or results of our labors, find work that energizes our talents, and thereby change our environment and ourselves for the better. Marxism's minimalist view of species-being includes the conviction that human fulfillment is intimately linked to the imaginative, unshackled use of productive capabilities. Labor is a distinctively human activity and overflows with value and significance. Only through free, creative activity can people realize their unalienated, species-being.

Imagine an artist, fully absorbed by what she is doing, who gains immense fulfillment from the process of creation, with full control over what she is designing. The gratified artist is working hard in the sense of investing enormous energy in her task, but she is so deeply engaged in her project that leisure time and passive distractions are unappealing. Her strenuous activity fills her soul. To labor for its own sake from passionate commitment is to experience unalienated work and to nurture species-being. Under such circumstances, we fully invest energy as a means of self-expression and self-creation. Marxism relentlessly charges that under capitalism workers are at the mercy of the small number of owners. The capitalist holders of the means of production dictate what is produced, how it will be produced, and what will happen after it is produced. The worker becomes a mere appendage, an instrument of production whose creativity is suffocated. Such workers, enjoying few if any other opportunities, toil only to satisfy survival needs. Their species-being shrivels from lack of nourishment.

Marx reminds us that to a significant extent we become what we do. How we expend our creative energies greatly influences the people that we are becoming. Our jobs are not merely peripheral to our lives. His distinction between alienated work and unalienated labor resonates with our intuitions and experiences. We have all luxuriated in unalienated labor that was strenuous and challenging, but fulfilling. We have all endured alienated work that was sheer drudgery and crushingly banal regardless of material reward. Independently of whether we are convinced by Marx's politics or his notion of species-being, he identifies a paramount aspect of structuring a meaningful, valuable human life: we must discover an outlet for our creativity that will promote our self-realization.

Exploitation

Understood broadly, "exploitation" arises when someone uses another person merely as an object for his own benefit, when he ignores the humanity of that person by treating the person as merely a means to his own ends. Understood in a narrower, Marxist sense, exploitation transpires when one class, the workers, produces surplus value that is wrongly controlled by another class, the capitalist owners. This sort of exploitation does not flow from explicit duress, physical threat, or other noneconomic force. Instead, capitalists leverage their enormously superior economic bargaining power over workers—their ownership of the means of production and the absence of real alternatives for workers—to exploit their employees.

On Marx's account, capitalists exploit the proletariat by siphoning off surplus value—profiting from the labor of workers by paying them only a relatively small percentage of the value their labor produces. Capitalists purchase workers' labor at its value, which is equal to a subsistence wage, and sell products at their value. Because the value workers create is greater than the value of labor power itself, surplus value sprouts. But workers do not receive the labor equivalent of what they produce. Also, workers' labor is "forced" in the sense that only limited and equally exhausting alternatives are available for workers who must satisfy their subsistence needs. Put simply, workers benefit owners; owners economically force, in the relevant Marxist sense, workers to supply that benefit; and owners wrongfully do not bestow equal, reciprocal benefits to workers.

Accordingly, workers produce value that is used to oppress and exploit them. Capitalists reinvest a portion of surplus value in the cycle of production that deepens the deprivation of workers by chaining them to the economic system that demeans their status. Workers, then, unwittingly reproduce their own oppression through their participation in the productive process: the more effectively they labor the more profoundly are they deprived. Oppression within the capitalist economic system is an ongoing feature of class struggle, which also includes the power of the working class, their labor.

Capitalists possess the means of production, and thereby have the power of control over investment of surplus value and the power to shape and supervise the productive process that also constitutes the conditions of labor. Workers lack independent access to the means of production and thus depend on capitalists to ply their skills and to earn sustenance wages. Capitalists depend on workers to animate the productive process and to create commodities that can be sold in the marketplace and generate surplus value. Also, capitalists depend on workers to purchase goods in the marketplace. The relationship between capitalists and workers, then, is one of mutual dependence and asymmetrical power in that workers possess power that remains subordinate to the amount held by capitalists. Still, respective power relations within capitalism are subject to recurrent negotiation and struggle. The capability of workers to unite in common cause always embodies prospects for large-scale social transformation or, at least, discrete changes in working conditions.

Capitalists have power over workers and exploit them because the proletariat need wages to secure the material necessities for survival but their opportunities are severely limited by the needs of capitalism, which are supported by ideological superstructure. Although owners do not literally hold a weapon to workers' heads and force them to become employees, the lack of an economic safety net, the similarity of other employment offers, and relatively high unemployment rates conspire to induce workers to accept what is offered. As such, the labor of the working class is subtly coerced because of their feeble bargaining power and desperate material situation. On this view, workers exert their labors under the control of capitalists, who set the terms of production and benefit disproportionately from the process. Moreover, the ideological superstructure is effective enough to obscure the oppression of workers and thereby to domesticate their potential resistance to the system. Only if workers could identity their genuine interests and realize the extent of their oppression could they potentially mobilize into a force for social change. But where capitalism successfully generates false consciousness it encourages the acquiescence of workers to their own oppression. By promoting oppressive relations as appropriate, natural, inevitable, and in the interests of everyone alike, capitalism secures its immediate future. The ongoing actions of these social agents maintain and reproduce social structures. While the system in place is always contestable and often contested—no ideological superstructure can render itself invulnerable to resistance—the forces in place are able to reconstitute, adjust social relations and structures, and thereby ward off serious opposition. Accordingly, Marx offers an elaborate explanation of how superiors secure the consent to and collaboration of subordinates in their own oppression, an analysis that goes far beyond Thrasymachus's description of how rulers enact laws and shape normative discourse. On Marx's view, it is only when the internal contradictions of capitalism explode it from within and the false consciousness of the proletariat withers away in the face of the stark reality of widespread deprivation that workers will solidify as a revolutionary class and cast off the yoke of capitalist oppression.

Marx insists that the antidote for economic exploitation and alienation is the arrival of communism, which he takes to be the final form of economics and society. But we need not buy a ticket on Marx's socialist bandwagon in order to extract legitimate insights from his writing.

Economic Base and Ideological Superstructure

One of Marx's more intriguing and ambiguous pronouncements concerns the relationship between a society's economic substructure ("the base") and its ideological superstructure ("the superstructure"). A society's mode of economic production includes its forces of production (natural resources, instruments and means of production, workers and their skills, raw materials) and its relations of production (the formal and informal organization of relations among people, or among people and commodities, in the productive process). The base consists, broadly speaking, of the constitutive elements of economic production. The superstructure consists of our political and legal institutions and our forms of social consciousness (what we think, believe, how we understand and experience the world).

For Marx, the development of the forces of production results in changes in the relations of production. There will come a time when the existing relations of production no longer effectively and efficiently allow the growth of the productive forces. This internal contradiction divides society and will result in the fall of the obsolete set of productive relations. New relations of production will triumph because only they facilitate the continued growth of society's productive forces. Thus, Marx provides an economic explanation for political revolution.

But what is his precise meaning about the relationship of the base and superstructure? Does Marx suggest that the economic base merely *influences* the ideological superstructure? If so, Marx's pronouncements seem tame. For who would deny that economic conditions exert some degree of influence on the way we think about and experience the world?

Does Marx assert that the economic base strictly *determines* the ideological structure? This interpretation holds that the base causes the superstructure, in the sense that our forms of consciousness and the institutions that embody them are the direct effects of the economic processes of material production. On this interpretation, the base is independent of and logically prior to the superstructure. But such an interpretation confronts daunting problems. First, it marginalizes human freedom by positing impersonal economic processes as the animating forces of history. Second, it fails to understand how the base is not fully autonomous from the superstructure in that a superstructure of property rights and legal categories is required for the coherent functioning and sanctioning of productive processes. Third, this interpretation ignores passages in the writings of Engels and Marx that distance them from it. For example, Engels rejected the crude reductionism of this interpretation when he stressed the "ultimate supremacy" or the "determination in the last instance" by the base. This suggests that elements of the superstructure register effects on the base.[6] Marx stated that the relationship of the base and superstructure is historical and complex, and that the superstructure is not merely the passive reflector of productive processes.[7]

Accordingly, the proper way to interpret "base determines superstructure" is somewhere between "influence" and "strict determination." Surely, Marx concludes that the economic base sets limits on the renderings of social consciousness: a society's dominant ideologies are constrained in that numerous possible superstructural elements will not be actualized because they are incompatible with productive processes. Thus, the base narrows the range of ideas and social practices that can gain currency in a society. Moreover, certain other superstructural elements will gain currency mainly because they facilitate the needs of the economic base. What pushes this interpretation beyond mere "influence" is the number of possible superstructural elements that are precluded and the number that are enabled by the economic base. That number exceeds what we would expect if the base merely influenced the superstructure, and it falls short of what we would expect if the base strictly determined the superstructure.

False Consciousness

If Marx is correct, capitalism mystifies social reality through "false consciousness," by which we misidentify the origins of our firmest beliefs. We are convinced these beliefs are derived independently from observations of human behavior, when they are actually produced by the needs of particular economic systems.

The term *false consciousness* suggests an inverted representation of reality which is systematically misleading and socially mystifying in that it misrepresents what are in fact the interests of the ruling class as the natural, common interests of everyone. (Shades of Thrasymachus!) This misrepresentation, which, according to Marxism, flows from superstructure, justifies, stabilizes, and reinforces the social and political status quo. A person who holds a view that is the result of false consciousness is unaware of the underlying motives and causal processes by which she came to accept that view.

The term *false consciousness* is used specifically when oppressed classes adopt the dominant prevailing ideology and perceptual prism. When these dominant ideas do not truly correspond to the experience of the oppressed classes, ideological distortion occurs. Such distortions have a functional explanation: they legitimate the ruling classes' monopoly on power by depicting current social relations as natural, appropriate, or inevitable. In this fashion, the interests of the ruling class misrepresent themselves as universal human interests. Thus, a particular class's perspective comes to prevail on the members of subordinate classes. There is often a tension, which can intensify into contradiction and eventually revolution, between the ideological prism acquired through socialization and the subordinate class's experiences accumulated in productive activity.

On this account, a belief is ideological only if it would perish upon the revelation of its causal origins. Because the relationship between false consciousness and nonideological perception cannot be interpreted validly as a species of the general relationship between illusion and truth, ideological distortion cannot be overcome solely by intellectual criticism. Ideological distortion is not the opposite of truth, but is, instead, a narrow or one-sided rendering of truth that functions to preserve the practices and privileges of the ruling class. Hence, false consciousness dissolves only when the internal contradictions of an economic system—especially evident when relations of production can no longer efficiently make use of developing technology—are practically resolved.

For example, in a capitalist society, economic competition is critical. Thus, our convictions supporting a thick theory of human nature that proposes that we are inherently self-interested are culturally induced by an economic system that needs workers to be self-interested; rewards such behavior; and provides disincentives for contrary actions. As a result, most workers act in self-interested ways and respond to material incentives to a significant extent. Observers who accurately perceive such widespread behavior may inaccurately conclude that human beings are inherently self-interested. They may further conclude that because of this thick theory of human nature the best economic system to champion is capitalism. If we are oblivious to this process, we will be convinced that our beliefs about human nature are independently derived from empirical observations. If Marx is correct, this is an example of false consciousness because we have failed to understand the process by which our conclusions about human nature were manufactured by the needs of capitalism itself.

As noted earlier, Marxism argues that the ways human beings think about, perceive, and experience their world ("ideological superstructure") are "determined" by the economic structures that surround them ("economic base"). Economic structures, other than communism, are riddled with internal contradictions: they contain the seeds of their own destruction. These internal contradictions are conflicting requirements that an economic structure must fulfill to continue to survive. To forestall their inevitable demise, economic structures must invade the consciousness of the masses and present themselves as necessary and natural. Thus, the survival needs of economic structures mold much of how we think about, perceive, and experience the world. Marx's economic analysis explains why Thrasymachus's account of how rulers establish and maintain power over the masses was too simple.

Let us return to the previous example. Capitalism requires workers and owners who are competitive, economically aggressive within rules, and motivated by material incentives. Capitalism rewards such behaviors. Most people, responding to positive reinforcement, accept the goals of capitalism as their own. Our ideologies reflect what we observe. The dominant ideologies—spread by politics, philosophy, literature, popular media, and the like—bray the message that most people are *naturally, perhaps inevitably,* competitive, economically aggressive within rules, and motivated by material incentives. Once these views solidify into common sense, they produce a supposedly independent reason to cling to capitalism: only capitalism conforms to fundamental human nature. In this manner, ideological superstructure mystifies reality and deepens our conviction that human beings are inherently self-interested, perhaps even selfish.

In this manner, capitalists (superiors) secure the acquiescence of the proletariat (subordinates), who unwittingly collaborate in their own oppression. As a result, capitalists do not need to exert their power over the proletariat recurrently; they do not need to express their desires to the proletariat at every discrete turn and demand obedience. Instead, through the magic of false consciousness, the members of the proletariat class are unable to identify their genuine interests as the social structure induces their consent to act and refrain from acting in ways compatible with the maintenance and deepening of their own victimization. By securing the acquiescence of the proletariat, as they internalize the values of the capitalist system, capitalists are able to effectively and efficiently wield power over them without having to monitor their victims recurrently.

Limitations of Marxism

When philosophical adversaries report conclusions or arguments that deny Marxism's central aspirations, they frequently are accused of promulgating the ideological distortions of false consciousness. In effect, Marxism too quickly charges that liberal-capitalists verify certain Marxist tenets by the very way these liberal-capitalists try to refute Marxism. This is not to say that the notion of false consciousness is without currency. There is much truth to the observation that certain views may be the unconscious, conditioned reflection of economic and social oppression; and that subordinate classes often become accomplices in their own torment by internalizing the dominant ideologies that contributed to their mistreatment.

But if applied relentlessly, the notion of false consciousness loses much of its critical bite. If the notion is advanced as a nonrefutable thesis, if all denials of Marxism are taken to be

affirmations of the doctrine of false consciousness, then the notion of false consciousness is trivial. Any subjective report that denies any basic Marxist conclusion seems too easily and automatically to stigmatize itself. Marxists dismiss the content of a view because it allegedly can be explained by its determinants. Moreover, such a posture demeans the experiences, and not merely the ideologies, of Marxism's philosophical rivals. In fact, subjective reports of one's

inner condition or of one's ideological commitments, are neither incorrigibly true nor self-refuting. Marxists can legitimately neither deny nor accept automatically the veracity of a perception or experience that undermines their conclusions. The challenge for a Marxist is to delineate without begging the question under what circumstances such reports and commitments do and do not reflect veridical perceptions correlated to wider experience.

Accordingly, the problem attending invocations of false consciousness is clear and persistent. On the one hand, accusations of false consciousness resonate because they underscore that the expressed preferences of members of subordinate classes arise to some extent from the dominant values embodied by social norms, practices, and institutions. As a result, the hegemony of those norms, practices, and institutions cannot be justified noncircularly by appeals to the expressed preferences of subordinates. On the other hand, invocations of false consciousness cannot be used to automatically stigmatize all those who dissent from the prescriptions of leftist critics as unwitting victims of and collaborators with the structures of oppression. If leftist critics of the status quo hurl accusations of false consciousness too promiscuously they invite countercharges of philosophical imperialism. They would also too facilely label the members of subordinate classes as utter gulls of the social system through which they are oppressed.

Marxism recognizes the structural basis of power-over, the mutual dependence of the constitutive parties, and the ongoing nature of negotiation between them. Thus, Marxism highlights class struggle and how power is reproduced and transformed within it. Marx underscores why and how classes, as opposed to discrete individuals, are the engines of social change, the loci of social conflict, and the constituents of society. The actions of members of classes are comprehendible only with reference to ongoing structural relationships.

Marxism underplays the independent role of militarism and territorial expansion in its analysis. Because of its relentless focus on economic causation and material oppression it wrongly reduces imperialism to economic phenomena: economic systems need to imperialize other countries to soften the effects of their own internal contradictions, which produce widespread, cyclical depressions and deprivations. On this account, wars of aggression arise from economic motives: to create new markets, to access a new inexpensive labor force, or to secure needed natural resources. Classical Marxists underplay the noneconomic sources of militarism that motivate state action. Unraveling the differences and overlaps between state power and economic power is crucial here. The most strident classical Marxists err in positioning the state as merely part of the epiphenomenal superstructure arising from the needs of an economic base. To argue that state power is relatively independent from and thus not reducible to the economic foundation is reasonable. The public institutions of the state and their functions cannot simply be reduced to the needs and functions of the private institutions of the economy.

Marxists also failed to foresee how capitalism could absorb numerous socialist ideas and policies while retaining its basic structure. Minimum wage laws, maximum hour laws, a progressive income tax, the rise of labor unions, and a host of regulations produced by significant governmental supervision have transformed capitalism yet allowed its basic principles to remain intact. Classical Marxism also too neatly conceives of social classes as fixed entities that serve as the main or only loci of social struggle. Within society, people embody a host of different, somewhat overlapping identities grounded in race, ethnicity, religion, educational level, geography, gender, and the like that cannot be absorbed easily into the limited categories of owners and workers.

Ideological Hegemony

Antonio Gramsci aspired to loosen Marxism's scientific and material inclinations and reinstate the importance of cultural and ideological change. He was inspired by Marxism's democratic impulses and by the need to translate ideas into political action.[8] But Gramsci distanced himself from Marx's scientific pretensions and convenient invocation of historical and economic laws.

Gramsci intended to sketch a new vision of politics empowering those hitherto on the margins of power and privilege. Although a committed communist, Gramsci nevertheless cast a critical eye toward the excesses of fundamental Marxist theory and Soviet practice. He avoided freezing his political thoughts in fixed doctrines or philosophical systems. Instead, he, reminiscent of Nietzsche, self-consciously wrote in fragments that invited future development. Most of his important work was written under censorship while he was imprisoned, so the precise meanings of many of Gramsci's fragments are inherently controversial. His access to material was limited while he was imprisoned and Gramsci was frustrated by his inability to consult all available sources. He evaluated his work concretely—Would it contribute to the political struggle against the dominant social order?—although he understood that prison life isolated him from the people on the margins who must translate his theory into political action. Gramsci did not take himself to be imposing abstract ideas on social reality. He was convinced that his work would have value only if the ideas arise from social reality and help realize a politics of inclusion.

Although the philosophical idealism of Benedetto Croce greatly influenced him, Gramsci criticized Croce for contributing to the defense of mainstream liberal-capitalist politics and for defining national character in terms of an intellectual elite class. Nevertheless, Gramsci also saw Croce as a promoter of intellectual reform who rejected religion, scientific dogmas, philosophical system building, and irrational myths. Gramsci also appreciated Croce's concise, clear literary style and historicism, which he took to be prime reasons for Croce's growing influence in Europe. Gramsci deepened his understanding that all human activity is political through his reading and analysis of Croce's writings.

Earlier Marxist thinkers insisted that the working class was an inherently revolutionary force, that capitalism's collapse was inevitable, and that the manner of collapse was predictable. Gramsci rejected these convictions. Instead, he believed that liberal-capitalist regimes were able to transform and reproduce themselves despite their persistent economic contradictions. They did this, according to Gramsci, by establishing ideological hegemony, which stabilized capitalism and reinforced its grip on citizens.

An ideological hegemony consists of values, cultural attitudes, beliefs, social norms, and legal structures which thoroughly saturate civil society. Whereas earlier Marxist theorists stressed the role of the state and the way economic forces molded dominant ideas, Gramsci emphasized the active role ideas play in class struggle and denied that a single cause, such as economics, could explain all social development.

Major social institutions—the state, legal systems, schools, workplaces, churches, families, media—transmit the dominant ideas and the practices they support. A nation's popular consciousness is thus transformed. The most solid ideological hegemonies receive general acceptance and come to be viewed as natural, appropriate, and perhaps even inevitable. In this manner, the ruling ideas become so deeply embedded in social relations that they are internalized by citizens as common sense. An ideological hegemony conceals the sources of its ideas and practices—particular power relations and specific historical circumstances—and presents itself as consisting of ahistorical truths.

For Gramsci, the state mobilizes both force and consent. As a forum of ideological and political dispute and a major medium through which the dominant classes lure popular consent, the state plays a major role in solidifying ideological hegemony.

But instead of relying mainly on the dominant Marxist analyses of economic base–ideological superstructure and state power, Gramsci introduces the notions of historical bloc and ensemble of relations. A historical bloc is formed by popular groups built around a common ideology that challenges the dominant set of ideas. Economic, social, and ideological forces combine to change social conditions. Social forces intrude on existing class domination and coalitions are formed to shift the ensemble of relations, the totality of social relations in historical context, to a new social order. While not ignoring the important role of economics in social change, Gramsci refused to view all cultural and ideological reality as caused only by economic factors.

Gramsci contrasted passive revolution with popular political struggle. Conducted mainly through state agency, passive revolutions respond to a perceived crisis by changing the economic structure from above. In contrast, popular political struggle requires the active participation of the masses, which must instigate a crisis of hegemony and develop a counterhegemony as prerequisites of successful revolution.

Gramsci's notion of hegemony refers to the intellectual and moral leadership that dominant groups exercise within civil society. Hegemony includes two dimensions: (1) the ideological structure that promotes the domination of the ruling classes, and (2) the political power and influence that classes are able to assert in combination. The first dimension refers specifically to the mix of force and acquiescence, say, the capitalist class can invoke to maintain and deepen its prerogatives; while the second dimension centers on class struggle where conditions can form counterhegemonies that can augur social transformation. Here, say, the proletariat have possibilities of forming political coalitions that can animate mass popular support, initiate revolutionary institutions, and shape a counterhegemony capable of energizing cultural and social change. As always, Gramsci relinquishes all claims to historical necessity, economic inevitability, and communism as the preordained, final form of society.

Popular political struggle requires a crisis of authority. Revolution must undermine the spiritual power of the ruling classes by penetrating the false appearances tied to the dominant order and by creating a new set of beliefs, cultural attitudes, and social relations. A counterhegemony must challenge and augur the collapse of the old authority patterns. At early stages of revolt, we can expect mass apathy, cynicism, and confusion as the gap between the promises and the performances of the dominant order widens. Next, we can expect overt, political forms of class struggle: the spread of antiauthoritarian norms, the development of new social relations, antiestablishment subcultures, new language codes, and emerging ways of life. State repression and force may follow. Such a response may serve to quell rebellion if the underlying counterhegemony is weak, or ennoble the rebels by drawing new supporters if the counterhegemony is strong. Successful revolution requires the unsettling of the old ensemble of relations and the transformation of civil society, which prefigures a new state system built on nonauthoritarian foundations. The revolutionary process will involve lengthy transition periods and much unpredictability. Such revolutionary strategies constitute a war of position in which the civil society of a developed nation is the object of attack. In contrast, in primitive societies Gramsci advised wars of movement in which the state is the object of frontal attack.

But what will energize a revolution? Marxists were divided between two answers: spontaneity and vanguardism. Advocates of spontaneity theory held that the working class would rise up to overthrow the state once capitalism could no longer mask its economic contradictions. A time would come when capitalism's relations of production could no longer efficiently use developing technology. Economic conditions would be so bleak that workers would no longer be mystified by the ideological superstructure and they would solidify into a revolutionary class. In contrast, advocates of vanguardism were less likely to view workers as an inherently revolutionary class. Instead, they stressed the role of the communist party in actively promoting and organizing political struggle.

Although Gramsci at various times was drawn to each of these models, his considered judgment was that each was fatally flawed. His relentless commitment to political inclusion undermined vanguardism by an elite force, while his equally strong conviction about the revolutionary role of ideas unsettled spontaneity theory. Instead, he advanced the notion of organic intellectuals.

Gramsci viewed traditional intellectuals such as writers, artists, philosophers, and the clergy as an independent social class typically divorced from social action. In contrast, he emphasized how all human action is inherently political and how all reflective human beings are intellectuals. Although not necessarily the bearer of special technical knowledge, working class intellectualism is woven into the fabric of everyday life. Gramsci was also convinced that there exists a general historical process that tends continually to unify the entire human race. Once he combined his inclusive vision of politics, his conviction that history tended to extend high culture, and his belief that all human action is political, his notion of organic intellectuals followed.

Thus, the underclasses must generate their own intellectual base, revolutionary consciousness, and political theories from self-activity. The solution to lagging revolutionary consciousness among workers is not reliance upon a vanguard elite class that seeks to impose a rebellious spirit externally. Nor is the solution blind insistence that communist revolution is inevitable and working-class consciousness will arise on cue at the appropriate historical moment. The solution is for workers to become revolutionaries through activity at job sites, in homes, and in civil life generally. Decades prior to contemporary feminism, Gramsci insisted that the personal is political. Again, Gramsci highlights the importance of extending democracy through ideas which translate to social activity. The revolutionary party must be a mass party rooted in everyday existence. It must be an agent of social change which coordinates historical forces already in motion. Most important, it cannot be a force of external imposition if it is to prefigure a classless, radically democratic social order.

Gramsci, perhaps more than any other Marxist thinker, understood that political ends are prefigured in the means used to achieve them. If the goal is a classless, sharply democratic society that absorbs the functions of the modern state, then revolutionary activity must itself assume that form. Rather than advancing a universal model of communism, as did Joseph Stalin, Gramsci counseled popular movements that paid careful attention to existing national character and differences in historical circumstances. Because he understood theoretical activity as a changing, dialectical part of mass struggle, he was sensitive to novel ideas, ambiguity, unevenness, and indeterminacy. His own work reflects little dogmatism and a robust sense of the inherent contestability of political strategies and ideas.

Gramsci presents a clear alternative to the historical materialism of Karl Marx, the vanguardism and state centralism of Vladimir Lenin, the spontaneity theory of Rosa Luxemburg, and the social democracy of Eduard Bernstein. He underscores the democratic impulses in Marxism: the need for workers to nurture and express their own critical consciousness; the importance of liberating ourselves from the constraints of false necessities; the practical advantage of viewing revolution as a series of human, active political events; and the role of consent in both sustaining and unsettling dominant political arrangements. Gramsci distanced himself from the scientism of Marxism: his historical bloc and ensemble of relations analysis alters the economic base and ideological superstructure model; he did not believe in the historical inevitability or clear predictability of communist revolution; and he viewed history as indeterminate. His political genius, though, goes beyond his commitment to Marxism. His theory contains lessons for social revolutionaries positioned on all points of the ideological spectrum. To understand his war of position as tied only to Marxism is to permit opportunities for social change to breeze past.

What is most attractive about Gramsci's political program is also most easily contested. His boundless, naive faith in the intellectualism of the masses cheers our egalitarian spirits, but has not ignited salutary cultural transformation; his aversion to violent revolution earns our sympathies, but ignores historical reality; and his reliance upon a war of position elates our democratic sensibilities, but may register, at best, only painfully slow social progress.

Perhaps Gramsci's greatest contribution is the cautionary tale his philosophy embodies for potential revolutionaries. His emphasis on ideological hegemony informs us that genuine political revolution must be preceded or at least accompanied by wider cultural change. Overthrowing an oppressive regime militarily will not automatically expedite the inauguration of the revolutionaries' preferred political structures. At times, powerful world nations such as the United States would be quite properly outraged at the excesses of totalitarian governments such as Iraq under Saddam Hussein. Leaders of such nations may allow themselves to be captured by a fantasy: if only we destroy the tyrant, the people will rise up, cheer democracy, and a new egalitarian republic will emerge. Where overthrow of the dictatorial leader promises to be relatively easy, the temptation to take action amplifies and seduces. In 2003, to a large extent, this process energized the invasion of Iraq. The good news was that overthrowing the tyrannical regime was even easier than anticipated. Although promising the "mother of all wars," Saddam Hussein generated the feeblest of all battles. His tyranny was deposed and he was captured with even fewer coalition casualties than expected.

However, the bad news was unsurprising for those who had studied Gramsci. Lacking democratic traditions and having endured centuries of oppressive theocracies and dictatorships, the citizens of Iraq lacked the cultural prerequisites for instituting an egalitarian republic. Predictably, ethnic and religious strife, which was previously moderated by tyrannical power, blossomed. Instead of tens of thousands of Iraqi taking to the streets singing paeans to democratic reform, longstanding resentments and internecine rivalries proliferated. The words of Gramsci whisper in our ears: without a significantly effective historical bloc that might create a counterhegemonic force, the established ideological hegemony will stymie successful efforts for radical social transformation. Regime change does not translate automatically to salubrious political conversion. As I write, more than a decade after the fall of Saddam Hussein, the volatile situation in Iraq is ongoing and coalition forces continue to search for a graceful exit strategy. Gramsci's cautionary tale remains vibrant.

Gramsci has had great influence, particularly in Italy, among leftist thinkers who are suspicious of the scientism of early Marxism, the tyrannical excesses of the Soviet model of communism, and the doctrinal posture of communist parties generally. Perhaps it is not merely a coincidence that for decades communists in Italy, inspired largely by Gramsci, gained consistent political influence through parliamentary means. A dispute will remain, however, whether this shows that political activity inspired by Gramsci's work is easily co-opted by liberal-capitalist regimes, or whether we are witnessing the building of a counterhegemonic force capable of eventually unsettling the dominant ensemble of relations in Europe. At present, we have a long way to go to achieve a new state and social system built on nonauthoritarian foundations. Hierarchy and division remain, smugly enjoying the bounty of their misdeeds.

Marxism and Power

The lessons of Marxism for power are numerous and profound. First, amplifying Thrasymachus and Machiavelli and anticipating Foucault, Marxism highlights why the most entrenched and enduring power relations are societal and structural, not those based on dyadic personal interactions. Second, oppressive power relations are those that alienate us from our species-being (human nature): those that diminish our possibilities for engaging in creative labor or our prospects for vigorously participating in political activities. Third, the most pernicious and effective relations of power are grounded in more than the coercive force possessed by the superior. Fourth, in such oppressive relations of power, superiors secure the consent and unwitting collaboration of subordinates largely thorough the mystification of ideological superstructure and ideological hegemony. Fifth, the false consciousness that thereby arises is never completely successful in obscuring the reality of economic conditions and political deprivation. Sixth, thus, possibilities for undermining and reversing oppressive power relations exist. Seventh, revolutionary change may occur because either (1) material conditions radically degenerate because of contradictions embodied by the economic structure or because of (2) cultural developments that nurture a Historical Bloc from which a compelling counterideological hegemony blossoms. Eight, a successful revolution would eliminate oppressive power relations; extend the personal power of citizens to engage in creative labor, which would energize their species-being, and in robust political activities, which would thereby subject the terms of social life to collective deliberation; and thus facilitate the use of social power in service of personal transformation and collective empowerment.

Marx and Gramsci focused their analyses on economic and political structures, and offered possibilities for healthy transformation of oppressive power relations. Although neither considered himself a moralist, their views invoked normative validity even if only implicitly.

Marx celebrated nonexploitive and unalienating economic conditions as necessary conditions for the type of creative labor that was required for human fulfillment. Gramsci identified vibrant political participation, woven into the textures of everyday life, as critical for human self-realization.

We shall now turn to contemporary thinkers and movements that confront the enduring themes of power, but in unique ways. Our first visit will be with the work of Michel Foucault, who will argue that power is virtually everywhere because it is presupposed in human relationships. Influenced greatly by Nietzsche, Foucault will unmask the workings of power in strange, obscure places.

PART THREE

VIII

Michel Foucault (1926–1984)

The Ubiquity of Power

I love power. But it is as an artist that I love it. I love it as a musician loves his violin, to draw out its sounds and chords and harmonies.

—Napoleon Bonaparte

At first glance, it is odd to include in a book on power a thinker who said the following: "[W]hat has been the goal of my work during the last twenty years? It has not been to analyze the phenomena of power, not to elaborate the foundations of such an analysis. My objective, instead, has been to create a history of the different modes by which, in our culture, human beings are made subjects. . . . I am no theoretician of power. The question of power in itself does not interest me."[1]

The critical qualifier, however, is "in itself." Because Foucault takes his paramount task to be the creation of a history of the different ways that human beings are constituted he must confront the notion of power, not because of abstract interest but because of the intricate connections he observes among establishing truth/knowledge claims, extant power relations, and the constitution of the self. Although an analysis of power is not his animating impulse, Foucault must confront power relations in order to understand how "human beings are made subjects." Accordingly, his inclusion in a book on power is required in order to more keenly grasp the wider effects of the phenomenon—how the results of our interactions in relationships of power make us the people we are becoming. This aspect of power Thrasymachus only glimpsed; Machiavelli intuited but did not fully develop; and Hegel and Nietzsche understood and elaborated upon. Foucault places the constitutive element of power at the forefront of his analysis.

First Renderings of Power

Foucault cautions against efforts to craft a general theory of power. Instead, he advises that we should focus on particular domains within which power resides and reveal how power structured them.[2] Perhaps Foucault's most famous example of disciplinary power is Bentham's panopticon, a circular structure of cells arranged such that no inmate can be certain that he or she is not being observed from a central watch tower. Under such circumstances, prisoners gradually police their own behavior through self-surveillance, which illustrates an especially effective and insidious form of domination. Human beings accept control of their own subjection: by being aware that they are visible subjects of monitoring; by assuming responsibility for the constraints of power; and by thereby becoming self-policing subjects, they collaborate with power through ongoing self-surveillance. In addition, Foucault analyzes disciplinary forms of power that are not explicitly within the political realm. For example, he describes how the physical body is a focus and vehicle of the interplay of power and knowledge exercised by the medical sciences, social workers, and modern psychologists.

Emphasizing the network of relations that constitute social power, Foucault concludes that

> [power] is never localized here or there, never in anybody's hands, never appropriated as a commodity or piece of wealth. Power is employed and exercised through a net-like organization. And not only do individuals circulate between its threads; they are always in the position of simultaneously undergoing and exercising this power. They are not only its inert target; they are always also the elements of its articulation. In other words, individuals are the vehicles of power, not its points of application. . . . The individual is an effect of power, and at the same time, or precisely to the extent to which it is that effect, it is the element of its articulation. The individual which power has constituted is at the same time its vehicle.[3]

Foucault's rendering of power is nuanced. Instead of portraying it as overtly oppressive, he stresses how it facilitates production. In addition, he emphasizes how power circulates throughout everyday social practices and is not simply imposed from above through state and economic policies. Finally, he downplays the role that personal beliefs and ideological distortion exert in establishing complex, shifting power relations. Accordingly, he concludes that social practices and productive gains are more important than beliefs and ideology for recognizing the workings of power. Modern power is more invidious than the oppression overtly wielded by earlier despotic regimes because it operates more ubiquitously, silently, and effectively, thereby rendering itself invisible to unreflective eyes. As such, Foucault distances himself in this regard from the ideological analyses of Marx and Gramsci.

Following Nietzsche, Foucault emphasizes the connection between power and knowledge. For him, knowledge is power in the sense that the exercise of power and the creation of truth are mutually sustaining: "We are subject to the production of truth through power and we cannot exercise power except through the production of truth."[4] At the level of society, oppression requires specific forms of knowledge and recognized truths in order to exist, while those specific cognitive foundations emerge in relation to the particular structure of oppression in place. Thus, power-over at the social level is wielded oppressively but is also constitutive of the established cognitive and cultural orders. Moreover, power-over and truth are partially constitutive of human beings in that they function to legitimate certain social roles that we occupy and that contribute to our identities. The processes that constitute a person as a subject of consciousness also shape that person as subjected to power.[5] On this account, the genealogy of the development of knowledge and truth claims becomes critical for grasping the nature and location of oppression. Foucault recognizes that he is constituted by *his* history, but he aspires to submit that history to critical interrogation, and liberate himself from its false necessity. (As with Nietzsche, however, Foucault must evade the self-referential paradox as the apparent universality of several of his claims coalesces uneasily with his own attacks on dogmatism, objectivism, and necessity.)

Foucault talks of his genealogical interpretations as histories of the present because his accounts are situated in the precise reality they seek to interpret and understand; they recount the past from the situated and interested standpoint of the interpreter and of an anticipated future. As such, genealogical method cannot claim to operate from the Archimedean perspective of an Ideal Observer. Like Nietzsche, Foucault attacks rationalism more thoroughly than thinkers such as Hegel and Marx whose critiques aspire to a more adequate rendering of reason. Foucault's genealogy cannot pose as science because it takes human sciences as implicated in the social webs of discipline and domination. (Of course, this suggests that Foucault's own method is an attempt to transform power relations and is, itself, an exercise of power.)

As opposed to merely ruling over subordinates, power regulates and normalizes human subjects by generating norms and imperatives in social discourses that seem detached from identifiable issuing agents. The connection of knowledge and power is critical here. Discourses of knowledge and normative validity are mechanisms of legitimating extant power relations. For Foucault, power and knowledge are not separate, nor are they equivalent. Instead, discourses of knowledge and normative validity create truth, construct and situate human subjects, while embodying power. In this fashion, Foucault places a contemporary gloss on the insights of Thrasymachus, Marx, and Gramsci on how the exercise of power shapes normative discourse.

As such, for Foucault what becomes solidified as "truth" is produced by multiple forms of constraint. Distinguishing between irrationality, deviance, and error, on the one hand, and rationality, normality, and accuracy, on the other hand, is part of the politics of the enterprise of knowledge and truth. For Foucault, truth is a regime that governs and its production arises within relations of power. In the contemporary disciplinary regime, coercion and force have been largely replaced by the bureaucracy of experts waving the banner of objectivity. By privileging certain types of discourse, distinguishing truth from falsity according to specified criteria, and by promoting certain methods for determining truth, the regime of knowledge confers pride of place upon those who can learn and use them effectively.

Foucault's earliest renderings of power are elastic and elusive. Power is nothing more or less than a host of relations and the context in which actions occur. As the entirety of influences on actions, Foucauldian power is not something an individual agent or identifiable group possesses and exercises over other agents and groups. Instead, power is the influencing of present actions by the results and interactions of previous and concurrent actions. Thus, he concentrates his discussion of power on actions rather than on agents. As such, Foucault's portrayal of power resists the definitions and descriptions I sketched in chapter I. For him, power is entirely relational so it is not *in and of itself* anything at all. Because power is not in this sense anything, interpreters of Foucault tend to make his rendering of power everything: "Foucault stressed three themes in his 'nominalist' analytics of power: it is immanent in all social relations, articulated with discourses as well as institutions, and necessarily polyvalent because its impact and significance vary with how social relations, discourses, and institutions are integrated into different strategies."[6]

But such a diffuse depiction of power seems uncongenial to another of Foucault's crucial claims: that power constitutes human subjects. We are *produced by* and *exist within* power relations and the context in which actions occur.

[I]t is . . . a mistake to think of the individual as a sort of elementary nucleus, a primitive atom or some multiple, inert matter to which power is applied, or which is struck by a power that subordinates or destroys individuals. In actual fact, one of the first effects of power is that it allows bodies, gestures, discourses, and desires to be identified and constituted as something individual. The individual is not, in other words, power's opposite number; the individual is one of power's first effects.[7]

Foucault, then, emphasizes power's capability to create, situate, and regulate human subjects as opposed to merely exercising force over antecedently constructed beings. His notion of "subjectivization" understands the human subject as both conjured into being and subjected by power. As the effects of power relations, human subjects are not simply the antecedent elements upon which power is exerted by some over others. As such, Foucault distances himself from viewing power as a commodity, object, or transferable substance. Instead, power is constitutive of human subjects and functions through relationships. Power operates from within and is dispersed from an intricate social web.

On this view, power constitutes human subjects through discipline, a vast array of techniques, such as surveillance, social hierarchy, reports, and evaluations administered by prisons, asylums, factories, the military, and schools, all designed to amplify an individual's productive force. Discipline domesticates the body by integrating into the prevailing social institutions and facilitating the internalization of the relevant norms of conduct. Another technology of constitution is governmentality, a fusion of government and rationality, designed to regulate more than to discipline. At this level, the entire national community is efficiently, effectively, and rationally managed. Whereas discipline attends more to individuals, governmentality focuses on the entire social body. Together they pervade the human subject, inducing him or her to internalize values and standards of behavior, while celebrating the dynamics of normalization.

To have such a, well, powerful influence one would suspect that power must be more than an omnipresent horizon encompassing the entirety of social relations and the context in which actions occur. But Foucault distances himself from the view that power is exercised by superior agents, consciously or not, to adversely affect the interests of subordinates. He takes behavior to be regulated impersonally. Instances of oppression (he would use the more traditional "domination") and coercion are not the essential elements of power. Of course, oppressive, dominating, intimidating actions,

and the like sometimes occur in the intricate network of relations that
constitute power, but these are simply possible results of the interactions
of previous and concurrent actions, and not definitive of the phenomenon
of power.

Likewise, Foucault, despite first appearances, does not *equate* power
and knowledge. For him, the two are reciprocal and thus distinct. Power and
knowledge are two dimensions of the context within which human beings
act and within which they are constituted. When Foucault intones that "it is
not possible for power to be exercised without knowledge [and] it is impossible for knowledge not to engender power,"[8] he means only that human
relations are informed by epistemology, or at least by expert judgment, and
that those relations and actions accompanying them constitute power. New
knowledge will thus generate new power as it will affect human relations
and accompanying actions, and power (the host of human relations and
the context in which actions occur) cannot be exercised unless informed by
knowledge of some sort: "[T]ruth isn't outside power, or lacking in power:
contrary to a myth whose history and functions would repay further study,
truth isn't the reward of free spirits, the child of protracted solitude, nor
the privilege of those who have succeeded in liberating themselves. Truth
is a thing of this world: it is produced only by virtue of multiple forms
of power."[9]

Accordingly, for Foucault, power directly affects actions, not individual agents or social groups. Power facilitates some actions and hinders
others. Because power is impersonal, rebellion or resistance is internal to
it. Resistance is directed at certain types of constraints on actions and by
attempting to mollify the strength of the constraints to which it is directed,
resistance is an aspect of relations of power. Thus, resistance is not aimed
at undermining power as such, but is instead an essential ingredient of
power's fluid context. Power is not a fixed, final phenomenon. Instead, the
dynamic of its relations affects the context in which it operates. Power is
mobile and unpredictable. Every act of resistance or compliance affects the
totality of relations and the context within which they operate. As power
relations multiply, so, too, do acts of resistance, which themselves generate
new power relations. In addition, Foucault is adamant that power can be
"exercised only over free subjects, and only insofar as they are free."[10] A slave
is a subject of domination and not a component of a power relation because
all of a slave's actions are coerced (in contrast to Hegel's depiction of the
lordship-bondage relationship). As such, the slave is completely constrained,
not merely limited in regard to *some* of his or her actions. Because there is
a physical relationship of complete constraint, the master-slave relationship

is not a power relationship that presents a range of options and alternate actions for the members of the relationship. Foucauldian power, though, does not leave agents in power relations with equally open choices among equally available alternatives: power has shaped the choices and actions of actors by having antecedently constituted them in various ways. (One might well conclude that Hegel's account of the lordship-bondage relationship was more acute and refined than Foucault's understanding of slavery.)

In any event, this is a paramount reason, along with the broad definition of power, why Foucauldian power is ineradicable and all-pervasive. Being strictly relational and embodying resistance of varying degrees to some of its extant constraints on actions, power is inescapable. But this bears dreary news only for those operating from a non-Foucauldian understanding of power. Such interpreters will conclude, wrongly, that Foucault is insisting that oppression, coercion, intimidation, and the like are necessary dimensions of human life and that resistance is futile because it is automatically feckless. Instead, a charitable reading of Foucault would highlight that for him human beings cannot have relations outside of power in that our interactions all take place within an environment of constraining and influencing actions in one way or another. To transcend power one would have to flee from human relationships, from the context in which they take place, and from the antecedent conditioning of earlier actions arising from power relations. The only available possibilities are solipsism, or escape to a deserted island, or enslavement (but only if we accept Foucault's account of master-slave relationships). As a result, for Foucault, an enterprise such as constitutional democracy depends upon the existence of the proper sorts of power relations.

Such a broad understanding of power allows Foucault to elude certain objections to his views—that he sees oppression as pervasive; that he must conclude that rebellion is futile because power relations are inevitable; and that the complicity of knowledge and power is pernicious and beyond transformation—but opens him to other, equally serious, problems. For example, can Foucault account for contrasts that we ordinarily are firmly convinced must exist: those between abusive exercises of power that are morally wrong and more benign exertions of authority; between salutary epistemological discoveries and those that are merely masks for increasing the power of superiors over subordinates; between occasions when exercising power facilitates the advancement of knowledge in service of the common good and times when power conjures knowledge claims in order to privilege its own prerogatives? In sum, Foucault seems unable to help answer the question that we find most pressing about power: How do we distinguish exercises of power that merit our allegiance and celebration from exercises of power that are abusive and chill the proper functioning of the social order? Complicating Foucault's ability to answer such questions is his apparent repudiation of the justification of all universal moral norms which, for him, can be demonstrated through genealogical analysis to arise from contingent, contestable power/knowledge relations.

Such conceptual difficulties lead Nancy Fraser to observe that

> [o]n the one hand, [Foucault] adopts a concept of power that permits him no condemnation of any objectionable features of modern societies. But at the same time, and on the other hand, his rhetoric betrays the conviction that modern societies are utterly without redeeming features. Clearly, what Foucault needs, and needs desperately, are normative criteria for distinguishing acceptable from unacceptable forms of power.[11]

What is clear is that exercises of power underwrite some knowledge claims while invalidating others; that abusive exercises of power sometimes validate knowledge claims that are otherwise unsound; that even sound knowledge claims can be manipulated to advance the interests of abusive power and that such power can at times even produce sound knowledge claims; and that rebelling against entrenched power is sometimes required in the service of truth. But can Foucault's account of power accommodate such apparently obvious phenomena?

Unsurprisingly, Foucault, following Nietzsche and the Frankfurt school of theorists, distanced himself from the Platonic notion of an unchanging metaphysical foundation from which objective truths arose.

> But if Foucault's project of a history of truth and of reason as the vehicle of truth resembles the Frankfurt theorists' in what it decries, namely a timeless, acontextual Reason that ignores its own values and interests, it differs markedly from their enterprise in what it fosters: not a historical Reason that unifies multiplicities in a developmental totality, but a plurality of counterpositions, of points of resistance, of styles of life—of "truth."[12]

In this regard, Foucault more resembles Nietzsche than the Frankfurt school. He connects the creation and acceptance of truth to ways of living that vary among different types of people; he aspires to evade problems of self-reference (Well, then, what authority do *your* prescriptions possess?) by casting suspicion upon, as opposed to logically disproving, certain truth claims by demonstrating their dubious historical origins or the questionable sorts of people whom they attract; and he offers new possibilities for believing, being, and acting in the world that flesh out the connections between knowledge, power, and self-constitution. All such efforts undermine the false necessity that the dominant understandings and social practices in place reflect the way things must be. In the manner of his ancient Greek heroes and his existentialist precursors, Foucault takes himself to be a contemporary parrhesiast rendering a vision of truth that connects theory and practice: "a truth one does or lives rather than [merely] says."[13]

We assume that Foucault must preserve common contrasts between power well-used and power abused; between knowledge that nurtures an increase in power-to and knowledge that is nothing more than a cover for the extension of oppression; and between the justified and unjustified use of power-over others. Yet Foucault stresses only the ubiquity of power and casts aside normative evaluation of it, perhaps because of his background view that universal moral judgments are themselves nothing more than the effects and vehicles of power.

But, certainly, more is required. Any critical project must retain a vantage point from which it can evaluate and not merely describe the workings of its subject. Otherwise, resistance and rebellion to extant power relations is difficult to explain unless one portrays the world as a Hobbesian state of nature in which human beings compete for the superior position in power relations in zero-sum contexts motivated only by self-interests while lacking independent normative appeal. On this gloomy view, one set of power relations is no better or worse (from a normative standpoint) than any other; moral assessment is misplaced because it is nothing more than one power game evaluating the outcomes of other power games. The result is that invocations of legitimate or rightful exercises of power are nothing more than rhetorical strategies and the exercise of power afflicts all claims to knowledge. If so, knowledge is merely power under a different name and cannot embody independent validity. More strikingly, Foucault's own work is nothing more than his thinly disguised attempt to exercise power and merits no more or less consideration than those, such as Platonic metaphysical realists, that he targets. Readers should merely self-consciously choose the side that will advance their own power objectives.

Such a picture of the world is conceptually bankrupt and phenomenologically untrue to reality. While the existence of power relations (power-over) in society is inevitable and widespread and such relations influence what comes to be taken as true, this does not disable normative evaluation.

What comes to be taken as true is not *merely* the result of a raw power struggles; power relations vary radically in their genesis, internal possibilities, and restraints; and the different effects of the exercise of power and the production of knowledge can be observed and evaluated as they register on the lives of human beings.

Foucault is most interested in the mechanisms by which domination secures the compliance of subordinates. He emphasizes the remarkable connection between power and knowledge: how claims to the possession of privileged knowledge sharply impact the lives of others. Foucault focuses on a series of domains in his quest to produce explanations of how forms of domination and the asymmetrical balance of forces operate wherever social relations exist; of the ways these power relations are structured; the forms they take; and the techniques upon which they rely. He is less interested in the individuals or groups who dominate as a result of the power arising from social relations. Most strikingly, Foucault concludes that human beings are both constituted by power and at the same time function as the vehicle of power.

Most important, the effectiveness of power is proportional to its ability to conceal its own mechanisms in the social practices that define daily life. As such, power both represses and produces. Power represses through prohibitions and constraints; its success depends on making subjects vulnerable to its effects by molding their desires and choices. Power produces by promoting pleasure, shaping forms of knowledge, facilitating certain discourses, and molding subjects by encouraging specific types of character, defining what is normal and abnormal, and rendering them capable and willing to embrace established values and practices of sanity, health, sexuality, and the like. Power, then, is productive in that it generates meanings, social order, and partly constitutes human subjects. Power and freedom are implicated in that human subjects can attain freedom only within a context of power that partially constitutes them. Human beings become subjects in at least two dimensions: subject to others "by control and dependence" and connected tightly to their "own identity by consciousness and self-knowledge."[14]

In contrast to some Marxist thinkers, for Foucault social conditioning is not simply the dissemination of the dominant ideas of the ruling class. Instead, such conditioning is more repressive because it engenders "the reciprocal confluence of common desires and corporeal dispositions."[15] Thus, as David Ingram observes:

> Scientific measurement, classification, and therapy modify strate-
> gies of detention, surveillance, conditioning, and spatial parti-

tioning that find increasing deployment in schools and factories, prisons and hospitals. Thus, scientific discipline conspires with strategic technique to create a new hierarchy of knowledge/power that instrumentalizes social relations both vertically and horizontally.[16]

Accordingly, the self is constituted by power relations that preclude the individual from knowing himself or herself without the distortions arising from those relations. The process thereby shrouds the individual from the contingencies and historical forces that shaped the self.

In his early work, Foucault genealogically analyzed social institutions that embodied hierarchical authority from the standpoint of his notion of power—a network of ubiquitous social relations in which we are all implicated always. Foucault underscored the constraints attending all social orders, all rational practices, and all institutionalized socialization. However, a feeling of hopelessness could arise if readers conclude that social power is inescapable. Worse, under Foucault's early work, what we might well consider the more important issues surrounding social oppression become less pressing: Who are the superiors who hold power? How do they benefit from its exercise? How do subordinates suffer as a result? The problem is that under Foucault's broadest understanding of power almost anything an agent does can be described as its exercise. In one sense, Foucault may be correct, but only trivially so: power-to is all-pervasive; but power-over understood as oppression is not all-pervasive. Accordingly, by denoting everything, the term *power* seemingly connotes nothing.

For example, Foucault describes the constitution of individuals as "one of the prime effects of power" and "the element of its articulation . . . its vehicle."[17] Taking this at first blush, we might conclude that ubiquitous, suffocating social forces shape each of us into people who merely reinforce and perpetuate the constraints of power in place. Even rebellion against the power of the status quo is implicated within it: "Where there is power, there is resistance, and yet, or rather consequently, this resistance is never in a position of exteriority in relation to power."[18] As such, the agency of subordinates seems either to evaporate or incline toward collaboration.

If so, Foucault grossly misleads. That every nation or large community must socialize its populace is undeniable. We learn the meaning of being a good citizen, of right and wrong, of the parameters of success, of cultural norms, and the like through the social institutions of family, school, religion, and media representations. This could hardly be otherwise. Thus, that existing social relations and institutions play crucial roles in forging our identities is beyond dispute. Later, individuals may play their part in continuing the process or in resisting it or in amending it. Thus, individuals situated within society retain agency after even the thickest existing socialization process. Foucault too facilely dismisses the beliefs, intentions, choices, and actions of socialized agents. His model of social interaction invokes asymmetrical oppression and disciplinary socialization too widely and too univocally. In so doing, extant social practices themselves become anthropomorphic forces that reign over human affairs: truth and even subjectivity are understood as and reduced to the effects of social power.

Thus, in his early writings, Foucault's work seemingly implies that there is no liberation from power, no ultimate escape from domination, and no way to judge between competing ways of life. Each society imposes its own most influential ideas and ways of life on its inhabitants and no independent way to adjudicate between these conflicting modes of living is available. The result is soul-crushing: power is everywhere; we are all formed largely by its effects; our ability to transcend power structures seems feeble or nonexistent; and the distinction between free actions and unfree actions apparently evaporates.

Foucault sums up his position thusly:

> [Each competing way of life advances its own] regime of truth, its "general politics" of truth; that is, the types of discourse which it accepts and makes function as true, the mechanisms and instances which enable one to distinguish true and false statements, the means by which each is sanctioned; the techniques and procedures accorded value in the acquisition of truth; the status of those who are charged with saying what counts as true.[19]

and:

> There are manifold relations of power which permeate, character-ize, and constitute the social body, and these relations of power cannot themselves be established, consolidated nor implemented without the production, accumulation, circulation, and function-ing of discourse. There can be no possible exercise of power without a certain economy of discourses of truth which operates through and on the basis of this association. We are subjected to the production of truth through power and we cannot exercise power except though the production of truth.[20]

At times, Foucault even speaks of power-over as an anthropomorphic agent: "Power would no longer be dealing simply with legal subjects over whom the ultimate dominion was death, but with living beings, and *the mastery it would be able to exercise over them* would have to be applied at the level of life itself; it was taking charge of life, more than the threat of death, that gave power *its access* to the body."[21] Such imagery mystifies the notion of power-over and has troubling metaphysical implications. Worse, it suggests that human beings are at the mercy of an external agent that is beyond human understanding and influence. Surely this cannot be what Foucault intended. Furthermore, in his early work Foucault describes power as all-pervasive, unavoidable, and only partially resistible. He adds that power constitutes human beings—it makes us who we are—yet its agency is beyond our control. So disciplinary practices such as psychoanalysis constitute patients as subject to the precise desires and preferences from which it supposedly aims to free them. In his early work, Foucault ignores the use of power-over in service of empowerment.

In sum, Foucault's early work confronts a host of questions: If power is so pervasive does it lose its distinctiveness? How are we to judge appropriate from inappropriate exercises of power and acceptable from unacceptable relations of power? What normative standards permit us to justify acts of rebellion and efforts to transform extant power relations? Why would we undertake such acts and efforts? How would we do so? And for what end? How and why is resistance implicated in power's basic constitution?

Later Refinements

In his later work, Foucault highlights the care of the self, the aesthetics of existence, and parrhesia. Along with his distinction between (1) rigid power relations that translate to domination and (2) power relations that are more open to revision and reversal, these elements may permit him to respond to critics who raise the objections and questions sketched above. In addition, those sympathetic to Foucault's work might distinguish between refusing to accept the purported justifications of universal moral norms that claim to apply at all times and everywhere and accepting local, provisional justifications of moral norms rooted in particular contexts at certain times. Saddling Foucault with a view that no one can coherently embrace, articulate, and practice—All normative claims are equally justified or unjustified—strikes fair interpreters as suspicious, if not utterly unwarranted.

Fortunately, in his later work Foucault distinguishes between "states of domination" (what I call "oppression") and "relations of power as strategic games between liberties" (what I call "paternalism," or "empowerment," or "influence").

> When one speaks of "power," people think immediately of a political structure, a government, a dominant social class, the master facing the slave, and so on. That is not all what I think when I speak of "relationships of power." I mean that in human relations . . . power is always present: I mean the relationships in which one wants to direct the behavior of another. . . . These relations of power are changeable, reversible, and understandable. . . . Now there are effectively states of domination. In many cases, the relations of power are fixed in such a way that they are perpetually asymmetrical and the margin of liberty is extremely limited.[22]

Now, Foucault makes clear that power as such is not evil because it need not be domination. To exercise power in strategic games between liberties, where power differentials can be reversed (or where subordinates can eventually sever themselves from the relationship after benefiting from it?) is not evil. The later Foucault shifts his focus to the human agency by which we transform ourselves and establish rules of conduct to make our lives "into an *ouvre* that carries certain aesthetic values and meets certain stylistic criteria."[23] The reverberations of Nietzsche are evident.

In his later writings and interviews, Foucault was well aware of the critical attack against his earlier work. He recognizes that human beings constitute themselves actively. We do so by practices of self, which are "patterns that [we find] in the culture and which are proposed, suggested, and imposed on [us] by [our] culture, society, and social group."[24] The danger here is that Foucault distances himself from some of his more radical, earlier claims, but in so doing domesticates his own position. That human beings are socialized—that society offers roles and practices that are culturally available; that we tend, over time, to internalize these offerings and accept them as our own, yet to experience them as freely chosen, is a commonplace. That our substantive sense of freedom arises from socialization and regulation registers no surprise.

But in his later interviews, Foucault clarified the paramount topics of his philosophical research: the connections between knowledge, power, and the constitution of human subjects: "Knowledge as the technique of power, power as the elaboration of the field of knowledge, knowledge as domination of the object."[25] He had analyzed the relationship between the human subject and discourses of truth through coercive practices such as psychiatry and the penitentiary systems, or in the context of theoretical or scientific practices such as language. In his later work, he studies the same topics by analyzing what he called "the practice of the self,"[26] which he traces back to the Greco-Roman era.

Most important, Foucault makes clear that relationships of power can be other than states of domination. First, he defines domination:

> There is a whole network of relationships of power, which can operate between individuals, in the bosom of the family, in an educational relationship, in the political body . . . [sometimes these are states of domination] in which the relations of power, instead of being variable and allowing different partners a strategy which alters them, find themselves firmly set and congealed. When an individual or a social group manages to block a field of relations of power, to render them impassive and invariable and to prevent all reversibility of movement—by means of instruments which can be economic as well as political or military—we are facing what can be called a state of domination. It is certain that in such a state the practice of liberty does not exist or exists only unilaterally or is extremely confined and limited.[27]

Next, Foucault insists that power is always present in human relationships that entail affecting the behavior of others. In relationships of power that are other than states of domination change, reversals and instability reign because the parties are free. In such relations of power—those that are other than states of domination—a measure of mutually recognized liberty must persist and the possibility of resistance by the subordinate party must be present. Thus, instead of advancing an understanding that power is ubiquitous and thus that full liberty is, practically speaking, impossible, Foucault's mature position is that "if there are relations of power throughout every social field it is because there is freedom everywhere. . . . One cannot impute to me the idea that power is a system of domination which controls everything and which leaves no room for freedom."[28] Accordingly, Foucault explicitly distinguishes between (1) relationships of power, understood as strategic games (that result when some people try to affect the conduct of others) between mutually recognized liberties and (2) states of domination.

Finally, Foucault ties practices of liberty to new relationships of power that permit care of the self. He contrasts the Greco-Roman era when Platonic, Epicurean, and Stoic philosophers celebrated the theme of care for the self with contemporary societies that view that theme suspiciously: "Caring for self was, at a certain moment, gladly denounced as being a kind of self-love, a kind of egoism or individual interest in contradiction to the care one must show others or to the necessary sacrifice of the self."[29]

The care of the self requires knowledge of one's self and of rules and principles of conduct which are also truths and regulations. Thus, Foucault restates the connections between knowledge, power, and the constitution of the self. On this model, to be free means not only to be not enslaved, but also to not be a servant to one's own immediate appetites. In the name of practices of liberty, one must establish a discipline or power over one's self. Foucault echoes the Socratic theme that "the good ruler is precisely the one who exercises his power correctly, that is, by exercising at the same time his power over himself. And it is the power over self which will regulate the power over others."[30] In sum, he is arguing that what I call oppression and what he terms domination arises from the failure to take proper care of the self, which produces a human subject who is enslaved by his basest, immediate desires. Perhaps surprisingly, here Foucault joins cause with Plato. In that vein, Foucault sees philosophy, the struggle of thought with itself, as a discipline that by its very structure challenges existing contexts of domination. The critical function of philosophy underscores the need to care for and master the self and to interrogate the assumptions and methods of the disciplines that produce society's dominant ideas: "What is philosophy . . . if it is not the critical work that thought brings to bear on itself: in what does it consist, if not in the endeavor to know how and to what extent it might be possible to think differently, instead of legitimating what is already known?"[31]

For Foucault, critical to the care of the self is the practice of truth-telling modeled on the ancient Greek parrhesiast. Like Socrates and the Cynics, the parrhesiast reveals the truth in order to tend to the souls of others and himself. Unlike the rhetorician who does not necessarily believe what he utters, or the prophet who speaks the truth as a mediator between a higher authority and an audience, or the sage who is not antecedently motivated to express his wisdom, or the teacher who is obligated to transmit knowledge but typically assumes no risk in doing so, the parrhesiast speaks the truth in order to manifest his beliefs, often at great personal risk[32] The purpose, then, of parrhesism is to advance a particular way of being and acting in the world. Foucault suggests, in my terms, that the parrhesiast exercises power-to in service of salutary self-transformation and exercises power-over, grounded in his or her superior knowledge and experience, in order to empower other people to transform themselves positively. In short, Foucault aspires to recapture Nietzsche's vision of life as a work of art.

Foucault notes three dimensions of philosophical discourse related to parrhesism: *alétheia* (forms of expressing the truth); *politeia* (structures and rules of governance); and *éthos* (normative principles guiding social relations). The parrhesiast insists that these three dimensions remain distinct but all three dimensions must be addressed if any of them are to be discussed. Again, Foucault underscores the inseparable connections between knowledge, power, and the constitution of the self.

Socrates was a grand parrhesiast in that he fearlessly spoke what he took to be the truth at great personal risk. His convictions that virtue arose from knowledge and that the proper cultivation of the soul is the primary human enterprise anticipated several Foucaultian themes. Socrates stressed the need for the appropriate political structures, embodied unique ways of expressing his convictions, and searched for appropriate normative principles and deep theoretical understanding. He eventually died for his beliefs and thereby became the ultimate exemplar of parrhesism. Crucial to this understanding is the way that Socrates crafted parrhesism into a distinctive way of life: his life manifested his convictions and doctrinal commitments. For Socrates, the search for truth is not merely an exercise in abstract thinking or a way to stimulate the intellect, but the only way to learn how to live one's life. His manner of living and self-knowledge amounted to "an aesthetic of existence" which involved "a practical proof, a testing of living and of truth-telling that yields a certain form to this rendering an account of oneself."[33] Socrates, then, represented a life of undivided rectitude, lived in accordance with normative principles that reflected and sustained a harmonious soul.

The Cynics eliminated the Socratic theoretical quest for deep theoretical understanding and basked in their role as deflators of the dominant social ideas. Cynical practice was explicitly outrageous, risky, and countercultural. The Cynics' philosophical convictions *were* their lifestyle. They challenged fellow travelers "to live radically different lives from those conforming to the received wisdom of their contemporaries."[34] They did not merely gnaw at the margins of social conventions, but relentlessly challenged and renounced the extant institutions, convictions, and dominant practices of all the cultures within which they dwelt. Their material minimalism, radical self-possession, dramatic displays of opposition, disdain of social honor, and self-assumed mission as scolds and guides for all humanity positioned the Cynics as impossible parrhesiasts to ignore.

In describing the connection between truth and power, Foucault often uses elocutions such as "the games of truth" or the "games of science." I have tried to avoid such expressions because they seem to trivialize the subject addressed. But he clarifies his use of the term: "When I say 'game' I mean an ensemble of rules for the production of the truth. It is not a game in the sense of imitating or entertaining . . . it is an ensemble of procedures which lead to a certain result, which can be considered in function of its principles and its rules of procedures, as valid or not, as winner or loser."[35]

He reiterates that the existence of power is not evil as such, and, again, that not all power relationships are states of wrongful domination. At their best, power relationships are strategic games where alterations, reversals, and transformations are possible because of the presence of mutual liberty. For example, Foucault describes the pedagogical institution:

> I don't see where evil is in the practice of someone who, in a given game of truth, knowing more than another, tells him what he must do, teaches him, transmits knowledge to him, communicates skills to him. The problem is rather to know how you are to avoid in these practices—where power cannot not play and where it is not evil in itself—the effects of domination which will make a child subject to the arbitrary and useless authority of a teacher, or put a student under the power of an abusively authoritarian professor.[36]

Regarding truth, Foucault develops Nietzsche's project: he does not claim to discover or invent something more foundational than the metaphysical (Platonic) notion of truth; instead, Foucault unveils the multiplicity of truths that the metaphysical notion of truth conceals and ignores. Thus, Foucault seeks to loosen the chains of necessity: past notions of truth and how they connected to power and the constitution of the self were ordered differently from contemporary ideas and practices that should not be viewed as natural and inevitable. Implicit in the process of socialization is a design for normalization, which, for Foucault circumscribes and impoverishes human possibilities. Thus, Joseph Rouse remarks that

> [t]he connection [Foucault] proposes between power and knowledge is not just a particular institutional *use* of knowledge as a means of domination. Foucault objects to the very idea of a knowledge or a truth outside of networks of power relations. The scope of his objection thus also encompasses the possibility of a

critical knowledge that would speak the truth to power, exposing domination for what it is, and thereby enabling or encouraging effective resistance to it.[37]

Evaluating Foucault

The problem in Foucault's early work is that it is unclear for what cause resistance to and liberation from the status quo can be championed. If there is no escape from a system of power and no grounds for concluding that a new system would be better in some sense than its predecessor then the peals of rebellion ring hollow. To object to domination requires that conditions of nondomination are possible and preferable. Foucault was seemingly impaled by his own doctrine, as he apparently lacked criteria to distinguish one regime of power from another, while he insisted on the inexorable links between power, knowledge/truth, and self-constitution.

However, Foucault clarifies much in his later work and it is highly doubtful that his position can be so easily undermined. For him, power is not merely something possessed and exercised by superior agents "because it is co-constituted by those who support and resist it. It is not a system of domination that imposes its rules upon all those it governs, because any such rule is always at issue in ongoing struggles."[38] The dynamics of power, then, are spread over complex social networks comprised of power relationships characterized by continual struggle: "Power is exercised only over free subjects, and only so far as they are free."[39] Moreover, not all such networks and relationships translate to domination. Some of the criticisms of Foucault included earlier in this chapter assume that he was committed to the conviction that all power relations are equal in that they all involve domination. This is not the case, and Foucault makes that clear in his later work.

Must Foucault's philosophy, because of its repudiation of epistemological foundationalism and its acceptance of the ubiquity of power, reject the possibility of transformative agency and appeal ultimately only to aesthetic sensibilities? I think not. Although Foucault does not make such recommendations explicit, I would argue that he can avoid the most severe and common objections to his philosophy.

First, his rejection of epistemological foundationalism need not fall prey to self-referential paradox and disable him from advancing positive prescriptions. Like Nietzsche, he does not logically disprove the truth and knowledge claims of the dominant order, but, instead, his genealogical and archeological critiques are designed to cast serious suspicion on the supposed naturalness, appropriateness, and inevitability of the dominant ideas. The purpose of such critiques, then, is to open possibilities and probe alternatives to the received order—all in the service of conjuring more glorious ways of life.

Second, Foucault must confront the paradox of progress: What progress can be made if power relations are inevitable and an ahistorical, objective vantage point of evaluation remains inaccessible? Do not all social orders socialize their citizens through mechanisms of discipline, control, surveillance, and punishment that aim at normalizing activity? Under Foucault's own presuppositions and conclusions, how can we evaluate one social order in relation to another? How can we construct a model social order toward which to strive?

The answer is often obscured by Foucault's rhetoric. But I offer the following on his behalf. Not all power relations degenerate into dominance. Some power relations are more easily reversible, permit greater degrees of mutual freedom, and are fairer games than others (such as those of dominance). We progress as we ascend to looser contextual structures which encourage their own destabilization, thereby giving currency to human possibilities. We are not engaged in self-defeating rebellion for its own sake, but transform power relations for a purpose: to liberate human personality. We never discover the Archimedean point that might arrest all future context smashing; we never create a nontranscendable context which is indisputably superior to its competition; but neither are we trapped by a democracy of conditionality. Criteria are available by which to evaluate various conditional contexts, criteria that distinguish pernicious dominance from fair games of power. Some conditional power relations are superior to others based on their flexibility and acceptance of destabilization. The contrast here is between rigid structures that resist attempts at destabilization and flexible structures that facilitate their own transformation. In rigid contexts, the distinction between context-preserving and context-transforming activities is relatively clear, while in more flexible contexts there is no firm distinction between the two activities. Presumably, context smashing itself does not turn into yet another routine because the process is neither ceaseless nor monotonous; progress, in the senses noted earlier, can be made.

Foucault's conviction in the inevitability of power relations arises from the benign observation that people will always try to influence and affect the beliefs and behavior of others. But not all power relations are equally desirable. Thus, those power relations that accelerate their own self-revision and allow more possibilities for destabilization are preferable to those that are fixed, solidified relations of dominance. Foucault, thus, could appeal to criteria beyond aesthetic sensibilities to distinguish salutary from destructive relations of power. Moreover, he can give a clear reason why these criteria bear merit: they facilitate better than their contraries the goals of self-care reflected in the Greco-Roman classical model. Foucault implores us to explore the diversity of our natures and to create modes of living that ameliorate the effects of power relations of dominance. Such a rejoinder to his critics allows Foucault to highlight, again, the connections among truth/ knowledge, power relations, and the constitution of the self.

Foucault intentionally never sets forth an explicit definition of "power" and he often speaks loosely when he invokes the term. For example, I have already demonstrated that trying to influence and affect the beliefs and behaviors of others is neither necessary nor sufficient for the possession or exercise of power. Thus, his notion of power is undoubtedly overly broad. In addition, on his own account, Foucault cannot claim to have entirely escaped the effects of his own disciplinary society; he is not quite Plato's philosopher fleeing from the cave, gaining special insights, and returning to educate the deluded masses who remain prisoners. Foucault probably exaggerates the ubiquity of disciplinary techniques in the maintenance of the modern state, while downplaying the ongoing role of the faithless trinity of violence, coercion, and legal sanction. More importantly, Foucault does not explicitly identify the principle or phenomenon that disciplinary power allegedly domesticates. In order to have a purpose and point, modern power must operate against some force or possibility. (Perhaps Foucault could cite freedom, human transcendence of dominant ideas and practices, and healthier modes of self-care as the targets of disciplinary power. But whose purposes are served, then, by relations of power of dominance and how do they originate?) Finally, one might well contest the defense I have offered on Foucault's behalf. Are the distinctions between relations of power of dominance and more flexible power relations; between context-preserving and context-transforming activities; and between rigid and flexible institutional structures substantive enough to provide a normative patina for Foucault's philosophical project? Is the notion of progress I have described and the enterprise of context smashing I have sketched enough to rescue Foucault from an indictment that his theory is "all hat, but no cattle" (an enticing form that lacks compelling content)? I must leave those judgments to readers.

Nevertheless, his analyses of the connections between power, knowledge/truth, and the constitution of human subjects are instructive in a host of ways. First, he reminds us that in modern societies power is less frequently exercised by individuals with special prowess and status and is, instead, more commonly exercised through impersonal administrative systems that operate in accordance with abstract rules. Disciplinary sexual practices, psychoanalysis, and other normalizing techniques employed by criminology, medicine, and sociology nurture human subjects that are both docile and productive. For Foucault, not even sexuality is a natural set of behaviors; instead, dominant sexual activity is the product of discourses and practices that constitute the surveillance and control of human subjects.

Second, the exercise of power requires the production of accepted knowledge and truth claims. The most effective power is embodied within a network of relations that secure the consent of subjects by luring them into internalizing dominate norms and values. Third, genealogical and archeological examinations demonstrate that dominant ideas and practices arise from specific historical origins that lack objective or foundational justifications. Fourth, disciplinary power is a set of techniques for governing human beings that simultaneously amplifies their capabilities (their power-to) and their controllability. Fifth, even power relations of dominance cannot extinguish the possibility of resistance and reversal. Sixth, in order to transform the self, human subjects must detach themselves from extant modes of being and behaving, and create new ways that are at least somewhat detached from the disciplinary order. The end sought is the loosening of the constraints of power relations of dominance. Finally, although much of Foucault's work is anticipated by the likes of Nietzsche, Marx, Freud, and Wittgenstein, Foucault's specific applications and development of their thinking—in domains such as sexual practices, prison punishments, conceptions of madness, and psychiatric counseling—illuminate and amplify their insights in concrete situations.

By now it should be clear that the problem of the nature and legitimacy of normative validity is at the center of debates about power. Distinguishing justified from unjustified exercises of power requires subjecting human actions to the tests of independent normative criteria. But how might we access such criteria in a diverse, contentious global community?

A contemporary of Foucault's, Jürgen Habermas, offers an answer arising from his efforts to refine the philosophical project of the Enlightenment period.

Jürgen Habermas (1929–)

The Power of Communicative Rationality

Silence is the ultimate weapon of power.

—Charles De Gaulle

Habermas rejuvenates the efforts of classical philosophers such as Socrates and Plato to confer a privileged place to normative validity in an analysis of power. However, unlike them, Habermas does not commit his analysis to the existence of enduring, mysterious metaphysical foundations. He begins his project by claiming that there are three different human sciences based on three fundamental cognitive interests, and understanding the nature of truth and nature of ourselves can provide a rational, universal basis for scientific and social norms. If Habermas's project is successful, it would provide an avenue to disaggregate the connection between truth/knowledge and oppression.

Human Sciences or Knowledge

The three human sciences correspond to three primary cognitive interests and three dimensions of social existence. The following chart outlines this correspondence.

Table 9.1. Correspondence in Human Sciences

Sciences or Types of Knowledge	*Cognitive Interests*	*Social Existence*
Empirical-Analytic (natural science)	technical	work
Historical-Hermeneutic (history, linguistics)	practical	interaction
Critical (psychology, art, philosophy)	emancipation	power

Empirical-analytic sciences express the human interest in controlling and manipulating our natural environment in order to survive. Through historical-hermeneutic sciences human beings shape themselves by clarifying the conditions of communication and language required to understand other people and social contexts. Critical sciences identify irrational and unjust features of social arrangements as a prelude to understanding the conditions under which nonalienated work and free interaction are possible.[1]

For Habermas, positivist accounts ignore the important and inextricable link between the sciences and human cognitive interests. Fundamental human interests shape the conditions of inquiry under which truth claims are made in these three areas. The three cognitive interests have "quasi-transcendental" status. That is, they are neither contingent, groundless facts nor ahistorical, transcendental foundations.[2] Such cognitive interests shape and determine the objects and forms of human knowledge. They are rooted in the conditions of self-constitution of the human species. Habermas's targets of criticism here are those who argue that there is only one type of knowledge, based on the model of the natural sciences and defined by the search for hypothetical-deductive theories and controlled observation and experimentation.[3] Habermas insists that a more comprehensive concept of rationality is required to give force to other deeply rooted human cognitive interests.

Sharply parting company with normative skeptics such as Thrasymachus, Habermas nevertheless also distances truth from exaggerated claims of objectivity, and distinguishes between different cognitive approaches characterized by varying configurations of "action, experience, and language."[4] He refuses to identify instrumental and strategic rationality as rationality as such. In his view, taking instrumental and strategic rationality as the vehicle of social oppression tells only part of the story. Capitalism has failed to develop adequately the different dimensions of rationality and thereby privileged the economy and government administration, the systems and institutions most prominent in wielding instrumental and strategic atonality. In Habermas's view, contemporary society has failed to pursue the full modalities of reason. In that vein, Habermas distinguishes objectifying (behavioral) approaches from interpretive (hermeneutical) from critical (genealogical or dialectical) approaches for understanding the human sciences. Unlike Foucault, who insists on the inextricability of knowledge and power, Habermas views only objectifying approaches as inherently directed to increasing control over human beings; interpretive approaches can extend intersubjectivity by facilitating mutual understanding. Habermas stresses the effects that speech acts can have on the actions of others, not in terms of gaining or exercising power over them, but more in terms of influencing them. Noncoercive discourse affects behavior in many cases more effectively than do exercises of power-over. Also, critical approaches can distance us from the dominant ideas that sustain extant social practices. For Habermas, societal norms are valid only if they are acceptable to all those affected by them as they take part in practical discourse. For Habermas, "a continuum obtains between power that is merely a matter of factual custom and power transformed into normative authority."[5] He thus distinguishes imperatives enforced by threats from commands underwritten by rationally compelling moral authority. Moreover, power may be exercised by personal prestige and influence devoid of threats and explicit force.

The problem for Habermas is whether his distinctions between transcendent reason and historical reality and between communicative and strategic actions can evade the self-referential paradoxes of reason. As with Foucault, Habermas struggles with a perplexing dilemma: any sweeping critique of ideology—as emanating from a contingent social reality that arises from the outcomes of power struggles and that lacks independent justification—undermines the persuasive force of the critic's own prescriptions; yet if theory embodies only aesthetic appeal it apparently relinquishes its critical bite.

The Basis for Social Norms

Habermas addresses the problem of independent justification directly. He argues that norms are presupposed and anticipated in the alienated forms of action and discourse under which we operate, just as our presently distorted human discourse presupposes and anticipates the "ideal speech" situation.[6] All communicative action presupposes a background consensus that involves four validity claims: (1) the comprehensibility of an utterance, the claim that each sentence employed conforms to the grammatical rules of the relevant natural language; (2) the truth of the propositional content, which is the claim that the speaker communicates a true proposition that represents a state of affairs; (3) the sincerity and veracity of the speaker, which is the claim that the utterer expresses his or her intention truthfully and sincerely; and (4) the legitimacy of the performative utterance, the claim that the illocutionary component of the speaker's utterance conforms to a mutually recognized normative background. This background consensus is generally taken for granted, but discourse arises when consensus is interrogated and no longer easily assumed. The aim of such discourse is to distinguish a merely accepted consensus from a rationally justified one. The basis of this distinction is argumentation itself, which itself lacks fixed decision procedures and incontestable criteria of evaluation.

But such argumentation is informed by the ideal speech situation, which is characterized by: (1) a lack of domination, hierarchy, internal neurosis, and external oppression; (2) the equality of participants as asserters and criticizers of truth claims; and (3) the absence of all power (in the sense of power-over) except the power of argument itself.[7] Such a situation requires the proper material conditions, as well as an ideal community and form of life. At present, such an ideal speech situation does not exist because of structural disturbances to communication, which include the ideologies of consumerism, sexism, racism, and technocracy. Unable to realize such ideals at present, we can only anticipate them.

David Ingram sums up Habermas's understanding as follows:

> *Communicative action* foregrounds the internalization of social roles and the acquisition of higher-order competencies for rational argumentation requisite for reflexive forms of learning. Such discourse, Habermas, believes, is always an immanent possibility for speakers who hold themselves rationally accountable. They must be prepared to justify their utterances if challenged, and they must do so rationally. This, in turn, implies a commitment to reach an impartial consensus on disputed knowledge claims and moral beliefs—a consensus that can be guaranteed only if each interlocutor has equal opportunities to speak, free from the external and internal constraints that distort communication and frustrate mutual understanding.[8]

Accordingly, the ideal speech situation is necessary for the adjudication of truth claims and it is defined by free dialogue in which there is a just and undominated atmosphere: people in the ideal speech situation both participate in and have equal access to the means of argument. As speech is essential to human life, Habermas contends that values that are presupposed by speech—such as freedom and justice in unconstrained dialogue—possess universal justification. By connecting science, the ideal speech situation, and norms in this way, Habermas aspires to provide an objective basis for cognitive judgments.[9] Those norms that violate the presuppositions of the ideal speech situation are thereby unjustified.

Habermas hopes to provide a practical orientation about what is right and just, yet to retain the rigor of scientific knowledge. The normative basis of his critical theory is implicit in the structure of the social action and the conditions it scrutinizes and interrogates. On this account, claims of reason are not external to life, but, instead, are immanent forces of social practices that are also criteria by which forms of life may be evaluated.

Clearly, Habermas's account is teleological in that it perceives a telos that is inherently and inextricably attached to human communicative action geared toward mutual understanding. Specifically, this telos, rather than adhering to classical understandings such as the inevitable progression of biological evolution or the unstoppable forces of history, includes a propensity to overcome systematically distorted communication.[10]

Habermas's "consensus theory of truth" includes the presentation of good reasons able to persuade participants in an ideal speech situation based only on the free force of the better argument.[11] Thus, Habermas emphasizes intersubjective norms accepted by a community of inquirers freed from pernicious forms of domination. The conclusions of such an intellectual conclave are not ahistorical, incontestable truths, but, instead, contestable, fallible judgments subject to further self-correction.

Concerns

Several criticisms might be lodged against Habermas's project. First, his illustration of the ideal speech situation is troubling. Habermas needs the ideal speech situation to elevate judgments from the merely contingent and arbitrary to the status of quasi-transcendental. But dangerous circularity looms. An ideal speech situation *requires* a background consensus which itself must be rational. But the intersubjective argument and debate needed to establish the rationality of the background consensus itself presupposes an ideal speech situation. In addition, in order to amount to more than merely an abstract ideal, an ideal speech situation requires concrete political realization—the establishment of the proper material conditions for the desired discourse. Yet, the concrete political realization again *presupposes* a rational background consensus that itself presupposes an ideal speech situation.

Also, notice here the ambiguity in the condition of freedom from pernicious domination. Habermas means, of course, that only the force of rational argument should prevail: there must be no unequal bargaining power, class subordination, radically unequal material distribution, physical coercion, and the like. Only the power of argumentation itself should generate substantive conclusions. But argumentation is engaged in by interlocutors who vary in persuasive power, education, personal charms, and rhetorical skills. Such inevitable inequalities among participants in rational debate, even in an ideal speech situation, amount to a kind of (unavoidable) distortion. Habermas implicitly assumes that the force of rational argument is restricted to ideas, principles, and premises and how they abstractly connect to conclusions. In fact, the same rational argument is often more or less persuasive depending on the character and skill of the person who advances it.

What would the alternative look like? A group of people equal in all respects, including the argumentational skills and attributes noted above, trying to persuade each other by the force of disembodied argument? Unless Habermas is committing himself to the force of pure, abstract argument, independent of who utters it or how it is uttered, the forces of rhetorical and personal distortion are inevitable. If, on the other hand, Habermas is committed, as he seems to be, to the force of disembodied argument, his prescriptions seems as contentless as those emanating from Kant's categorical imperative and Rawls's original position.[12] For if all participants in the ideal speech situation are equal in all respects, including persuasive and rhetorical skills, then they are indistinguishable from one another and seemingly merge into a glob of Pure Reason submitting to the authority of disembodied argument, thereby parodying any claim to Habermasian genuine intersubjectivity.

Second, the conditions themselves of the ideal speech situation may well include implicit and disguised appeals to substantive moral and political theory. Habermas either ignores these or claims that they flow from the formal conditions of reason presupposed in speech. The former tack is disingenuous given Habermas's objections to other thinkers who in effect put the rabbit *in* the hat (implicitly assuming from the outset what the thinker purports to prove), while the latter tack is too reminiscent of the countless Kantianisms from which he seeks to escape.

Habermas's consensus is intended either to be actual, one that could or will come about, or theoretical, one that should come about given the requirements of rationality. If the first, then he does not take seriously the differences among people; and if the second, then he seems to have constructed a warmed-over transcendentalism subject to the usual litany of complaints spewed at Kantianism, some of which have been lodged by Habermas himself. In fact, Habermas seems not to have shed the Enlightenment adoration of a pure, neutral, disembodied reason by which conflicting truth claims might be adjudicated. In addition, he accepts as unproblematic the notion that domination must be purged from the ideal speech situation. Yet argumentation is relevant at the outset to determine what does and does not constitute pernicious domination. Habermas seems to think that universal consensus is already in place on *that* issue, but that is far from clear.

Third, Habermas tells us that in ordinary normative discourse, we perceive and experience certain (partial) frameworks as self-evident. But when ordinary discourse breaks down and is itself interrogated, what types of reasons can provide the standard for judging? Habermas can rely only on the alleged procedures or the normative presuppositions of discourse, while ignoring explicit invocation of substantive grounds that might adjudicate the disputes arising from the breakdown of ordinary discourse. This consequence of his theory underscores Habermas's proclivity for privileging the illocutionary act involved in asserting normative claims, rather than the substantive content of the judgments that are fixed firmly in those illocutionary acts. By suggesting that it is the procedures and presuppositions of argument that function as the main foci of justification, Habermas is seemingly committed to the view that standards of validity emerge as the *conclusions* of argumentation, rather than function *within* argumentation as (at least one) criterion of choice.

Fourth, Habermas does not distinguish carefully between the human agency involved in adhering to and discovering truths and norms related to our technical cognitive interest and that required for our emancipatory cognitive interest. That is, he suggests that the rationality claims of a science will motivate us to accept them based, at least partially, on their ability to facilitate universal interests. Thus, our technical interest is best served by those methods and standards that seem to permit us to control and manipulate our natural environment, where control and manipulation serve universally. The universal rationality of these methods and standards motivates their acceptance. But our emancipatory cognitive interest, contra Habermas, seems to require a quite different motivation. For there our individual interests are often in conflict. Just as Hobbes did not foresee clearly that for a self-interested individual the social contract was not the best improvement over a state of nature—for the best situation from the perspective of pure self-interest occurs where all others are obeying social norms but "I" disobey them without response from the central authority—so, too, Habermas fails to see clearly that the rationality of a moral or political norm is insufficient to motivate moral and political action unless a person is antecedently committed to the general good or collective social benefit.[13]

From the vantage point of, say, Nietzscheans, Habermas could be understood as yet another scion of the Enlightenment who privileges consensus over disagreement, and who succumbs to an irresistible impulse to build a theory in order to legitimate intersubjective judgments. While disavowing ahistorical, incontestable foundations, Habermas's transcendental urge is too overwhelming for him to avoid substituting another, quasi-transcendental ground for moral and political choice. As such, Habermas may be simply a newer model of an old, long line of thinkers who aspire to unveil the allegedly purely rational background presupposed in deliberation and normative choice.

From the critical vantage point, Habermas embodies a pernicious rationalist tendency. He seems to equate social problems and deficiencies with mistakes in one or more of the three areas of cognitive understanding. Thus, he casts his argument with those classical thinkers who believed that if we only knew more or could reason better or could dismiss pesky cultural prejudices, a better vision of political association would emerge. Critics may have less faith in pure cognition and its ameliorating effects on the polity. For example, neo-Marxists would take changed material and social conditions as a more important point of departure for serious progressive politics than improved reasoning, which they would take to be largely ideological (in the pejorative sense).

Habermas and Power

As he developed his main philosophical themes, Habermas adjusted his position and directed his attention more thoroughly to the nature of power, communicative rationality, and distinguishing claims of normative validity from exercises of social and administrative power.

As always, Habermas's faith resides in undistorted communication that is free of structural constraints that prevent or hinder participants from an equal opportunity at rational discourse. Such communication "can release prospective meanings latent in world views, as well as already existing interests which have been denied expression by the suppression of generalizable interests."[14]

Hannah Arendt's rendering of power highlights the human capability of acting cooperatively to attain common aims. Such power is not embodied by a particular person and ceases to exist when the relevant group of human beings disperses. Hers is an explicitly normative version of power, where force to accomplish ends is linked to positive value. For Arendt, a government that oppresses the people is not powerful but weak. Such a structure has a limited shelf life and will surrender to internal revolution or external conquest, or it will try to solidify its prerogatives through explicit tyranny.

Habermas interprets Arendt's understanding of power to rest on the formation of a common will through communicative rationality directed toward
understanding and agreement. Power, on this view, is "the communicatively
produced power of common convictions [arising from] reciprocal speech or
unconstrained communication."[15]

Habermas uses Arendt's notion of communicative power as the springboard to outline how social and administrative power are legitimated through
public discourse that embodies normative standards. Communicative power
is grounded in collective agreement, a consensus attained through the formation of the collective will guided by communicative rationality. The resulting
norms provide a framework within which strategic social and administrative
power can be exercised less oppressively than otherwise. Communicative
power exercised from within a public arena that is organized fairly can soften
social power differentials. For Habermas, the moral norms arising from the
process of communicative rationality embody context-transcending validity
and should be institutionalized in the political and legal structures that frame
social action. These norms, again, arise from intersubjective communicative
rationality conducted under proper conditions. In this fashion, Habermas
hopes to have established conditions such that truth and knowledge can
be sheltered from the contamination of social power exercised oppressively.

Communicative Rationality and Language

Habermas takes the alleged presuppositions of language to reflect its essential
nature which is the medium of communicative rationality. Argumentation
is fundamentally illocution in that the best argument embodies the highest
persuasive force. The ideal speech situation is the engine of human progress
and contrasts to the distorting influences of the media of money and power.

Unlike Foucault who stresses the actions arising from power relations
as paramount for constituting the human subject, Habermas emphasizes
intersubjective experience grounded in rational communication. For him,
human beings are socialized into a rationally communicative lifeworld:
"Identity is produced through socialization, that is, through the fact that
the growing child first of all integrates into a specific social system by
appropriating symbolic generalities; it is later secured and developed through
individuation, that is, precisely through a growing independence in relation
to social systems."[16] Unlike Foucault, Habermas does not highlight relations
of power as major constituents of the self. Instead, he underscores socialization occurring within a process of rational communication and relations

of mutual recognition. Whereas Foucault recognized the descriptive character in his analysis of power, Habermas, as always, stresses the normative grounding of his.

Of course, human beings proceed through socialization that does not reflect an ideal speech situation. Thus, socialization must occur within a context of power relations. But Habermas is not alarmed by this admission. Amy Allen captures his position well:

> First, [Habermas] assumes that the social controls that have to be internalized are rational and the authority of the parents who enforce them is legitimate; thus they are unobjectionable from a normative point of view. Second, he assumes that the outcome of this process is the capacity for autonomy, a capacity that allows the individual subject to reflect critically on and assess the validity of the norms, relationships, practices, institutions, and so forth, into and through which the individual has been socialized.[17]

To regard the paternalistic and transformative exercises of power by a parent over a child as unobjectionable is one thing, but the processes of socialization go well beyond what takes place in a caring family. Habermas too easily embraces a process that is often distorted by oppressive power relations and the ideological conditioning that supports them. To observe that individuals can subsequently reflect critically upon their socialization and assess the validity of the norms they learned, too facilely ignores how the oppressive exercise of power can control ideological agendas and render the genuine interests of subordinates opaque. The deeper problem for Habermas is that his philosophy requires a sharp distinction between validity and the effects of power, and this seemingly seduces him into an overly sanguine portrayal of the socialization process. That validity is connected to power—in that what comes to be viewed by a culture as valid is inextricably connected to the workings of power relationships—seems intuitively obvious. But it does not follow that validity is merely the end of the causal workings of power relations. By distinguishing legitimate and illegitimate exercises of power more acutely, Habermas could elevate power to a more prominent place in his philosophy without violating his pursuit of universal norms. That he does not do so is a shortcoming of his position.

Habermas narrows the notion of communicative action in this way: the deliberative process should restrict itself to illocutionary speech aimed not merely at strategically luring participants to certain desired behavior (which would be perlocutionary persuasion), but, instead, toward understanding and agreement that engender intersubjective relations noncoercively (or, more precisely, noncoercively coercively by means of the best argument that warrants our allegiance). One clear problem is whether such discourse can genuinely establish the desired intersubjective relations or whether such relations are presupposed, they must already be in place, prior to engaging in the discourse. Habermas seems to ignore the preconditions required for participants to enter the salutary discourse he conjures.

But let's brush this technical problem aside for the moment. In addition, Habermas's ideal speech situation is exclusionary from its beginning. Instead of requiring extensive public participation, he requires only that the points of view of everyone be *represented* in the rational decision-making process. This ignores the process values of participation itself for those engaging in rational discourse. As Gramsci might remind him, even if "my" desired outcome wins the day and is established as part of the consensus of everyone, if I did not actually participate in the process leading to that result I do not benefit as thoroughly as I might have.

Communicative rationality and the moral norms it produces are designed to justify and frame political and legal institutions that mollify social power differentials. But the communicative process producing the required norms should be justified noncircularly. That is, what comes first—the framework for communicative rationality that produces the required norms or a context already rich with norms that defines the process of communicative rationality? A critic may well object that any process of communicative rationality must presuppose a context (which includes a host of moral norms) in order to proceed. If so, on what basis were these norms legitimated? If an apologist for Habermas appeals to a prior process of communicative rationality, then we curry the specter of an infinite regress of moral norms preceded by a process of communicative rationality preceded by another set of moral norms, and so on. In fact, social agents generate moral norms from extant contexts even though the resulting products typically aspire to or assume transcendent authority. In addition, the substance of moral norms is produced at a time and in a place that does not reflect an idealized starting point or procedure. As such, social power cannot neatly be excised from the process of deliberation or from communicative rationality in general.

> While consensual basic norms underpin the creation of material norms, public discourse rarely leads to consensual moral outcomes in this substantive sense. Rather, in benign circumstances,

societal argumentation in the public sphere is likely to generate a higher level of rationality in public discourse and hence the application to norm-setting processes of a variety of perspectives claiming moral validity. Insofar as they are opposed, not all can be "right" in the ultimate sense of [Habermas's] discourse ethics. In certain cases, some initially have a real but disputed moral force and *may* then acquire universal institutional validity. Examples are minority rights in a democracy or some basic precepts of social or gendered justice. . . . In the real conditions of public discourse, moral claims are raised without the possibility of an exhaustive procedure of validity testing that would satisfy the adequacy conditions of moral argumentation.[18]

Habermas is also somewhat untidy in identifying shared understandings and meanings with agreement. A group of citizens may well share the same understandings and meanings, but not agree to the same normative rules or social institutions. But suppose a community, following Habermas's prescriptions, could arrive at a consensus of everyone through the representative process. Would this result be an unambiguous benefit? The arrival of overwhelmingly acknowledged "truth" may well entrench bland orthodoxy and be accompanied by the surrender of robust discourse. Vigorous political activity requires a diversity of voices and judgments, not genuflection in the presence of the dominant ideas. Where dogma and doctrine prevail, unconstrained dialogue struggles mightily. Habermas's nifty slogan of "noncoercive coercion" may mask the beginnings of implicit tyranny and explicit conformity, both of which suffocate the energy of normative debate and intersubjective exchange. Accordingly, whether "truth" underwrites rationally uplifting politics or whether it facilitates oppression is contestable and undoubtedly a function of social context.

Communicative Power

Habermas distinguishes communicative power as a normative, justified force from potentially oppressive administrative and social power. Properly designed laws should delineate the sphere of communication aimed at understanding from the potentially coercive power of the state. Communicative power arises "only in undeformed public spheres . . . only from structures of undamaged intersubjectivity found in nondistorted communication."[19] Administrative power arises from the state's exercise of authority through an instrumentally rational process. The two sources of power are both connected and separated by law, which transforms the communicative power developed in informal public spheres and in deliberative governmental branches into administrative power exerted by the state. In addition, Habermas describes social power as "a measure for the possibilities an actor has in social relationships to assert his own will and interests, even against the opposition of others."[20] Habermas concludes that the three sources of power permit us to "interpret the idea of the constitutional state in general as the requirement that the administrative system, which is steered through the power code, be tied to the lawmaking communicative power and kept free of illegitimate interventions of social power (i.e., of the factual strength of privileged interests to assert themselves)."[21] In addition, administrative power must not reproduce itself without being informed by communicative power bearing normative justification. If so, administrative power does not directly address normative justifications; being instrumentally rational, it merely legitimates its decisions by pointing to the normative justifications embodied by communicative power.[22]

Habermas aspires to minimize two problematic results: administrative power amplifying itself without reference to the normative justifications and reasons arising from communicative power, and social power being directly translated into administrative power. For him, robust political institutions must transform communicative power into administrative power. Accordingly, he invokes a principle of the separation of state and society such that social power cannot be directly translated into administrative power "without first passing through the sluices of communicative power formation."[23]

But how are we to judge whether the exercise of administrative power has been infected by the noxious effects of unequal social power and without the cleansing tonic of normative justification arising from communicative power? Habermas appeals to an ideal of a communicatively structured lifeworld: undistorted by oppressive relations, an undeformed public sphere that is structured by undamaged subjectivity.[24]

Critical to Habermas's project, then, is a communicative rationality that is uncontaminated by the effects of merely strategic or instrumental action, rationality, and power. But his notion of social power ignores how the human subject is constituted by relations that often embody oppression. Social power as "a measure for the possibilities an actor has in social relationships to assert his own will and interests" requires that agents be in a position to distinguish their genuine interests from mere preferences that have been heavily socialized through oppressive power. If social power plays an inevitable role in constituting the human subjects engaging in communicative rationality it remains unclear how that discourse can be free from distortion, which is required for it to generate the normative resources crucial to Habermas's project.

Habermas's account of communicative power is ambitious and commendable. Building upon the work of Arendt, he hopes to structure power that is neither oppressive nor noxiously coercive. Habermas describes the social and structural conditions that genuinely nurture individual autonomy. But his remedy to the excesses of established versions of power-over severs the construction of moral norms from real world conditions and stresses formal legitimacy to the detriment of substantive context. In truth, the moral norms arising from communicative rationality cannot be completely sheltered from the effects of social power differentials.

Valid Norms

Habermas aspires to, among other things, distinguish validity claims from (mere) power claims. By appealing to communicative rationality he hopes to establish the normative foundations of a critical theory of society. His conception of communicative reason is rooted firmly in the ground of universality. Communicative reason striving for understanding embodies a normative binding force that is noncoercively coercive. Unlike coercion as such, it does not exert pressure in service of exercising or increasing the power of superiors over subordinates; but it exerts force in terms of highlighting the best argument that must command the allegiance of those committed to rationality.

Habermas distinguishes criteria of success, whereby parties reciprocally influence each other in a purposive fashion, from criteria of understanding, the presumed original mode of language use whereby consensus is the primary aim of discourse. Instrumental action occurs when an agent acts to bring about a desired end. Strategic action is a type of instrumental action such that an agent acts to induce other people to do things that facilitate the agent's ends. The ends of instrumental rationality and strategic action are determined independently of reaching consensus. As a result, the systems of wealth and social power—the results of instrumental rationality and strategic actions—reflect and sustain patterns of actions in which agents mask their ends. A salutary society should prevent these networks of instrumental and strategic actions from intruding into its "lifeworld" (the everyday reality we share with others in domains such as family, culture, informal political life, mass media, and voluntary associations where communication and discourse prevail) and contaminating its functions. Oppression within social systems arises because the actions of citizens fall prey to the thick, antecedent patterns of instrumental and strategic reasoning that are seemingly impenetrable.

Habermas asserts that the instrumental or strategic use of language and its aim at success is parasitic on the original mode of speech which is oriented toward reaching understanding by recognizing and accepting validity claims. His central tool here is the distinction between illocutionary acts, which openly declare their aims, and perlocutionary acts, defined by "the peculiarly asymmetrical character of concealed strategic actions."[25] Illocutionary acts are self-identifying; the descriptions of their effects do not refer to a context of teleological action that goes beyond the speech act; their results are internally connected with speech acts; and their aims can be attained only if they are expressed. Perlocutionary acts are such that their aims, at best, must be inferred by the listener from context; their effects are external to the meaning of the utterance; and their aims can be attained only if the speaker refrains from expressing them.[26] Illocutionary speech acts embody only one kind of success: reaching understanding. Perlocutionary speech acts conceal the intentions and aims of the strategic agent. In general, social action is oriented either toward reaching understanding through illocution or striving for success through perlocution. For Habermas, perlocutionary persuasion is a strategic behavior geared toward individual success, whereas illocutionary understanding is oriented toward agreement and consensus.

Exceptions to this categorization are commands or imperatives that openly declare illocutions but do not seem aimed at understanding; instead, commands are oriented toward success and claim a special force. Accordingly, commands, at first blush, are a type of power claim. But Habermas finesses this problem by concluding that commands, although action-oriented toward success also aim at understanding in the sense that they assert normative authorization. That is, imperatives do not earn our allegiance because of the position or status of the utterer but because of the normative validity they embody: for example, "Wear a helmet when riding a motorcycle" embodies a claim to normative validity grounded in personal safety. The imperative aims at both success, taken as compliance with the command, and understanding, taken as acceptance of the underlying claim to normative validity. Imperatives that explicitly lack a claim to normative validity—for example, an armed hoodlum screeches, "Give me your money or I will take your life"—embody a coercive or oppressive power claim and constitute limiting cases to Habermas's general view. Still, even here, Habermas, probably unwisely, ascribes illocutionary force to "*all* imperatives" and explains them all "in terms of the pattern of normatively authorized requests."[27] Thus, imperatives that lack a claim to normative validity are parasitic on the standard case of commands that embody such a claim. In so doing, Habermas effaces his formerly bright line between (mere) power and normative validity. By accepting, in effect, a continuum between normatively authorized force (noncoercive coercion) and starkly oppressive power, Habermas seemingly permits oppression to seep into normative validity.

For Habermas, actions emerge from speech acts. When agents use discourse to generate actions they justify those deeds on the basis of arguments purportedly grounded in good reasons. Such justifications are validity claims, which embody a normative status in that they apply universally (to all agents), they produce duties toward other language users, and are rational in that they are linked to sound arguments and good reasons. On this account, the primary function of discourse is to arrive at understanding by bringing about consensus. Thus, any utterance that is valid, any utterance that is true, and any norm that is right is amenable to rationally motivated consensus. In this vein, Habermas advances the discourse principle, a weaker principle arising from his theory of communication, and the principle of universalizability, a stronger principle that tests the validity of moral norms by assessing their universalizability:

> *Discourse Principle*: Only those action norms are valid to which all possibly affected persons could agree as *participants in rational discourse*.[28]

> *Principle of Universalizability*: A norm is valid when the foreseeable consequences and side effects of its general observance for the interests and value-orientations of *each individual* could be *jointly* accepted by *all* concerned without coercion.[29]

Habermas distinguishes norms, which are rules of behavior grounded in the communicative rationality of the lifeworld, from values, which shape our preferences, interests, and desires. Whereas values are largely cultural and historical, norms are universalizable. Brushing aside whether values and norms can be so neatly distinguished, the discourse principle can determine only which norms are not valid as it provides only a necessary condition of validity: that all possibly affected persons could agree as participants in rational discourse. To fail this test is to reveal the invalidity of a norm, but to pass this test establishes only that a norm has fulfilled a necessary condition of validity. The principle of universalizability provides both necessary and sufficient conditions of validity (at least if we understand "when" to mean "if and only if"). To pass this test is to establish the validity of a norm.

Habermas designs the principle of universalization as the test for whether a set of particular values and interests merits elevation as a valid, generalized norm. Habermas anticipates that critics will object that the principle of universalization invites contingent, ethnocentric intuitions to masquerade as timeless conclusions. That is, when answering the question posed by the principle of universalization we will supply answers arising from our situated, limited understandings and take these answers to be much more than they are. Habermas responds with his transcendental-pragmatic argument: the principle of universalization is an "inescapable presupposition of [an] irreplaceable discourse and in that sense universal."[30] By that he means that the principle of universalization is a necessary presupposition of any moral argument and therefore unavoidable: in order to participate in any argument, the parties must assume that they all take the discussion to be a mutual search for truth such that the rational force of the better argument must prevail.[31]

The justification of the principle of universalizability is murky. The notion of communicative rationality and the discourse principle are thin reeds upon which to rest the principle of universalizability. Beyond that technical problem, how many candidates would survive the stringent test posed by the principle of universalizability? The generality of bromides such as "do good" and "avoid evil" surely pass the test, but their ability to adjudicate serious moral conflicts is severely limited. If two of the functions of norms are resolving moral conflicts and weaving together the social fabric of a community, then the few general norms surviving the test of the principle of universalizability may be insufficient. Finally, a critic might object that passing the test of universal acceptance is neither a necessary nor a sufficient condition of validity: some norms may be valid even though not everyone affected by them accepts them because their rejection arises from people who misidentify their genuine interests, while other norms might be generally accepted but not be valid because the grounds of acceptance are insufficient or arise from radically false beliefs. We must not forget the lessons of Thrasymachus, Machiavelli, Marx, Gramsci, and Foucault about the effects of ideological distortion on the constitution of human subjects.

But an apologist for Habermas might rejoin that he always distinguishes between what human beings would and do agree to in practice and what is in principle amendable to agreement. That is, the principle of universalizability is not intended to reflect what human beings in fact would agree to in the real world, an agreement that is contaminated by numerous distorting influences, some epistemological and some the unfortunate results of differentials in social power. Instead, the principle of universalizability describes norms that are in principle amendable to consensus arrived at under ideal conditions of communicative rationality. Accordingly, under the principle of universalizability, in order to be deemed valid a norm must *merit* the uncoerced assent of all those concerned; it need not be *actually* agreed to by everyone in the world that we know.

This rejoinder is effective, but opens Habermas to a further criticism. How, exactly do we determine the merit of a norm without begging the critical substantive questions? How can the merit of a norm be derived absent some substantive normative presuppositions that are built into the ideal conditions of communicative rationality? Do we genuinely derive the merit of norms or must we antecedently determine their merit by the way we structure our initial conditions of choice? Accordingly, a critic might well conclude that Habermas is less the magician who pulls the rabbit (a conclusion about the merit of a norm) out of his hat and more the magician's assistant who stuffs the rabbit in the hat.

Foucault's objections to Habermas's ideal speech situation are telling:

> The idea that there could exist a state of communication which would be such that truth games circulate without obstacles, without constraints and coercive effects, seems to me utopian . . . a society cannot exist without power relations, if one understands them as strategies through which individuals try to lead, to influence the behavior of others. The problem is therefore not to try to dissolve them in the utopia of a completely transparent communication, but to build the legal rules, the technics of management and also the moral, the ethos, the care of the self, which will help, in these power games, to play with the minimum of domination.[32]

In addition, Habermas argues that "reasons count only against the background of context-dependent standards of rationality . . . reasons that express the results of context-altering learning processes can also undermine established standards of rationality."[33] But if good reasons compel our allegiance because of the context of rationality from which they arise, how are the contexts themselves accepted for good reasons? Human subjects become reasonable by internalizing such contexts, but prior to doing so they must, to avoid circularity, be at least somewhat unreasonable. Accordingly, human subjects must internalize contexts of rationality without appeal to independently good reasons. If we internalize contexts of rationality arbitrarily or from the effects of social power, then subsequent discourse is conducted among those antecedently influenced and shaped by social power. Even if Habermas is correct in thinking that our assertions of truth commit us to presupposing that they can be justified under ideal conditions, what we take to be ideal conditions must embody a context that we already embrace. Again, our notion of ideal conditions, then, is not an independent legitimating agent, but already presupposes a context that is historically situated, not ahistorically transcendent. Perhaps our truth claims aspire to such transcendence, but they arise from within historical contexts.

Habermas intuits part of the problem and suggests that the effects of social power are necessary but not sufficient for the internalization process: "[The internalization process] is usually not repression-free; but it does result in an authority of conscience that goes hand in hand with a consciousness of autonomy."[34] Moreover, law supplements morality by "relieving the individual of the cognitive burdens of forming her own moral judgments";[35] by providing an external inducement to conform to norms; and by its preeminence as a justifying institution. Still, in the real world, law may well be contaminated by the effects of social power, which is sometimes pernicious, and by its independent authority translate those effects to citizens during the socialization process. To object that Habermas, unlike Foucault, has an overly sanguine view of how the human subject is constituted is reasonable. In order to uphold normative legitimacy in discourse and decision making, Habermas struggles mightily to insulate the individual citizen, communicative rationality, and the enterprise of reason itself from the contaminating effects of social power. But in every corner of discourse, subject constitution, and the construction of legal and political institutions we find social power intruding. Although noxious social power may not be ubiquitous, it is widespread enough to gravely threaten Habermas's purification process.

Foucault continues his attack that Habermas's celebration of unconstrained consensus is utopian by adding:

> I don't believe there can be a society without relation of power, if you understand them as means by which individuals try to conduct, to determine the behavior of others. The problem is not of trying to dissolve them in a utopia of a perfectly transparent communication, but to give one's self the rules of law, the

techniques of management, and also the ethics, the *ethos,* the practice of self, which would allow these games of power to be played with a minimum of domination.[36]

Constitutional Democracy

For Habermas, constitutional democracy is a political procedure that controls and limits power because the institution embodies procedures that embody the pragmatic presuppositions of discourse. As such, democracy facilitates communicative action embodying rational agreement to control money and power, the forums that govern systematic integration. Money and power are outside forces that distort communicative discourse if left unchecked.

For Habermas, in liberal capitalist societies power arises from the relations of production: "Has the class struggle organized politically and through unions had a stabilizing effect only because it has been successful economically and has visibly altered the rate of exploitation to the advantage of the best organized parts [industrial wage earners] of the working class?"[37]

Strikingly, Habermas's notion of constituting human subjects dismisses the role of the nation-state. Traditionally understood as critical for shaping a common identity, nurturing a sense of belonging, and mollifying social, cultural, and economic differences among disparate citizens, the nation-state aspires to make the abstract idea of the common good tangible. Yet, Habermas considers national identity to be passé, an outdated cultural artifact; instead, he champions the "constitutional patriotism"[38] of multicultural society. His aversion to the nation state is twofold. First, in his view the nation-state is exclusionary and distances those who lack the same language or ancestry. This can lead to the oppression of minority groups within the state. Second, the emotional identification with such relatively closed communities is "independent of and prior to the political opinion and will formation of citizens themselves."[39] Thus, nation-states are immune from collective deliberation, from reason, and become part of the arsenal of administrative and social power. Invocations of the "fatherland" and "motherland" are compelling slogans by which administrative and social power brokers manipulate the will of the masses.

Again, Habermas is vulnerable to the objection that he fails to understand how the human subject is constituted. Invariably inclined to view human beings as unencumbered, abstract reasoners, he privileges communicative rationality at the expense of the constituents of self that most command our allegiance. Families, cultural traditions, and national heritages are valuable because of their role in constituting personal identity. Human beings are valuable, and without social attachments and connections, some of which rise involuntarily, we would all stand alone, naked before a terrifying and seemingly all-powerful universe. Not to belong to a nation, tribe, or parents—to be stripped of our metaphysical constituents—is to be nobody. We draw strength from and are constituted by our inherited legacy, and to be uprooted, to belong to no place, is the great tragedy of displaced persons, refugees, and aliens. Such people suffer grave and frightening identity crises because they have relinquished some of their most valuable characteristics, those pertaining to membership and belonging. Our inherited legacy thus fulfills necessary psychological functions. Although Habermas creases the mark when he charges that administrative and social power brokers often invoke national identity and patriotism in service of their oppressive agenda, he fails to illuminate why that is possible: the critical role that national identity and patriotic allegiance have played and continue to play in constituting human subjects. That an otherwise valuable constituent of the self can be manipulated and abused is an important cautionary tale, but to conclude that its manipulation and abuse destroy its value is unnecessary and imprudent.

Despite my misgivings, Habermas contributes significantly to the literature on power in several ways. First, he refines and underscores an insight of classical philosophers such as Socrates and Plato: we must filter administrative and social power through the prism of valid norms in order to soften the possibilities of oppression. Second, he amplifies Arendt's insights and constructs a theory of communicative rationality that underscores the "noncoercive coercive" power of sound arguments grounded in good reasons. Third, unlike Thrasymachus, he refuses to succumb to the seductions of an insipid relativism that tolerates too many conflicting positions on the theoretical level but acts quite differently on the practical level. Fourth, unlike the early work of Foucault, he offers a rationale for resistance to purveyors of oppression who distort the conditions required for communicative rationality. Although Habermas's grandest aspirations embedded in his project are unrealized—indeed, perhaps all philosophers must fail in the end—he exemplifies an enduring spirit that animates the search for more wholesome forms of human association.

Theories of power are best observed in action—in their practical efforts to transform societies and create institutional structures geared to fulfilling paramount human interests. To view philosophy in action, we must examine contemporary feminist thought.

X

Feminism

The Power of Collective Transformation

I do not wish them [women] to have power over men; but over themselves.

—Mary Wollstonecraft

Feminists aspire to undermine oppressive exercises of power over women and to develop strategies for the collective empowerment of women that would animate gender equality. To those ends, feminist thought regarding power embodies at least four distinct but overlapping themes:

1. *Ending Patriarchal Oppression.* Under the assumption that patriarchal societies are defined in part by inequalities arising from the disparity in power among men and women, and that a more equal society requires that such disparities be eliminated, some feminists argue that power is inconsistent with feminism's commitment to social transformation.[1]

What feminists rile against is one use of power-over: oppression. Power-to, understood as the dispositional capabilities of individual agents to affect outcomes, cannot and should not be eliminated. In fact, the collective action of reformers to soften social inequalities requires an increase of their power to affect events. Moreover, feminists aspire to elevate the systemic and constitutive notion of social power from patriarchal renderings to conceptions that are more egalitarian.

Understood as a call to end oppression, this feminist theme appears at first blush to be banal. For who favors oppression? Perhaps a few unrepentant fascists and self-styled tyrants in training would embrace the spread of oppression—as long as they were the oppressors—but who else? In addition, even these stalwarts of wrongful domination would clothe their policies and convictions in more acceptable garb: they would claim their harsh principles and views were required by some higher purpose than merely squashing the opportunities and possibilities of the masses. Thus, finding someone who explicitly advocates for oppression and who perceives oppression as serving critical social ends is as difficult as rounding a square. To oppose oppression amounts to no more than reaffirming an analytical truth once oppression is properly understood as a wrongful exercise of power over others such that superiors affect adversely the interests of subordinates.

Perhaps worse, the slogan "the end of oppression" suggests that the less privileged in society are powerless and thus inferior agents. Anna Yeatman observes that

> [w]hen a movement understands itself as representing those who are powerless, the victims of the powerful, it neither permits itself responsibility for, nor engagement in the affairs of the world. It maintains an innocence of worldly affairs, and in particular an innocence in regard to power. It does not confront the truths that power inheres in all relationships, that any interpretation of reality is itself a manifestation of power, and that those who are relatively powerless still participate in power.[2]

In fact, the apparently empty call to "end oppression" is only a starting point for feminism's major project. The paramount issues surrounding oppression form the launching pads for social transformation: How might we distinguish legitimate from illegitimate exercises of power? What social practices and policies are patriarchally oppressive and why? How do such practices and policies arise? How can they be identified? How can they be changed? What concepts and exercises of power are compatible with feminism's ideal of an egalitarian society? In addressing such questions, what began as an obvious opposition becomes a complicated process of identification, explanation, and reformation.

Furthermore, a host of underlying matters makes the answers to the questions posed more complex. For example, assuming most, if not all, extant societies are patriarchal in a pejorative sense and that they have and do disadvantage women significantly it follows that our notions of "power" themselves may be contaminated with male bias. Also, under this assumption, the reformist programs of feminists are hatched in a patriarchal context. Will such "reforms" genuinely pave the way to gender equality? Or, given the context of their genesis, are they more likely to either reinforce or, at least, merely reshape existing privileges and prerogatives?

These underlying concerns mirror the paradoxes that pervaded our discussions of interests and of false consciousness. What a person explic-

itly understands as being in her short- and long-term interests—the fulfillment of what she prefers now and in the long run—is shaped by her
social context. If that social context is radically flawed, the assumption
from which feminists begin their critique, then the short- and long-term
interests expressed by subordinates in such a context are immediately suspect. Contaminated by the pernicious socialization of patriarchal societies,
the explicit understanding of what is in their interests may lead women to
only reinforce the precise privileges and prerogatives that oppress them. In
sum, a victim of oppression may explicitly extol preferences that are not in
fact in her genuine interests (understood as fulfillments that would advance
her objective well-being). Thus, feminists must be careful when answering
the questions about identifying oppression, explaining its sources and possibilities for change, and advancing programs of reformation that they are
not inadvertently serving the interests of their oppressors.

Recalling the lessons of Marx and Gramsci, part of the cultural phenomenon of oppression is the process by which a privileged group's—in this
case, a segment of upper class males—perceptions, values, and experiences
become solidified as universal standards. Having primary access to inter-
preting and communicating events, elite men disproportionately influence
cultural understandings. For example, in law the standard of "the reasonable man," often used in jurisprudential interpretation, is aptly named. This
standard views and examines a sequence of events from the vantage point of
reasonable, educated men but takes itself to embody universal significance.

As the result of such cultural imperialism, "oppressed individuals often
more or less fully accept and identify with the negative cultural images of
their own group as the basis of their own self-image . . . affirming the
cultural values of oppressed groups may serve to maintain or even reinforce their oppression, at least to the extent that those values result from
identification with and attachment to a negative cultural self-image on the
part of the oppressed."[3] Again, we confront the possible conflict between
genuine and extant interests.

2. *Redistributing Power.* Another branch of feminist thought takes
power to be a resource, a social good, that requires redistribution in service
of egalitarian social reform. On this view, the problem is not that men have
power, but that they have too much power to the detriment of women.
Alternately, we could speak of women having too little power in relationship to men. Thus, the solution to the excesses of patriarchal societies is to
redistribute power more equitably.[4]

This view does not directly invoke oppression. That is, it does not
advocate that if power-over is exercised oppressively by both men and wom-
en, but equally, then the harmful effects of wrongful domination will be

balanced. Instead, this view raises the possibility that if power-to was more equally distributed among men and women, then gender oppression would decrease and perhaps even wither away. If the dispositional capabilities of individual men and women, and each gender taken collectively, were equal in that each group could affect outcomes to the same degree, then neither group could oppress the other to a significant extent. Thus, a more equitable redistribution of power-to along gender lines would result indirectly in the end of gender oppression. On this view, power-to is a valuable, desirable resource whose more equitable distribution will have worthy transformative social effects.

But some of the background imagery of this position is problematic.[5] First, it portrays power as a commodity, an object to be possessed and distributed much like any material good. As such, it seems to ignore the wisdom of Foucault and others that power is part of dynamic relationships; that power is partially constituted by resistance; and that power admits of reversals. Second, this position speaks of power as mainly or solely dyadic. The view speaks most directly of the dispositional capabilities of individual agents, while marginalizing the systemic and constitutive aspects of social power. By not addressing the broader social context that molds our notions of power, our possibilities for attaining power, and our relations of power, the position under discussion overly simplifies both the problem of and the solution to oppression. Third, this position portrays power as a scarce resource that should be shared more equitably, whereas, if Foucault is correct, it is in fact the dynamic foundation of virtually all possible actions and interactions.

Although such concerns are legitimate, they may be allayed by amending or supplementing the redistribution of power thesis. The insight of the position centers on its vision of enhancing the capabilities of women to affect outcomes as a prelude for a transition to a more egalitarian society. This insight does not depend on regarding power as a commodity that is possessed and distributed like material goods. Although power-to is not necessarily relational, it is often so, and it is typically nurtured within a larger societal context. Thus, those committed to increasing the powers of women must pay careful attention to relational and societal environments. The redistribution of power thesis, if not taken too literally, does not automatically oversimplify the problem of and the solution to oppression once such clarifications are recognized. If we take this position as claiming only that increasing the power of women is a necessary, but not a sufficient condition of ending patriarchal oppression, then its insight glistens. Although the imagery it invokes does invite the objections lodged, the redistribution of power thesis can accommodate the required amendments without compromising the trajectory of its primary insight.

3. *Using Power-To for Collective Transformation.* A third branch of feminist thought emphasizes collective transformation as a group effort in enhancing the capabilities of women to affect outcomes.[6] I have referred to collective transformation throughout this work as the third major use of power-over: empowerment wherein superior parties act to affect positively the outcomes and/or interests of subordinates with the aim of favorably transforming the subordinates by controlling or limiting the alternative choices or actions available to the subordinate. However, feminists who advocate collective transformation are likely to resist the hierarchical imagery and benevolent control that my rendering conjures even if nobly motivated. They would understand their recommended process as a mutual effort among equals, instead of a top-down enterprise conducted among benevolent superiors and grateful subordinates. The illustrations of empowerment I offered earlier, such as teachers to students and parents to children, might well be seen by some feminists as uncongenial to their final purpose and untrue to their prescribed method of consciousness raising.

Accordingly, feminism's notion of collective transformation is distinct from my rendering of the use of power-over for empowerment. We can agree that both conceptions aim at increasing the power of those who would benefit greatly by such efforts and in so doing transforming them positively. Whereas my depiction assumes the existence of well-meaning, relatively powerful people—superiors in knowledge and experience—aiding the positive transformation of those of lesser knowledge and experience, the feminist conception portrays a mutual quest among equals to collectively transform themselves and others. Feminists advocating collective transformation might well see my rendering of nonoppressive power-over as arising from the contaminated dustbin of patriarchal imagery.

For my part, I would want to distinguish how people become powerful from how they use their power once it is attained. I can join hands with feminists in celebrating those who use their power to increase instead of diminish the power of others. Thus, both conceptions of power explicitly reject oppression and explicitly advocate the positive transformation of self and others. Feminists highlight reciprocity and mutuality among numbers of people joined in common cause as a way of becoming powerful, while the conception of power-over exercised for purposes of empowerment begins from the standpoint of those already holding a power advantage grounded in knowledge and experience.

Moreover, mythologizing feminist consciousness raising as an illustration of the egalitarian, nonhierarchical, collective nurturing of mutual power
is too facile. As Yeatman points out:

> Feminist consciousness-raising is not intrinsically democratic. Even
> though it is structured by a democratic form of turn-taking in
> discussion, it functions in terms of face-to-face relations oriented
> by the desire to find what it is the members of the group have
> by way of experience and feelings in common. This is a total-
> izing politics which can easily be made over to particular kinds
> of moral blackmail and personal tyranny.[7]

Finally, we must acknowledge, again, that efforts at collective transformation are often shaped and structured by oppressive power relations. Thus,
Amy Allen argues that

> [o]nce we conceive of power in relational terms, then not only
> does it no longer make sense to think of domination or oppression
> as a lack of some sort of stuff or good called power but it also
> no longer makes sense to think of empowerment as a process
> of gaining or acquiring that same stuff. Rather, just as domina-
> tion and oppression are understood in terms of social, cultural,
> economic, and political relations that impede self determination
> and self-development, empowerment must be understood in terms
> of social, cultural, economic, and political relations that foster
> and promote these same capacities . . . if we acknowledge that
> modes of empowerment themselves do not take shape outside
> relations of domination and oppression but instead are shaped
> and structured by them, then we must face the difficult issue
> of how to distinguish between modes of empowerment that are
> emancipatory and those that serve to reconfirm or reconsolidate
> systems of oppression.[8]

In any event, feminism's collective transformation conception of power
includes but goes beyond dyadic power relations. Grounded in collective
deliberation and action, this conception aspires to soften if not eliminate
power-over by amplifying the power-to of women. Perhaps prefigured in
Socrates's philosophical methods, which aimed at helping instead of harm-
ing the interlocutors with whom he bantered, Arendt's notion of legitimate
power as collective action, and overlapping Habermas's ideal of consensus

arising from collective deliberation under salutary conditions, feminism's call for power as collective transformation distances itself from oppression while acknowledging that power-to is a relational social good that must be won. Accordingly, we can understand this feminist conception as a distinct use of and way of gaining or amplifying power-to. *Power-to is exercised for purposes of collective transformation when a plurality of agents voluntarily enter into a mutual quest among equals to affect positively their shared outcomes and/ or interests and collectively transform themselves such that their individual and collective capabilities to affect outcomes (their aggregate power-to) are enhanced.*

4. *Using Power-Over for Empowerment.* As detailed earlier, power relations are not always oppressive. Even in their traditional roles, women have exercised power in order to enhance and transform the lives of others.[9] In the most patriarchal contexts, women have possessed and exercised considerable power over others. In fact, Nancy Hartstock argues that women gain different experiences of the exercise of power than men from their tradition social role and consequently they occupy a distinctive standpoint from which to understand power.

> The female experience not simply of mothering (but more broadly the general education of girls for mothering, and the experience of being mothered by a person of one's own gender) is one in which power over another is gradually transformed by both the powerholder and the being over whom power is exercised into autonomy and (ideally) mutual respect. . . . Thus, the point of having power over another is to liberate the other rather than dominate or even kill her.[10]

Accordingly, Hartstock contrasts, in the terms I am using in this work, power-over for empowerment and transformative purposes with power-over exercised oppressively (which she identifies as a male view of power-over). The exercise of power-over for empowerment or other transformative purposes includes three elements: (1) the superior (in this case a mother) exercises power over the subordinate (in this case a child) not to control or oppress, but to benefit the subordinate; (2) the exercise of power is part of a program aimed at eliminating the extant asymmetrical power relation— that is, the transformation of the subordinate into a fully capable person renders the existing power relation inappropriate; and (3) the result is the formation of a mutual, reciprocal relationship between the parties no longer accurately characterized by the locution of power-over. Unlike paternalistic exercises of power that often seek to retain the subordinate in a condition of dependency, transformative exercises of power seek the elimination of the power relation. In that respect, paternalism typically reflects and reinforces a stable relationship, while transformative exercises of power are dynamic and unsettle the status quo. Therefore, the notion of exercising power over others for empowerment and transformative purposes can be used by feminists more generally to establish that not all power relations are equally oppressive, that the truth/knowledge that emerges from power relations is not equally contaminated, and as one way of distinguishing salutary power relations from destructive power relations. In sum, a normative base that can prevent feminists from stumbling into the swamp of abject relativism is available. Accepting the pervasiveness of power relations need not disable critical reflection or prevent critics from constructing a positive program of reformation.

However, the exercise of power transformatively must be clarified further. First, transformative power is not a unique type of power. Instead, it falls under the rubric of power-over: exercising power transformatively is a distinctive use of power-over. Second, exercising power transformatively underscores how those who are otherwise oppressed by power retain much power-to and even power-over in the subcontexts of their general subordination. Within that retention of power reside possibilities for unsettling general subordination and nurturing different overall relations of power. Once again, we observe that subordinates in an oppressive social context still possess resources for resistance and rebellion. Third, we may tend to idealize the mother-child or teacher-student relationships in dangerous ways. While I have stressed the possibilities for unsettling extant power relations and resisting the dominant order, other more pernicious possibilities lurk: mothers and teachers deeply socialized into and by the dominant social order may use power transformatively to sustain and reinforce the generally oppressive context from which their social roles arise. Thus, the *content* of the transformation emerging from this use of power and not its mere occasion is critical. To the extent that parenting or teaching nurtures accommodation with the generally oppressive social order it can transform children and students into little more than unwitting stooges to their continued victimization. To genuinely empower subordinates, superiors must recognize the general power relations that situate and define their roles. If the wider social context is oppressive, then the content of empowerment must be reformative. Fourth, in that vein, within the power relation itself what presents itself and is understood by the parties to be a transformative use of power may, instead, amplify the dominance of the superior party and the dependence of the subordinate. The satisfactions and fulfillments that the superior party (in this case the mother or teacher) experiences during the course of her relationship with the subordinate may subconsciously impel her to actions that solidify that relationship rather than rendering it obsolete. Fifth, the transformative use of power-over must be extended beyond the common examples of parenting and teaching if it is to provide the ballast for a normative evaluation of power relations generally.

Overlapping Themes

The four themes sketched converge on a crucial point: virtually all feminist thinkers agree that relationships offer opportunities to empower and transform others in positive ways. Whether people use their capabilities and exercise power-to for collective transformation or use power-over for empowerment, the main legitimate use of power is not to denigrate but to amplify the lives of other human beings. In a social world where any invocation of the term *power* is most likely to be heard by others as a reference to wrongful domination, the granting of privilege of place to collective transformation and empowerment is no small accomplishment. Power can no longer be conceived in purely negative terms or be viewed as inherently pernicious. In addition, feminism offers a starting point that can distinguish legitimate from illegitimate exercises of power.

In that vein, although the four feminist themes outlined here remain distinct, their areas of overlap demonstrate the trajectory of feminist thinking regarding power. First, power-over exercised oppressively is the paradigm of illegitimate action. Second, power-to, understood as the capability to affect outcomes, is a social good that is typically relational, usually exercised in a wider social setting, and can be amplified by collective action. Third, identifying, explaining, and reforming oppressive, illegitimate exercises of power require some commitment to normative reasoning. Fourth, feminism's commitments to normative reasoning and to the ideal of an egalitarian society require, among other things, accessing the genuine interests of women while women continue to live within an oppressive social context. Fifth, enhancing the capabilities of women to affect outcomes, increasing their power-to, is a prelude for a transition to a more egalitarian society: the empowerment of women is a necessary, although not sufficient, condition of ending oppression. Sixth, the concept of "power" itself plays an important role in determining the boundaries of legitimate and illegitimate action. Seventh, some forms and uses of power are desirable, namely power-to and exercises of power that are positively transformative of self and others, while other forms and uses of power are illegitimate, namely power-over generally and uses of it that are oppressive. Even power-over used for empowerment should be examined carefully because of its hierarchical and unequal origins (although the mother-child relationship and other contexts in which subordinates are unable to access or evaluate their own interests rationally are exceptions many feminists explicitly recognize).

Echoing Marx, Gramsci, and Foucault, most versions of feminism acknowledge explicitly that the most pernicious forms of power do not arise from the overt exercise of violence wielded by a clearly identifiable ruler. Moreover, feminisms stress Foucault's insight about how power constitutes subjects: instead of operating on antecedently constructed women, oppression is critical in creating socially acceptable gender models that undermine women's equality. Wendy Brown and Joan W. Scott elaborate upon feminism's debt to Foucault:

> What feminism surrenders consequent to Foucault's critique is the idea that women's subordination is the consequence of power held in a straightforward fashion by men or the state, wielded in commands or laws, and operating to repress women's innate strength or true nature. It sacrifices the notion of patriarchy as a total system, rooted in a single cause and operating through a coherent machinery. . . . [Feminism thus derived also surrenders] a formulation of resistance that imagines seizing power or imagines finding a place "outside power," a strategy of resistance independent of the powers that constituted it.[11]

The Paradox of Identifying Genuine Interests

Some feminists embrace objective foundations, arising from the liberated subject rooted in "women's experiences," as the basis for identifying genuine interests and the ground for their theory of emancipating power. The politics of personal life retain pride of place and, à la Foucault, they illustrate the ways that oppressive, patriarchal power employs versions of knowledge/truth and the technologies of medicine, social work, and psychology to subjugate women. In addition, such analyses open the way to strategies of resistance to such oppressive institutional structures.

For example, Sandra Bartky illustrates how the disciplinary technologies energize a host of distinctively feminine modes of appearance through dietary and fitness programs, advice on how to present oneself by walking and talking in certain prescribed ways, and promoting ways of styling hair and wearing cosmetics.[12] The subtlety here is that oppressive power reinforces its advantage over women by enhancing their victims' power-to in carefully circumscribed areas. Women gain new abilities, attach themselves to and take pride in embodying certain identities, and measure themselves on their sexual attractiveness. If this account is persuasive, patriarchal power slyly amplifies the subordination of women not by directly seizing power from women but by enhancing particular kinds of power-to, which in a general way boomerang against their users. By forming the female subject in certain ways, the oppressive power structure can maximize its own prerogatives. As ever, this process does not arise from a conscious conspiracy or the strategies arising from the agreements of an explicit congregation of self-described oppressors.

But many allegedly socially constructed situations confronted by women invite conflicting interpretations. Let's continue with the example of feminine physical appearance. Women in reasonably affluent societies are socialized into a beauty culture, reinforced by the cosmetic industry that lures them into placing high value on their physical appearance. One straightforward feminist analysis of this phenomenon is that patriarchal privileges are sustained by diverting women from developing their higher capabilities and by consigning them to focus on relatively trivial matters such as their physical attractiveness to men.

But Bartky points out that the situation may not be so simple:

> The persistent need I have to make myself "attractive," to fix my hair and put on lipstick—is it the false need of a "chauvinized" woman, encouraged since infancy to identify human value with her attractiveness in the eyes of men, or does it express a basic need to affirm a wholesome love for one's body by adorning it, a behavior common in primitive societies, allowed [women] but denied to men in our still puritan culture? Uncertainties such as these make it difficult to decide how to struggle and whom to struggle against, but the very possibility of understanding one's own motivations, character traits, and impulses is also at stake.[13]

Perhaps an answer can be derived from assessing the degrees to which the feminine focus on physical attractiveness has precluded women from developing their higher capabilities. The attention to *la bella figura* is not of itself a mark of oppression. However, if cultivating physical attractiveness becomes the sole or primary route for women to secure a sense of personal worth within society, then the prospects of alienation and exploitation arise. When women embody needs and satisfactions that within their societal context affix them to subordinate social roles, then they have internalized values contrary to their genuine interests. With the internalization of the dominant, oppressive values, those in subordinate positions exercise dominion over themselves; they become their own oppressors and free their masters from continual surveillance over them. Accordingly, the question is not whether concern for physical attractiveness is a mark of subordination as such, but whether it serves the interests of the oppressor in the particular societal context at issue. Where the primary employment opportunities for and the main sources for self-worth of women involve their compliance with conventional standards of physical attractiveness, the obvious conclusion is that the beauty industry serves the prerogatives of an oppressive patriarchy. Where employment opportunities and possibilities for self-worth are more widespread, the concern for physical attractiveness may be less pernicious.

Following the lessons of Foucault, the ubiquity of disciplinary power facilitates its anonymity, which it turn contributes to the conclusion that the production of the more typical versions of "femininity" are either biologically natural or socially voluntary. To the extent to which prevalent ideals of physical attractiveness are prominent causal factors in inclining women to become docile appendages to men, the beauty industry serves the interests of patriarchal oppression. As Foucault advised, that identifying clearly the perpetrators of the relationship between a social phenomenon and oppression is difficult or even impossible should not obscure the causal connection.

How might feminists resist nuanced oppression where it occurs? How might they respond in social contexts where distinctively feminist modes of appearance contribute substantively to oppression? First, the victims must experience the process as oppressive and not as empowering. Reflective thought must raise consciousness such that women understand the consequences. Second, alternate images of the female subject must be promoted: strength, intelligence, and athleticism may be offered as desirable feminine bodily attainments. Third, feminists offer an alternate epistemological outlook that highlights the standpoint of the oppressed and includes a specific theory of power. In that vein, Hartsock argues:

> [W]e need a theory of power that recognizes that our practical daily activity contains an understanding of the world . . . a "standpoint" epistemology [grounded in] the claim to material life . . . not only structures but sets limits on the understanding of social relations, and that, in systems of domination, the vision

available to the rulers will be both partial and will reverse the real order of things.[14]

However, some feminists raise concerns about the foundationalist epistemology grounding this vision. If the identity of women is constructed under social conditions that are patriarchal, appeals to the "standpoint of the oppressed" invoke a perspective within that oppressive context. Can such a perspective, then, genuinely serve as an antidote to patriarchy? Or is it merely a reaction from the subordinates within a set of oppressive power relations that lacks legitimate claims to epistemological authority? In fact, the appeal to epistemological privilege may itself be a remnant of patriarchy. As Wendy Brown observes:

> [The feminist claim to epistemological privilege] betrays a preference for extrapolitical terms and practices: for truth . . . over politics; . . . for certainty and security . . . over freedom; . . . for [scientific] discoveries over decisions [choices]; for separable subjects armed with established rights and identities over unwieldy and shifting pluralities adjudicating for themselves and their future on the basis of nothing more than their own habits and arguments. . . . [The claim to epistemological privilege seeks] knowledge accounts that are innocent of power, that position us outside power, that make power *answer* to reason/morality and prohibit demands for accountability in the other direction. . . . Could we learn to contest domination with strength and an alternate vision of collective life, rather than through moral reproach?[15]

The problem identified is familiar: From what vantage point can feminism elude charges that its prescriptions are simply another series of power claims that lack inherent legitimacy? If feminists claim that the standpoint of the oppressed is uncontaminated by power they confront the objection that their standpoint emerges from what they antecedently insist is oppressive and from the foundationalist epistemology that animates patriarchy. If feminists cast aside all appeals to foundationalist epistemology and accept unsqueamishly that their alternate prescriptions are inherently political and implicated with their own aspirations for power, then on what basis can they conclude that their prescriptions are superior to those emanating from patriarchy? The question is one of legitimacy: How can an aspiring reformist demonstrate that her alternate vision is superior to the extant dominant order without falling prey to the philosophical excesses that the existing regime has employed to reinforce its advantage? If a reformist discards the philosophical baggage—such as appeals to foundationalism, truth purified of power, and a perspective that transcends power relations—employed by patriarchy, then how can she demonstrate the legitimacy of her alternative vision? If she uses the philosophical baggage employed by the patriarchy to legitimate her alternate vision, how can she show that she has escaped the context of her subordination? Does not the "standpoint of the oppressed" arise from experiences and interests women form as subordinates in patriarchal power relations, and does not that standpoint rely on an essentialist female subject that feminists otherwise disparage? In addition, each woman is constituted by various class affiliations beyond her gender such as race, social and economic level, religion or lack of religion, educational level, professional status, family context, and the like. From this olio of often conflicting class affiliations can a univocal "standpoint of the oppressed" be fairly constructed?

The problems may appear intractable, but they are not. Just as Foucault, in my view, can elude many of the common objections raised against him in these areas, so too, can feminists. A workable feminist program might proceed as follows: First, unsettle the veil of patriarchal mystification through consciousness-raising exercises and information. Much of this can be done through immanent critique, by demonstrating that the extant social order fails to fulfill its own promises because its practices do not reflect its theory and stated ideals. The aim is to unmask the character of oppression and the conditions of subordination, and to demystify as ideological (in a pejorative sense) competing interpretations that purportedly justify such power relations. In that vein, the dominant social order's pretension to be authoritative because its prescriptions emerge from a neutral, disinterested vantage point must be debunked. In fact, the prescriptions of the dominant order emerge from a partial, interested perspective that reflects and sustains oppression. Second, accept the proposition that power relations are pervasive and that what emerges as truth/knowledge is not independent of power. Third, understand that accepting that proposition need not degenerate into the hopeless conclusion that all truth claims are equally vacuous or that no legitimate prescriptions and alternate visions can emerge. That all normative prescriptions flow from interpretations that are partial and interested does not imply that they are all equally worthy or unworthy. The social processes by which prescriptions come about, the results they produce, and the nature of the power relations that produced them (oppressive, paternalistic, or transformative) are critical to such an assessment, as is the extent to which they fulfill the promise of widely shared cultural ideals and thereby elude objections emerging from immanent critique. Fourth, distinguish salutary power relations from destructive power relations; perhaps in the manner I have done so on behalf of Foucault. By unsettling the obtuse idea that all power relations must be or are equally oppressive, and that the truth/knowledge that emerges from power relations is equally contaminated, social critics lay the groundwork for legitimating their own assertions. Fifth, construct a positive program that accepts the diversity among women's interests—relinquish the "the standpoint of the oppressed" and essentialist appeals to the feminine—that allows for intra-mural political disputation that does not aim at establishing new dogmas and certitudes. Instead, such a program would aspire to ongoing debate, tentative solutions, and accelerated self-revision in the light of how theory and practice play out in the world.

In concert with such ideas is the feminist portrayal of the role of motherhood. Many argue that the reproductive and child-rearing social roles of women are the pivot of their marginalization in the public realm. Often those in positions of authority are less willing to hire women whose careers may be interrupted by childbearing and -rearing, and to view them as only secondary economic producers in the family unit. These perceptions trans-late into women earning less money than men in comparable jobs and the prevalence of glass ceilings that limit women's advancement to the upper levels of corporate and political life.

While this account has much intuitive appeal and empirical support, it sometimes is offered too simplistically. More women are breaking through glass ceilings; the more frequent availability of day care facilities for young children and the establishment of parental leave policies soften the problem to some degree. In addition, mothers possess considerable power over their children and within the home that should not be discounted. As Jean Baker Miller observes:

> One instance [of women's influence] is in women's traditional role, where they have used their powers to foster the growth of others—certainly children, but also many other people. This might be called using one's power to empower others—increasing the other's resources, capabilities, effectiveness, and ability to act.[16]

In most cases, feminists begin by undermining the authority of extant regimes of power: what present themselves as neutral, disinterested findings are in fact the partial, interested conclusions of dominant social groups exercising and reinforcing their privileges and prerogatives. Some feminists go farther and insist that claims to objectivity are themselves masks for oppression.[17] Here a dose of insight from Habermas is helpful. Habermas is sensitive to the theoretical weakness of much leftist critique of mainstream normative justification and social practices: instead of employing immanent criticism that manifests how contemporary practices do not fulfill the criteria of their purported justificatory norms, leftist critics eviscerate the constitutive norms of liberalism so relentlessly that they disable the possibility of offering constructive alternatives. In short, they too often reject the required commitments to truth, rationality, and freedom that are presupposed by robust criticism.

Feminist justification need not reflect the categories—such as a commitment to metaphysical realism, an invocation of the correspondence theory of truth, and the identification of experts embodying epistemic superiority—that often underwrite mainstream justificatory schemes. But feminists who embrace a feckless relativism are unwise and counterproductive to their own cause.[18]

To the extent that feminists identify human practices or characteristics that exist in all societies and thereby embody cross-cultural explanatory force they risk charges of "essentialism," the view that there is a set of attributes that are necessary to the identity and function of human beings or of women or men. Given that feminists have identified essentialism as one of the culprits in establishing noxious gender roles in modern cultures, they are reluctant to embrace it in their reformatory agenda. In addition, when theorists purport to discover such practices or characteristics they are often unwittingly constructing their supposedly cross-cultural elements by projecting the dominant perceptions and practices of their own society while ignoring the genealogy of how such structures come into being. However, the alternative to essentialism seems to be specific, local analyses of patriarchal oppression that apply only to particular times and places. Such analyses make the construction of general reformative policies and practices more difficult.

Replacing the underpinnings of the dominant ideas—the commitment to objectivity and supposedly impartial analyses—by privileging the oppositional "feminist perspective" invites obvious objections. Does such a perspective exist given the numerous differences among women in socioeconomic class, ethnicity, race, religion, sexual orientation, age and the like? Would the feminist perspective simply be yet another projection of partial interests amplified into a general understanding? Why do the "oppressed" embody special access to reality and truth? How can their perspective be uncontaminated by the participation of women in the oppressive relations of power partially constituting the extant social order? Do not the "standpoint of women" and the "feminist perspective" exude an essentialism that feminists otherwise disparage?

Perhaps the best way to avoid such objections is to work backward. First, identify power relations in particular societies that through process and procedure disadvantage women as a class. Second, trace the genealogy of these power relations in order to capture general trends that might be arrested in the future. Third, instead of assuming and applying an alternate version of essentialism to women, analyze the existing essentialism that has been applied to them in order to reveal its role in reinforcing beliefs and practices that serve oppression. Fourth, recognize the indisputable fact that women, like men, participate in racial, class, religious, and sexual social relations that often facilitate various kinds of oppression. On this reading, the feminist perspective and the standpoint of women would not represent a set of univocal conclusions that mirrors a privileged insight into reality. Instead, such expressions would signal a procedure and research agenda adopted by feminists to identify and undermine the oppressive power relations embodied by the extant social order. The goal would not be the end of power relations—for that would be impossible—but their transformation in the manner sketched on behalf of Foucault previously: power relations that are more easily reversible, that permit greater degrees of mutual freedom, that are flexible and accept destabilization, that facilitate better than their contraries the goals of self-care, that enhance the capabilities to affect outcomes (enhancing the power-to) of all their constitutive parties, and that aim at transforming exercises of power-over are recommended. In addition, relations that seek the empowerment of subordinates without taxing the care and resources of superiors in counterproductive ways would be prized.

A dose of Nietzschean wisdom is recommended. All interpretation is partial and although we should strive to "see with many eyes"—viewing social phenomena from numerous often conflicting vantage points—we cannot be everywhere. Human beings cannot ascend to an Archimedean point, perceive reality from a detached perspective, and grasp reality once and forever. So, too, human beings cannot be serially detached, hop merrily and commitment-free from one perspective to another, and thereby garner a privileged perception of social reality.

Feminists confront another paradox regarding the concept of power-over as empowerment or positive transformation. On the one hand, this notion seemingly provides an outlet to enhance the power-to of subordinates while deepening the personal relationships between the parties. As we have seen numerous times, the exercise of power-over another need not be oppressive and may, instead, augur personal growth. Power relations of this sort should be initially attractive to feminists committed to enhancing the capabilities of others, particularly of their sisters, and to resisting oppressive power relations. On the other hand, a danger of stressing power as transformation is that feminists who do so may, ironically, reinforce the more pernicious consequences of patriarchal oppression. The ideals of sacrifice, caring for others, and self-effacement have commonly played a critical part in the traditional feminine societal role. The concomitant feminine virtues of patience, meekness, and service have solidified that social role.

Bartky highlights the ambiguity in the common social practice of women subjectively feeling empowered and productive by providing caretaking services to others, especially to men. Her remarks indirectly sound a caution: perhaps women should examine more closely even their exercises of power that aim at transforming and empowering others, at least insofar as those others are men. In her view, too often the subjective feelings of power that women experience as they exercise their agency on behalf of others have the long-term effects of deepening their own oppression.

> Women run real risks of exploitation in the transactions of heterosexual caregiving. . . . All too frequently, women's caregiving involves an unequal exchange in which one party to this exchange is disempowered by the particular inequalities that characterize the exchange itself. This disempowerment . . . lies in women's active and affective assimilation of the world according to men; it lies in certain satisfactions of caregiving that serve to mystify our situation still further. . . . The *feeling* of out-flowing personal power so characteristic of the caregiving woman is quite different from the *having* of any actual power in the world. . . . She imagines herself to be a great reservoir of restorative power. This feeling of power gives her a sense of agency and of personal efficacy that she may get nowhere else. . . . Women's provision of emotional sustenance to men may *feel* empowering and hence contradict, on a purely phenomenal level, what may be its objectively disempowering character.[19]

In addition, Iris Marion Young lodges a related point when discussing the oppressive dimensions of economic exploitation:

> Women's oppression consists not merely in an inequality of status, power, and wealth resulting from men's excluding women

from privileged activities. The freedom, power, status, and self-realization of men is possible precisely because women work for them. Gender exploitation has two aspects, transfer of the fruits of material labor to men, and the transfer of nurturing and sexual energies to men.[20]

To the extent that feminists celebrate power as positive transformation of others they may unwittingly tighten the chains of their own oppression. By describing such caregivers as "powerful," feminists may be indirectly running a public relations campaign for the continuation of their own subordinate societal role. In addition, the purportedly superior role in a transformative power relationship typically requires more effort and contribution of resources than does the purportedly subordinate role. Finally, when women fill the purportedly superior role in a generally patriarchal context they may end up disempowering themselves more than succeeding in empowering those in the purportedly subordinate role. Most dangerously, women in such roles may feel empowered while being in fact disempowered by their contributions in service of others. How might feminists avoid such problems while continuing to value power as personally and collectively transformative instead of oppressive?

Although the concerns expressed are legitimate, to exaggerate their force would be imprudent and, worse, might well paralyze the reflection and action required for positive reformation of the status quo. This chapter rejects the conclusion that all power relations are equally oppressive and sketches normative criteria to distinguish legitimate from illegitimate exercises of power. In addition, although feminists must be cautious about imputing genuine interests to others that conflict with their extant interests, the effects of pursuing preferences often provide strong evidence of whether doing so advances a person's objective well-being (for example, given the effects of smoking cigarettes and their addictive qualities, the case that smoking advances a person's objective well-being and is in one's genuine interests is difficult to make in the vast majority of cases.) Finally, statistical evidence is available in a host of areas that compares and contrasts the life prospects of men and women in various cultures. Such evidence is useful in identifying, analyzing, and changing existing relations of oppression.

Causes and Remedies of Gender Oppression

What are the causes of patriarchal oppression of women and how is such oppression remedied? Feminist explanations of the oppression of women range widely, from economic exploitation; harmful political conditioning that nurtures the acceptance of menial social roles; the entrenched history of general patriarchal prerogatives; women's reproductive role that disadvantages them in pursuing and advancing in prominent positions in the public sphere; the power differentials between the class of men and the class of women that arise from and reinforce some of the other sources of oppression mentioned; and the pernicious effects of married, heterosexual, monogamous, private sexual relations. Of course, not all of these explanations are mutually compatible, and intramural disagreements about the more likely and more effective sources of oppression exist among feminists.

The suggested remedies of oppression correlate with the suspected sources. They range from: the total separation of women from men, including female boycott of heterosexuality; the decommodification of the female body, which would require major changes in social conditioning and media presentations; a biological revolution, for example, widespread acceptance of artificial reproduction that would liberate women from a significant amount of childbearing and -rearing; the economic independence of women from men; pay for women who provide domestic and socially necessary services in the private sphere; the obliteration of distinction between "men's work" and "women's work"; full access for women in the public sphere, particularly in those prestigious positions that define political and social power; and the elimination of capitalism. Again, not all of these proposals are mutually compatible and feminist disagreements about the better paths to pursue are connected to commitments to the more likely sources of oppression.

In any case, feminists evaluate heterosexual relations generally and power relations in particular by a test consisting of questions such as the following: Are the traditional roles of male dominance and female submission absent? Are women politically victimized by their participation in the relationship? Do women have the power and capability to control access to and define themselves? Again, power relations generally and heterosexual power relations in particular should nurture mutual freedom; facilitate self-realization and self-determination; amplify the capabilities to affect outcomes (enhancing the power-to) of all their constitutive parties; aim at personally and collectively transforming positively all participating parties; and in the case of exercises of power-over for purposes of empowerment, subordinates should benefit without exhausting the emotional resources of superiors counterproductively.

Final Words

Nearly all men can stand adversity, but if you want to test a man's character, give him power.

—Abraham Lincoln

The philosophers of power address all the paramount issues surrounding power relations:

The Pervasiveness of Power-Over. Thrasymachus introduces this theme when he identifies might as the root of our general normative understandings. If he is correct, law, as the most powerful instrument of social control, structures most social relations; these laws reflect the will of the most powerful in that society, who, acting in their own perceived self-interests, create and promulgate epistemology (truth and knowledge claims) that supports normative conventions that disproportionately benefit them; while the masses, succumbing to habit and propaganda and fearing retribution for noncompliance, become alienated from their own genuine interests as they internalize the values of those who are most powerful. As such, Thrasymachus anticipates the more refined analyses in this regard of Marx and Gramsci.

Foucault adds two crucial dimensions to this topic: power relations are a necessary aspect of social life and the effects of such relations percolate throughout the fabric of society in more complicated ways than imagined by previous thinkers. Nietzsche had earlier offered a reason why this must be: the will to power is the fundamental human motivation. If so, then understanding power-over only in terms of dyadic social relations is inadequate to capture the phenomenon. While such relations will always exist and exert considerable influence, they cannot define the workings of power-over. If Nietzsche and Foucault are correct, even if Thrasymachus overstates or misidentifies the necessary connection between power exercised oppressively and a society's normative understanding, the effects of power-over nevertheless structure a society's theory and practice for better or worse. What becomes critical to a society's health is how power-over is predominantly exercised.

The Manner in Which the Powerful Lure the Less Powerful into Acquiescing Unwittingly to Their Continued Victimization. As sketched above, the basic elements of this process are implicit in Thrasymachus's position. But Marx and Gramsci fully explained how ideological superstructures, arising from the needs of economic systems or created independently to support particular political regimes, generate false consciousness that mystifies citizens from perceiving and acting upon their genuine interests. Put simply, the needs of an economic system or a political regime require the widespread acceptance of certain ideas about human nature, the proper forms of social relations, the appropriate structure of the family and workplace, and the like; to that end, the economic system or political regime transmits that ideology and, more importantly, rewards compliance with it; as a result, the bulk of citizens, responding to positive reinforcement and avoiding punishment for noncompliance, model the behavior supported by the ideology; this process further legitimates the ideology and the economic system or political regime from which it arose; in addition, citizens, responding to positive and negative reinforcements, habit, and messages from social media, internalize the values embodied by the ideology; as time passes, these values become to be viewed widely as appropriate, reasonable, and perhaps even inevitable. Insofar as this process of legitimation disproportionately benefits the powerful to the detriment of the less powerful, a false consciousness sets in whereby most citizens misidentify the source of their values and have difficulty identifying and acting upon their genuine interests. Instead, their short-term desires and long-range preferences become aligned roughly with the needs of the very economic system or political regime from which the dominant ideas arose.

In this manner, the oppressive system in place lures the less powerful within it into acquiescing unwittingly to their continued victimization. The payoff is that superiors within the system need not monitor the activities of the subordinates systematically and closely or make their desires known explicitly to them at each turn. Instead, once subordinates internalize the values of the system, as reflected in the dominant ideologies, they discipline themselves to conform to the dominant ideas. The analyses of Marx and Gramsci become essential points of departure for the contemporary understandings of power offered by Foucault, Habermas, and feminism.

The Relationship between Social Context and the Power of Individuals within That Context. Foucault, Habermas, and feminism best illustrate this theme, which reminds us that the power of individuals is often structured by and a function of societal context. The teacher-student and employer-employee relationships are examples that have meandered throughout this work. In such cases, an entire social network of understandings is required to establish that teachers and employers have certain power over students and employees, respectively. The point here is that even in seemingly straightforward dyadic power relations, social context is often crucial. Recall that Hegel described his lordship-bondship relation in an essentially precivilized context. That is why he makes no mention of the wider social context that might have structured the relationship. As such, Hegel's depiction is an anomaly from the general connection between the power of some individuals over others and the social background that shapes that relationship.

The Sense in Which the Accumulation of Power Is a Primary Motivator of Human Action. Whether, as Nietzsche insisted, amassing power is the prime human motivation is less important than recognizing it as a common animator of human thought and action. Although Nietzsche is popularly interpreted as proclaiming that the will to power embodies the desire to attain power over others and exercise it oppressively, I have argued that this notion is not a necessary part of his position and that stressing it only jeopardizes a sound understanding of what he intends. Nietzsche emphasizes, instead, that the will to power is an ongoing second-order desire to pursue first-order desires, to confront obstacles to the fulfillment of first-order desires, and to overcome those obstacles through struggle. As such, Nietzsche places continual agonistic conflict at the cornerstone of a fulfilling human life. No final achievement can quench the insatiability of a robust will to power. Growth, increased strength, and relentless pursuit define the human journey. Process values, as we undergo recurrently the three metamorphoses (the camel, the lion, and the child) of the human spirit, distinguish the refinement of the human subject. In effect, we are all artists striving to continually paint or sculpt the grandest self of our imaginations. This process requires the actualization of more and more of our higher potentials, which is triggered by an ever-increasing power-to and a carefully exercised power-over. Accordingly, the accumulation of power is tied to notions of self-fulfillment, self-direction, and self-constitution in service of Nietzsche's perfectionist ideal. To the extent that we embody a generous amount of power-to we can neutralize the effects of social and dyadic power-over to constitute our being. Nietzsche's ideal is one of a grand striver who refuses to harbor illusions of a final serenity or release from the process of life and, instead, pursues the journey and relishes the process as definitive of his or her existence.

Nietzsche refines some of Thrasymachus's intuitions and anticipates much of Foucault's analysis of social power. Most important, he forces us to distinguish carefully among the different possible exercises of power-over and the reasons why human beings might aspire to accumulate power-to. Even if we reject some of his more extravagant claims about human motivation and the nature of the world, Nietzsche draws some of the earliest explicit connections between the desire for power, the nature of social relations, and the constitution of human subjects.

The Possibilities for Undermining the Experience of Oppression through Disciplining the Human Will. The Stoics celebrate what they take to be the most important form of power-over: the disposition and capability of exercising power over oneself in service of personal fulfillment. For Stoics, the only type of power worth possessing is the capability of disciplining the human will. Through the proper cultivation of habit and acute understanding of what is normatively natural for us, human beings can at once undermine the effects of exercises of oppression, attain the human good, and constitute the self, worthily. The Stoics bear glad tidings: even the seemingly lowliest among us has it within his or her capability to accomplish all of this without any increase in material resources and in spite of the reactions of a hostile world. Once we abrogate our biological inclinations to make excuses and assume full responsibility for the people we are becoming, we begin the process of positive self-transformation.

Although the Stoics' renderings of the human good and the proper constitution of the self are uninspiring, they force us to confront our own complicity, witting or not, in the pernicious aspects of exercises of oppression and the maintenance of unhealthy power relations. We are rarely defenseless victims, without resources or avenues of resistance, of the workings of social oppressors. Only when we confront our options, self-consciously choose our manner of existence, and actively undermine the designs of those conspiring against our genuine interests can we attain a measure of self-sufficiency that marks a life lived well and freely.

The Subtleties and Nuanced Reversals Attending Dyadic Power Relations. Hegel's analysis of the lordship-bondage relationship demonstrates that possessing and exercising power over others is not as glamorous as it first appears. In fact, if Hegel is correct, oppression has worse consequences for the superior in the relationship than it does for the subordinate. Hegel implicitly assumes two cornerstones of Socratic philosophy: vice is its own punishment and what a person does affects significantly his or her internal condition. The superior becomes indolent and alienated from his own self as he becomes primarily a consumer who experiences the natural world only through the labors of the subordinate. The subordinate, after several phases of the relationship have played themselves out, exercises his agency and comes to fuller self-understanding and self-realization through creative labor. Several lessons about living and power emerge: those who conceive of *la dolce vita* as one of limited exertion, maximum consumption, and ultimate leisure have misconstrued the ingredients of human fulfillment—they are too reminiscent of what Nietzsche will later call last men; anticipating Marx, Hegel insists that only through creative labor can human agency discover satisfaction and self-development; the dynamics of dyadic power relations admit of reversals and surprises as the agency of oppressors shrivels while the agency of subordinates amplifies; and full human self-recognition and self-understanding require equal, reciprocal human relations that preclude the exercise of power-over oppressively. Hegel implicitly prefigures the feminist ideal of exercising power-to and power-over in service of individual and collective positive transformation.

The Prerequisites for Large-Scale Social Reformation. Classical Marxism concluded that when the extant relations of production could no longer effectively and efficiency use the forces of production, economic conditions would worsen to the extent that workers would pierce through false consciousness (viscerally, not through rational demonstration), solidify as a class, and rise up and crush capitalism (either through violent revolution or parliamentary process). On this view, certain economic prerequisites were required to energize the social struggle auguring social reformation. Later Marxists, such as Lenin, replaced the emphasis on economic prerequisites with organized insurrections instigated by a vanguard of professional revolutionaries, the communist party. On this model, in order to solidify into a class committed to and capable of affecting social transformation, workers need the leadership of an elite political cadre antecedently geared to massive social change. Gramsci replaces both models with his view of organic intellectuals, who have learned the art of political participation by weaving it into their everyday lives and who begin the process of crafting an ideological hegemony that could undermine and replace the extant dominant ideas. In addition, the nature of the social and political ends sought should be prefigured in the means used to attain them.

The point here is that at the level of political power, regime change is a necessary but not a sufficient condition of salutary social transformation. Even if aspiring revolutionaries (or foreign forces) have the military power to unseat the perceived tyranny in place, genuine social transformation requires much more. Entrenched, large-scale political power rests upon more than the particular superiors in place and the form of government they manipulate. Every longstanding tyranny depends upon more than its monopoly of the instruments of coercion. Accordingly, revolutionaries must attend to and diffuse the cultural conditions that reflect and sustain the tyrannies they hope to unseat. Failure to do so may still allow the revolutionaries to defeat the tyrant, but will not automatically generate the social transformation to which they aspire.

The Manner in Which the Effects of Power Constitute the Human Subject. Thrasymachus tells us that it is good to be an oppressor: better to be a hammer than a nail. But his conclusion flows from his background views of human motivation (we all act only from self-interest), of the world (a zero-sum context), of what fulfills human beings (satisfying their material and tangible interests), and of the nature of our normative understanding (merely internalizing principles that have been codified into law, but which arise from the volitions of the powerful). In spite of the contestability of his background views and his unappealing conclusion that oppressors gain and their victims lose, Thrasymachus sets the stage for all discussion about the relationship between power relations and the constitution of human subjects.

Socrates and the Stoics disagree with Thrasymachus. Committed to the position that a person's internal condition is paramount and that virtue is its own reward and vice is its own punishment, Socrates and the Stoics reject the view that the victims of oppression are harmed. Poverty, material deprivation, and lowly social status—often the results experienced by the victims of oppression—are not harms because they do not automatically affect a person's internal condition and connection to the human good, which is centered on virtue. On the contrary, it is the oppressor who has harmed his soul by exercising power unwisely and viciously. Thus, Socrates and the Stoics prefigure Hegel's analysis of how exercising power oppressively over others constitutes human subjects.

Machiavelli, too, touches upon this topic when he discusses the responsibilities borne by political leaders who must "risk their souls" in the discharge of their official duties. Using power oppressively, transformatively, and paternalistically, as the situation requires, chief political leaders must at times transgress the imperatives of conventional morality. Doing so will dirty the hands and stain the souls of these leaders even when they perform the best available action, all things considered. Thus, Machiavelli addresses the connection of the effects of exercising power and the constitution of political superiors. He also discusses the link between the effects of exercising power and the constitution of political subordinates. If political superiors exercise their power over their citizens wisely and well then the masses will be constituted positively: their civic *virtù* will be individually and collectively enhanced.

Nietzsche' makes the link between the will to power and the constitution of the self the foundation of his philosophy. He ranks people in accordance with the values they embody and the strength of the wills to power they evince. In general, the stronger the will to power the closer one comes to approximating Nietzsche's perfectionist ideal (although much more is required). Nietzsche's disparagement of last men arises mainly from the feebleness of their will to power and their muted agency.

Marx and Gramsci, when discussing matters such as alienation and exploitation and the process by which false consciousness arises, also enter the conversation of how oppression registers palpable effects upon subordinates and superiors. Implicitly echoing the advice of Hegel, both theorists insist that only egalitarian, reciprocal social relations will maximize human flourishing.

Foucault receives enormous credit—probably far more than he deserves—for discussing how power constitutes human subjects. He stresses that instead of operating on antecedently constructed people, oppression is crucial in creating human subjects by constructing socially acceptable models to emulate. Fair enough. But the major theorists of power who preceded Foucault were hardly committed to a contrary position. Foucault's insight is in the pervasiveness of power, which allows him to remind us that virtually every power relation that we are presently considering now involves people who are partially constituted by the effects of a previous series of power relations. Thus, Foucault makes explicit what was implicit in the work of most of the philosophers of power discussed herein.

Feminism builds on the work of the earlier philosophers, especially on the work of Foucault, and begins with analyses of how power exercised oppressively creates socially acceptable gender models that have undermined women's equality. In addition, feminism grapples with the problem of women identifying their genuine interests while choosing within a patriarchal context and under the mystifying effects of false consciousness (to at least some degree).

The Ways Power-Over can be Exercised for Empowering Subordinate Parties. Socrates presumably employed his dialectical method—grounded in asking questions seemingly impossible to answer conclusively (for example, What is Justice? What is Piety? What is Knowledge?), followed by the offering of tentative solutions by his interlocutors, solutions that were dismantled by Socrates's cross-examination, only to be replaced by better tentative solutions that were undermined by deeper Socratic cross-examination, and the process could continue in principle ad infinitum—in order to improve the internal condition (by tending to their souls) of discussants committed to philosophical analysis. In the course of his examinations, Socrates enjoyed and exercised a great power differential over his interlocutors. He was gifted in the dialectical method and had considered thoroughly the issues at hand prior to approaching his foils. Often, in the Platonic dialogues, Socrates seems to treat the discussants ungraciously, dismissively, even condescendingly. At first blush, we are tempted to conclude that Socrates, as portrayed in the dialogues, is a cognitive oppressor, a person who exercises his superior capabilities in his area of expertise to reduce and humiliate those who are less capable.

However, such a conclusion ignores the motivation animating Socrates's philosophical activity: to benefit those with whom he engaged. Convinced that virtue equals knowledge (to know the good is to do the good), that virtue is its own reward (to be virtuous is to nurture and reflect a well-ordered internal condition that defines health and happiness), and that only a disordered internal condition constitutes genuine harm, Socrates used the dialectical method and his cognitive power over others to benefit their souls by striving for sound epistemology that would trigger virtuous action.

Now, most of Socrates background assumptions are highly contestable. In addition, we must wonder whether those who engaged in philosophical conversations with him were in fact always better off for the experience. But a charitable interpretation of Socrates's reasons for philosophizing with others must conclude that he sought to use his power over them for the purpose of empowering them: to make them better at the dialectical method and thus more likely to attain the harmonious internal condition that constituted and mirrored a life lived well. If nothing else, Socrates distances us from automatically identifying the exercise of power-over with oppression.

In that vein, the much-misunderstood Machiavelli advises his ideal political leaders to exercise power over their citizens in multiple ways: sometimes oppressively, at times paternalistically, but in the long term transformatively. The well-ordered republic flourishes only after its political leaders have used power creatively to establish and increase the civic *virtù* of the masses. Doing so empowers the masses to affect positively political and social outcomes. Again, if nothing else, Machiavelli softens our crude conviction that exercising power over others must be oppressive.

How Power-To Can Be Exercised by a Plurality of Agents in an Egalitarian Fashion for Positive Personal and Collective Transformation. Although anticipated to some degree in the work of earlier thinkers of power, particularly in the writings of Gramsci, the notion that power-to can be exercised by a group of agents in an equalitarian manner in order to transform positively individuals and classes of people is the distinctive contribution of contemporary feminism to the literature of power. On this model, superiors are not exercising power over subordinates in order to benefit them. Instead, a plurality of agents act democratically and reciprocally to nurture the common good.

As always, critics may contest whether this or that attempt at such a project truly lives up to the theory and practice of the ideal. But the more important point is that this conception of the exercise of power embodies an inspiring normative content and provides another image of how power can be exercised creatively.

Distinguishing Justified from Unjustified Exercises of Power. Underlying all such matters—at least insofar as we desire to go beyond merely describing the workings of power and we aspire to evaluate and reform unworthy power relations—is the vexing problem of how to distinguish wrongful from permissible, and justified from unjustified exercises of power. Conventional wisdom maintains that the adjudicating criteria must embody normative validity. But specifying the nature of normative validity is highly problematic and seemingly inherently contestable.

Moreover, an unrepentant skeptic persists. The Platonic character Thrasymachus claimed that such criteria are unavailable and thus all exercises of power fall into the same category: the exertion of might in order to establish what cannot otherwise be rationally discovered or created. At least in the domain of value, Thrasymachus was convinced that those having an advantage in power-to (the disposition and capability to affect outcomes) act in accord with their perceived self-interest to set the terms of social life. Accordingly, Thrasymachus conceived of the world in zero-sum terms: a person is either a social winner or a social loser; we have no criteria we might consult to evaluate exercises of power other than those created by other exercises of power; and human motivation is both simple and brutal. That any of us thinks otherwise is itself nuanced testimony to the mystifying effects of power used effectively and recurrently. To speak of justified exercises of power in order to distinguish them from unjustified exercises of power is simply wordplay that has no basis in reality. What we will take to be "justified" power will be nothing more than uses of might upon which our collective values confer an imprimatur. But those values lack independent authority; instead, they conspire with the most powerful elements in society to obscure the truth. Thus, human beings are advised to accumulate power-to as a prelude to exercising power-over. The only alternate, for Thrasymachus, is to submit to oppression, either consciously or subconsciously. The character Thrasymachus, then, represents all those who have insisted, do, and will insist that appeals to normative validity are a sham and that the effects of power cannot be purified by filtering them through an independent authority or neutral evaluating principles.

The Platonic character Socrates objected strongly to Thrasymachus's worldview and sketched an elaborate metaphysics to support his conclusions that independent, objective normative standards adjudicated between all conflicting value claims. If Thrasymachus represents one extreme in the debate about normative validity, then Socrates champions the other extreme. Socrates understands that the only true power is that underwritten and endorsed by the impersonal Forms subsisting in a transcendent realm. Beyond the extravagance of his metaphysics, Socrates struggled mightily to access and identify the precise normative prescriptions that could ground his method. The realm of genuine values remains remote in a Socratic universe. But Socrates brings the effects of the transcendent realm of values down to earth when he connects it to the internal condition of human beings. Virtue is its own reward and vice is its own punishment because the quality of our choices and actions registers itself on the condition of our souls. Our internal condition is objective and we cannot escape the consequences of our deeds. Accordingly, those who exercise power oppressively harm themselves tangibly. In a sense, Socrates anticipates Hegel by illustrating how oppressive power relations affect superior parties negatively. The glitter of exerting one's will over others can be alluring, but those who are seduced into tyranny ultimately destroy themselves. If Socrates is correct, then our sense of justice is vindicated: regardless of external appearances, the cosmos is rational and just, because the principle of desert reigns. But as much as we hope that Socrates is correct do we not suspect that he is not?

Machiavelli has a more complicated take on all this. He accepts Christian values as authoritative, but insists that a statesman must transgress their imperatives under certain circumstances. Machiavelli is the thinker who identifies the conflict within morality itself between (1) prescriptions arising from the impartial perspective of the Ideal Observer and (2) the obligations flowing from the partial vantage point of the human beings occupying specific social roles. Statesmen cannot value all human life or all human interests equally (as would an Ideal Observer) and simultaneously fulfill their partialist duties to their countrymen. Because Machiavelli takes normative principles to be absolute in a special sense: they must be overridden at times because of the conflict within morality, but even when doing so is wise and partially excused (because the action is evil well-used) a remainder of wrongfulness persists. Thus, for Machiavelli the line between legitimate and illegitimate exercises of power cannot be drawn sharply, at least in those circumstances, such as those who occupy important social offices, where the conflict between impartial imperatives and partialist duties is inevitable. Whereas Thrasymachus insisted that normative validity was a hoax and Socrates was convinced that normative validity was foundational and authoritative, Machiavelli concluded that normative validity embodies an internal ambiguity. In response to this ambiguity, our assessments of exercises of power must be more complex. Machiavelli strikes a disturbing chord of realism that at once confirms the practicality and exposes the fragility of our considered political and moral judgments.

Nietzsche views all sweeping accounts of normative validity suspiciously. Any invocation of value that clothes itself in universality, objectivity, and foundationalism is, as Thrasymachus intuited, an exercise of power lacking independent authority. Nietzsche is more interested in establishing how the quest for power defines the human condition. The will to power—understood as a second-order desire to have desires; to confront obstacles to the fulfillment of first-order desires, and to overcome those obstacles—animates human existence.

The content of our first-order desires, which cannot be supplied by the will to power itself, determines whether we pursue only power-to or exercise power-over in one or more of the three most common ways. Still, Nietzsche implicitly accepts a thin notion of normative validity (although he would never accept describing his view with that expression). He offers a value scheme that distinguishes weak from robust wills to power; that contrasts the life and character of the last man from those of higher human types; that posits a highest value, *amor fati* (the love of fate, which he takes to be a maximally affirmative attitude toward life); that celebrates the lives of higher human specimens as the justification for the entire race; and that champions elitist, aristocratic institutional structures. Although Nietzsche must admit that his value scheme arises from a particular perspective and thus cannot claim universal authority, he does present a partial, provisional way to adjudicate the content of first-order desires that energize the will to power.

Accordingly, Nietzsche's sketch of normative validity has limited application and cannot fulfill the designs of those who seek to construct a bright, authoritative line between justified and unjustified exercises of power as such. Yet Nietzsche challenges the moorings of our extant normative understandings.

Stoics highlight what they take to be the most important exercise of power: disciplining one's will to make oneself invulnerable to oppression.

Power over oneself, in that sense, is the fundamental normative unit. By distinguishing what is totally under our control from what is not, by pursuing preferred indifferents only with the proper attitude, and by accepting nonpreferred indifferents serenely, individuals can dissolve the chains of oppression that others may think they possess over them. For Stoics, once people understand the contours of virtue and what is normatively natural for their fulfillment they can not only distinguish justified from unjustified exercises of power but also neutralize the effects of oppression. Although Stoics grossly exaggerate our power to discipline our wills in such a fashion, they teach us that subordinates have more personal power to soften or reverse oppressive power relations than is commonly believed. The Stoics distance us from the solace of easy excuses and force us to assume responsibility for the people we are becoming.

Hegel's psychological analysis of dyadic power relations is grounded in a normative principle: human flourishing and genuine freedom require both asserting the self and affording recognition, in its fullest sense, to others. Human beings require both a measure of independence and an acceptance of a healthy dose of dependence. The ideals of self-sufficiency and radical independence, then, are illusory and unhealthy. Because of the requirements of human fulfillment, oppressive power relations are not what they seem. Such relations, by their very structure, admit of reversals, rebound to the detriment of the superior party, and undermine the full development of human identity. If Hegel is correct, we can distinguish justified from unjustified exercises of power on the basis of his normative principle: Does this power relation include forced inequalities of superiors and subordinates? Or does it construct affirmative, reciprocal, sustaining social relationships? Does the power relation allow both parties freedom that is mutually recognized and thereby nurture the full self-consciousness of both parties? In a more detailed fashion than provided by Socrates, Hegel underscores how exercising power oppressively is counterproductive to human fulfillment and how it registers unwelcomed effects on superiors in dyadic power relations.

Despite his occasional protestations against philosophy, Marx, as he must, also appeals to a normative principle to distinguish justified from unjustified exercises of power. Grounded in economics and his thin notion of human nature, Marx's normative principle is unalienated labor. Exercises of social power that restrict possibilities for creative labor and that tighten the suffocating environment of alienated work oppress the human spirit and are thereby tainted (even if historically inevitable). Although Marx's principle is limited because it covers only one area of power relations, he teaches us that the most entrenched and enduring power relations are societal and structural, not based on dyadic personal interactions. Also, the most oppressive power relations arise from the needs of internally contradictory economic systems that persist longer than they otherwise might because social superiors are able to secure the acquiescence and unwitting collaboration of social subordinates to their own continued victimization through the pernicious machinations of ideological superstructure. The worst effect of such oppression is alienation from our higher potentials as human beings endure diminished possibilities for engaging in creative labor. As such, Marx anticipates Foucault in demonstrating the effects of workplace oppression in constituting human subjects.

Gramsci accepts the basic structure of Marxism but distances himself from its claims of historical inevitability. In addition, he identifies robust political participation rather than unalienated labor as the core of human fulfillment. (Alternately, one might interpret vigorous political participation as Gramsci's preferred form of unalienated, intellectual labor.) Thus, for Gramsci, unjustified social power relations, among other things, stifle full political participation, while justified power relations facilitate such activity. As with Marx, Gramsci's domain of analysis of power relations is limited, but within that realm he refines Marx's notions of false consciousness and ideological superstructure, and offers a broad outline for bloodless revolution. Accordingly, Gramsci, prefiguring Habermas, locates normativity in the conclusions of egalitarian political disputation.

Foucault's early work was less concerned with evaluating power and more concerned with describing power and demonstrating its connection to constituting human subjects. His later work, however, in my view, appeals to normative criteria that might distinguish justified from unjustified exercises of power. Power relations that are not wrongfully dominant (1) are more easily reversible and permit greater degrees of mutual freedom; (2) encourage their own destabilization, thereby giving currency to human possibilities; and (c) facilitate the care of the self, including the practice of truth-telling modeled on the ancient Greek parrhesiast. Foucault concludes that human subjects must detach themselves from extant modes of being and behaving, and create new ways that are at least somewhat detached from the disciplinary order. The end sought is the loosening of the constraints of power relations of wrongful dominance. Although we can never eliminate power relations—nor should we aspire to even if we could—we can construct healthy power relations modeled on the criteria sketched above.

Habermas distinguishes justified from unjustified exercise of power on the basis of his principles of discourse and universalizability. He tries to purify knowledge and truth claims, to the extent possible, from the effects of wrongful domination. His ideal of communicative rationality is grounded in normative force that is "non-coercively coercive." Unlike coercion as such it does not exert pressure in service of exercising or increasing the power of superiors over subordinates; but it exerts force in terms of highlighting the best argument that must command the allegiance of those committed to rationality. Habermas's faith, then, rests in undistorted communication that is free of structural constraints that prevent or hinder participants from an equal opportunity at rational discourse. His is a contemporary rendering of an Enlightenment project directed at undermining the authority of principles and institutions arising from oppressive relations of power. Habermas speaks to our faith in reason as the adjudicator of normative disputation. Still, we may wonder if human reason is enough.

Although directed explicitly at remedying the oppression of women, feminist thought distinguishes justified from unjustified exercises of power by assessing their effects on self-development and self-determination. To the extent that power constrains or hinders the self-development and self-determination of individuals or groups it increases the likelihood that it is unjustified. The power of collective transformation, where power-to is exercised by a plurality of agents voluntarily entering a mutual search among equals for individual and collective positive growth, contrasts with wrongful domination. Feminists, then, conjure a compelling ideal of power exercised creatively in service of undermining oppression.

The vast majority of our philosophers of power, then, converge in celebrating an increase in power-to that is placed in service of positively maintaining or transforming oneself and others. We find minor intramural disagreements about the nature and specificity of human fulfillment and about what is required for salutary change. For example, does human fulfillment center, broadly, on self-determination and self-development (feminism), or on the prerequisites for the attainment of full human self-consciousness (Hegel), or on the proper discipline of the individual will (Stoicism) and cultivation of the proper internal condition of the soul (Socrates)? Or does human fulfillment require an antecedent faith in and gratitude for life in its totality (Nietzsche)? Or does human fulfillment require, more specifically, increased opportunities for unalienated labor (Marx) or on fuller political participation (Gramsci)?

Does positive social change demand the proper sort of economic (Marx) or political system (Gramsci, Machiavelli), or does positive change depend on discovering authoritative principles emerging from a vantage point of ideal communicative rationality (Habermas) or grounded in the metaphysics of the cosmos (Socrates) or arising from the proper care of the self (Foucault)? Or can individuals transcend their social context by exercising their wills to power reflectively and iconoclastically (Nietzsche)? Our answers to such questions will complete the puzzle and permit us to discover or construct standards of normative validity that can distinguish between justified and unjustified exercises of power, and between healthy and debilitating relations of power, whether dyadic or social.

But in the background of such debates lurks Thrasymachus, still convinced that all such questions and proffered solutions are vanities. For in the end and at the beginning, he insists that might (power-over exercised subtly but oppressively) determines what we come to believe is right (our general normative understandings). The Chalcedonian sophist bellows that winners not only write histories that conform to their preferred narratives, they also exert disproportionate influence in sculpting societal values. Our illusions otherwise are as false as they are necessary. The echoes of Thrasymachus's skeptical laughter resound.

Notes

Chapter I. Concepts of Power

1. See, for example, Steven Lukes, *Power: A Radical View*, 2nd ed. (New York: Palgrave MacMillan, 2005); Thomas E. Wartenberg, *The Forms of Power* (Philadelphia: Temple University Press, 1990); Jeffrey C. Isaac, *Power and Marxist Theory* (Ithaca: Cornell University Press, 1987); Stanley I. Benn, "Power," in *The Encyclopedia of Philosophy*, ed. Paul Edwards, vol. 6 (New York: Macmillan, 1967); Robert A. Dahl, "The Concept of Power," *Behavioral Science* 2 (1975): 201–15; Peter Morriss, *Power: A Philosophical Analysis*, 2nd ed. (Manchester: Manchester University Press, 2002). These works have greatly influenced this chapter.

2. See, for example, Benn, "Power," 424–26.

3. See, for example, Dahl, "Concept of Power," 201–15.

4. Steven Lukes, "Introduction" in *Power*, ed. Steven Lukes (New York: New York University Press, 1986), 9.

5. See, for example, Charles Tilley, "Domination, Resistance, Compliance . . . Discourse," *Sociological Forum* 6 (1991): 593–602.

6. Lukes, *Power: A Radical View*, 29, 125–51.

7. Lukes, "Introduction," 4.

8. See, for example, Lukes, *Power: A Radical View*, 85–88.

9. Hannah Arendt, *On Violence* (London: Allen Lane, 1970), 44, 52, 51.

10. Ibid., 48–49.

Chapter II. Thrasymachus (ca. 459 BC–ca. 400 BC) and Socrates

1. Plato, "Republic," trans. Paul Shorey, in *Plato: Collected Dialogues*, ed. Edith Hamilton and Huntington Cairns (Princeton: Princeton University Press, 1973), 575–844.

Chapter III. Niccolò Machiavelli (1469–1527)

1. Raymond Angelo Belliotti, *Niccolò Machiavelli: The Laughing Lion and the Strutting Fox* (Lanham, MD: Lexington Books, 2009), 63–98.

2. Isaiah Berlin, *Against the Current* (Princeton: Princeton University Press, 2001), 43–44.

3. Ibid., 44.

4. Belliotti, *Machiavelli*, 63–98.

5. See, for example, Michael Walzer, "Political Action: The Problem of Dirty Hands." *Philosophy and Public Affairs* 2 (1973): 160–80.

6. Raymond Angelo Belliotti, *Machiavelli's Secret: The Soul of the Statesman* (Albany: State University of New York Press, 2015).

Chapter IV. Friedrich Nietzsche (1844–1900)

1. See, for example, Walter Kaufmann, *Nietzsche: Philosopher, Psychologist, Antichrist*, 4th ed. (Princeton: Princeton University Press, 1974), 242, 246–47; Maudemarie Clark, *Nietzsche on Truth and Philosophy* (Cambridge: Cambridge University Press, 1990); John Richardson, *Nietzsche's System* (Oxford: Oxford University Press, 1996); Alexander Nehamas, *Nietzsche: Life as Literature* (Cambridge: Harvard University Press, 1985). I argue for my favored interpretation in Raymond Angelo Belliotti, *Jesus or Nietzsche: How Should We Live Our Lives?* (Amsterdam: Rodopi Editions, 2013).

2. Belliotti, *Jesus or Nietzsche*, 126–31.

3. Raymond Angelo Belliotti, *Happiness is Overrated* (Lanham, MD: Rowman and Littlefield, 2004), 82–88.

4. Philippa Foot, *Virtues and Vices and Other Essays in Moral Philosophy* (Oxford: Oxford University Press, 1979), 85.

Chapter V. Stoicism

1. Richard McKeon, "Introduction to the Philosophy of Cicero," in Marcus Tullius Cicero, *Selected Works*, trans. Hubert M. Poteat (Chicago: University of Chicago Press, 1950), 48–49: Raymond Angelo Belliotti, *Roman Philosophy and the Good Life* (Lanham, MD: Lexington Books, 2009), 61–71.

2. John Sellars, *Stoicism* (Berkeley: University of California Press, 2006), 64–70.

3. Stephen A. White, "Cicero and the Therapists," in J. G. F. Powell, *Cicero: The Philosopher* (Oxford: Clarendon Press, 1999), 239.

4. Tad Brennan, *The Stoic Life* (Oxford: The Clarendon Press, 2005), 99.

5. Ibid., 98.

6. Ibid., 144.

Chapter VI. Georg W. F. Hegel (1770–1831)

1. Georg Hegel, *Philosophy of Mind*, trans. William Wallace and A. V. Miller (Oxford: Clarendon Press, 1971), 172.

2. Georg Hegel, *Phenomenology of Spirit*, trans. A. V. Miller (Oxford: Oxford University Press, 1977), 234.

3. See, for example, Thomas E. Wartenberg, *The Forms of Power* (Philadelphia: Temple University Press, 1990), 121–28.

4. Hegel, *Phenomenology of Spirit*, 118.

5. Ibid., 118–19.

6. Frederick Neuhouser, "Desire, Recognition, and the Relation between Bondsman and Lord," in *The Blackwell Guide to Hegel's Phenomenology of Spirit*, ed. Kenneth Westphal (Oxford: Wiley-Blackwell, 2009), 50.

7. Hegel, *Philosophy of Mind*, sec. 431, 436.

Chapter VII. Marx (1818–1883) and Gramsci (1891–1937)

1. Karl Marx, "Contributions to the Critique of Hegel's Philosophy of Law," in Marx and Engels, *Collected Works*, vol. 3 (New York: International Publishers, 1976), 192.

2. Karl Marx, "Economic and Philosophic Manuscripts of 1844," in *Collected Works*, vol. 3, 333.

3. Ibid., 332–33.

4. Karl Marx, *Das Kapital*, trans. Samuel Moore (Seattle: Pacific Publishing Studio, 2010).

5. Karl Marx, "Critique of Hegel's Doctrine of the State," *in Early Writings*, trans. Rodney Livingstone and Gregor Benton (New York: Penguin Books, 1992), 176.

6. See, for example, Richard Schmitt, *Marx and Engels: A Critical Reconstruction* (Boulder: Westview, 1987), 36; Jorge Larrain, "Base and Superstructure." In *A Dictionary of Marxist Thought*, ed. Tom Bottomore (Cambridge: Harvard University Press, 1983), 44; Raymond Angelo Belliotti, *Justifying Law* (Philadelphia: Temple University Press, 1992), 147–50.

7. Larrain, "Base and Superstructure," 43; Belliotti, *Justifying Law*, 148.

8. Antonio Gramsci, *Selections from the Prison Notebooks*, ed. and trans. Quinton Hoare and Geoffrey Nowell-Smith (London: Lawrence and Wishart, 1971).

Chapter VIII. Michel Foucault (1926–1984)

1. Michel Foucault, "How Much Does It Cost for Reasons to Tell the Truth," in *Foucault Live: Interviews, 1966–1984*, ed. Sylvere Lotringer (New York: Semiotexte, 1989), 254.

2. See, for example, Michel Foucault, *Power/Knowledge: Selected Interviews and Other Writings, 1972–1977*, ed. Colin Gordon (New York: Pantheon Books, 1980).

3. Michel Foucault, "Disciplinary Power and Subjection," in *Power*, ed. Steven Lukes (New York: New York University Press, 1986), 234.

4. Ibid.

5. See, for example, Michel Foucault, *The History of Sexuality*, vol. 1: *An Introduction*, trans. Robert Hurley (New York: Pantheon Books, 1978).

6. Bob Jessop, "From Micro-powers to Governmentality," *Political Geography* 26 (2007): 34–40, 35.

7. Michel Foucault, *Society Must Be Defended: Lectures at the College De France, 1975–76*, ed. Mauro Bertani and Alessandro Fontana (New York: Picador, 1997), 29–30.

8. Foucault, "Prison Talk," in *Power/Knowledge*, 52.

9. Foucault, "Truth and Power, in *Power/Knowledge*, 131.

10. Michel Foucault, "The Subject and Power," Afterword to Hubert L. Dreyfus and Paul Rabinow, *Michel Foucault: Beyond Structuralism and Hermeneutics*, 2nd ed. (Chicago: University of Chicago Press, 1983), 221.

11. Nancy Fraser, *Unruly Practices* (Minneapolis: University of Minnesota Press, 1989), 33.

12. Thomas Flynn, "Foucault as Parrhesiast," in *The Final Foucault*, ed. James Bernauer and David Rasmussen (Cambridge: The MIT Press, 1988), 112.

13. Ibid., 113.

14. Foucault, "Why Study Power?" Afterword to *Michel Foucault: Beyond Structuralism and Hermeneutics*, 212.

15. David Ingram, "Foucault and Habermas on the Subject of Reason," in *The Cambridge Companion to Foucault*, ed. Gary Gutting (Cambridge: Cambridge University Press, 1994), 220.

16. Ibid., 221.

17. Foucault, "Two Lectures," in *Power/Knowledge*, 98.

18. Foucault, *The History of Sexuality*, 95.

19. Foucault, "Prison Talk," in *Power/Knowledge*, 38.

20. Foucault, "Disciplinary Power and Subjection," 229–30.

21. Foucault, *The History of Sexuality*, 142–43.

22. Michel Foucault, "Interview," in *The Final Foucault*, 11–12.

23. Ibid., 19.

24. Ibid., 11.

25. Garth Gillan, "Foucault's Philosophy," in *The Final Foucault*, 38.

26. Foucault, "Interview," in *The Final Foucault*, 2.

27. Ibid., 3.

28. Ibid., 12–13.

29. Ibid., 4–5.

30. Ibid., 8.

31. Michel Foucault, *The History of Sexuality*, vol. 2: *The Use of Pleasure*, trans. Robert Hurley (New York: Pantheon Books, 1978), 9.

32. Flynn, "Foucault as Parrhesiast," in *The Final Foucault*, 103–104.

33. Ibid., 108, 109.

34. Ibid., 110.

35. Foucault, "Interview," in *The Final Foucault*, 16.

36. Ibid., 18.

37. Joseph Rouse, "Power/Knowledge," in *The Cambridge Companion to Foucault*, ed. Gary Gutting (Cambridge: Cambridge University Press, 1994), 99.

38. Ibid., 109.

39. Foucault, "How Power is Exercised," in *Foucault: Beyond Structuralism and Hermeneutics*, 221.

Chapter IX. Jürgen Habermas (1929–)

1. Jürgen Habermas, *Knowledge and Human Interests* (Boston: Beacon Press, 1968), 308–10.

2. Ibid., 196–97.

3. Ibid., 309.

4. Thomas McCarthy, "The Critique of Impure Reason," in *Rethinking Power*, ed. Thomas E. Wartenberg (Albany: State University of New York Press, 1992), 128.

5. Jürgen Habermas, "A Reply," in *Communicative Action*, ed. Axel Honneth and Hans Joas (Cambridge: MIT Press, 1991), 239.

6. Habermas, *Knowledge and Human Interests*, 317; *Theory and Practice* (Boston: Beacon Press, 1973), 1–40; *Legitimation Crisis* (Boston: Beacon Press, 1975), 102–17; *Communication and the Evolution of Society* (Boston: Beacon Press, 1979), 1–68.

7. Ibid.

8. David Ingram, "Foucault and Habermas on the Subject of Reason," in *The Cambridge Companion to Foucault*, ed. Gary Gutting (Cambridge: Cambridge University Press, 1994), 225.

9. Habermas, *Knowledge and Human Interests*, 317; *Theory and Practice*, 1–40; *Legitimation Crisis*, 102–17; *Communication and the Evolution of Society*, 1–68.

10. See, for example, Richard Bernstein, *Beyond Objectivism and Relativism* (Philadelphia: University of Pennsylvania Press, 1983), 195.

11. Habermas, *Communication and the Evolution of Society*, 18–35.

12. Moral thinkers such as Kant and Rawls are sometime viewed as attempting a task both impossible and undesirable: in an effort to purify reason from distorting influences, they extract rationality from social and historical context, and hope thereby to discover Reason in a disembodied, impersonal form.

13. See, for example, Roger S. Gottlieb, "The Contemporary Critical Theory of Jurgen Habermas," *Ethics* 91 (1981): 280, 287.

14. Robbie Pfeufer Kahn, "The Problem of Power in Habermas," *Human Studies* 11 (1988): 361–87, 375; Habermas, *Knowledge and Human Interests*, 274–300.

15. Jürgen Habermas, "Hannah Arendt's Communication Conception of Power," *Social Research* 44 (1977): 3–23, 6.

16. Jürgen Habermas, "Moral Development and Ego Identity," in *Communication and the Evolution of Society*, 74.

17. Amy Allen, "Discourse, Power and Subjectivation," *The Philosophical Forum* 40 (2009): 1–28, 18.

18. Patrick O'Mahony, "Habermas and Communicative Power," *Journal of Power* 3 (2010): 53–73, 61.

19. Jürgen Habermas, *Between Facts and Norms* (Cambridge: The MIT Press, 1998), 148.

20. Ibid., 175.

21. Ibid., 150.

22. Ibid., 150, 484.

23. Ibid., 169–70.

24. Ibid., 148.

25. Jürgen Habermas, *The Theory of Communicative Action*, vol. 1 (Boston: Beacon Press, 1985), 294.

26. Ibid., 290–92.

27. Gerhard Wagner and Heinz Zipprian, "Habermas on Power and Rationality," *Sociological Theory* 7 (1989): 102–109, 107.

28. Habermas, *Between Facts and Norms*, 107.

29. Jürgen Habermas, *The Inclusion of the Other*, ed. Ciaran Cronin and Pablo De Greiff (Cambridge: Polity Press, 1998), 42.

30. Jürgen Habermas, "Discourse Ethics," in *Moral Consciousness and Communicative Action*, trans. Christian Lenhardt and Shierry Weber Nicholson (Cambridge: The MIT Press, 1990), 84.

31. Ibid., 88–89.

32. Michel Foucault, "Interview," in *The Final Foucault*, ed. James Bernauer and David Rasmussen (Cambridge: The MIT Press, 1988), 18.

33. Habermas, *Between Facts and Norms*, 36.

34. Ibid., 67.

35. Ibid., 115.

36. Foucault, "Interview," 18.

37. Habermas, *Legitimation Crisis*, 57.

38. Jürgen Habermas, "The Postnational Constellation and the Future of Democracy," in *The Postnational Constellation* (Oxford: Polity Press, 2001), 74.

39. Habermas, *The Inclusion of the Other*, 115.

Chapter X. Feminism

1. See, for example, Carole Pateman, *The Sexual Contract* (Stanford: Stanford University Press, 1988), 207–19; Marilyn Fyre, *The Politics of Reality* (Freedom, CA: The Crossing Press, 1983), 98–105.

2. Anna Yeatman, "Feminism and Power," in *Reconstructing Political Theory*, ed. Mary Lyndon Shanley and Uma Narayan (University Park: The Pennsylvania State University Press, 1997), 147.

3. Amy Allen, "Power and the Politics of Difference: Oppression, Empowerment, and Transnational Justice," *Hypatia* 23 (2008): 156–72, 164.

4. See, for example, Susan Moller Okin, *Justice, Gender, and the Family* (New York: Basic Books, 1989), 136.

5. See, for example, Iris Marion Young, *Justice and the Politics of Difference* (Princeton: Princeton University Press, 1990), 31–33.

6. See, for example, Sarah Lucia Hoagland, *Lesbian Ethics* (Palo Alto: Institute of Lesbian Studies, 1988), 114–18; Jean Baker Miller, "Women and Power," in *Rethinking Power*, ed. Thomas E. Wartenberg (Albany: State University of New York Press, 1992), 241–48.

7. Yeatman, "Feminism and Power," 146.

8. Allen, "Power and the Politics of Difference," 167, 169.

9. See, for example, Virginia Held, *Feminist Morality* (Chicago: University of Chicago Press, 1993), 136–37.

10. Nancy Hartsock, *Money, Sex, and Power* (New York: Longman, 1983), 257.

11. Wendy Brown and Joan W. Scott, "Power," in *Critical Terms for the Study of Gender*, ed. Catharine R. Stimpson and Gilbert Herdt (Chicago: University of Chicago Press, 2014), 344.

12. Sandra Lee Bartky, *Feminism and Domination* (New York: Routledge, 1990), 15–21.

13. Ibid., 18.

14. Hartsock, *Money, Sex, and Power*, 171–72.

15. Wendy Brown, "Feminist Hesitations, Postmodern Exposures," *differences* 3 (1991): 63–84, 69, 76–77.

16. Miller, "Women and Power," 189.

17. See, for example, Catharine A. MacKinnon, "Feminism, Marxism, Method, and the State: An Agenda for Theory," *Signs* 7 (1982): 515–44.

18. See, for example, Nancy Fraser, *Unruly Practices* (Minneapolis: University of Minnesota Press, 1989), 182.

19. Bartky, *Feminism and Domination*, 117, 116, 115, 114.

20. Iris Marion Young, "Five Faces of Oppression," in *Rethinking Power*, ed. Thomas E. Wartenberg (Albany: State University of New York Press, 1992), 183.

Bibliography

Allen, Amy. "Discourse, Power and Subjectivation." *The Philosophical Forum* 40 (2009): 1–28.

———. "Power and the Politics of Difference: Oppression, Empowerment, and Transnational Justice." *Hypatia* 23 (2008): 156–72.

———. *The Power of Feminist Theory.* Boulder: Westview, 1999.

———. "Rationalizing Oppression." *Journal of Power* 1 (2008): 51–65.

———. "The Unforced Force of the Better Argument." *Constellations* 19 (2012): 53–368.

Arendt, Hannah. *On Violence.* London: Allen Lane, 1970.

Aurelius, Marcus. *Meditations.* Edited by Martin Hammond. New York: Penguin Books, 2006.

———. *The Meditations.* Translated by A. S. L. Farquharson; introduction by R. B. Rutherford. Oxford: Oxford University Press, 1989.

Bachrach, Peter, and Morton S. Baratz. "Decisions and Non-decisions: An Analytic Framework." In *Political Power: A Reader in Theory and Research,* edited by Roderick Bell, David V. Edwards, and R. Harrison Wagner. New York: Free Press, 1969.

———. "The Two Faces of Power." *American Political Science Review* 56 (1962): 941–52.

Ball, Terence, "Power, Causation, and Explanation." *Polity* 8 (1975): 189–214.

———. "Two Concepts of Coercion." *Theory and Society* 15 (1978): 97–112.

Barnes, Barry. *The Nature of Power.* Cambridge: Polity Press, 1988.

Barry, Brian, *Power and Political Theory.* London: Wiley, 1976.

Bartky, Sandra Lee. *Feminism and Domination.* New York: Routledge, 1990.

———. *"Sympathy and Solidarity" and Other Essays.* Lanham, MD: Rowman and Littlefield, 2002.

Belliotti, Raymond Angelo. *Dante's Deadly Sins: Moral Philosophy in Hell.* Oxford: Wiley-Blackwell, 2011.

———. "Do Dead Human Beings Have Rights?" *The Personalist* 60 (1979): 201–10.

———. *Happiness Is Overrated.* Lanham, MD: Rowman and Littlefield, 2004.

———. *Jesus or Nietzsche: How Should We Live Our Lives?* Amsterdam: Editions Rodopi, 2013.

——. *Justifying Law: The Debate over Foundations, Goals, and Methods.* Philadelphia: Temple University Press, 1992.

——. "Machiavelli and Machiavellianism." *Journal of Thought* 13 (1978): 293–300.

——. *Machiavelli's Secret: The Soul of the Statesman.* Albany: State University of New York Press, 2015.

——. *Niccolò Machiavelli: The Laughing Lion and the Strutting Fox.* Lanham, MD: Lexington Books, 2009.

——. *Posthumous Harm: Why the Dead Are Still Vulnerable.* Lanham, MD: Lexington Books, 2012.

——. *Roman Philosophy and the Good Life.* Lanham, MD: Lexington Books, 2009.

——. *Seeking Identity: Individualism versus Community in an Ethnic Context.* Lawrence: University Press of Kansas, 1995.

——. *Stalking Nietzsche.* Westport: Greenwood Press, 1998.

——. *What Is the Meaning of Human Life?* Amsterdam: Editions Rodopi, 2001.

——, and William S. Jacobs. "Two Paradoxes for Machiavelli." In *Terrorism, Justice, and Social Values,* edited by Creighton Pedan and Yeager Hudson. Lewiston, NY: The Edwin Mellen Press, 1990.

Benhabib, Seyla, Judith Butler, Drucilla Cornell, and Nancy Fraser. *Feminist Contentions,* edited by Linda Nicholson. New York: Routledge, 1995.

Benn, Stanley I. "Power." In *The Encyclopedia of Philosophy*, edited by Paul Edwards, vol. 6. New York: Macmillan, 1967.

Berlin, Isaiah. *Against the Current.* Princeton: Princeton University Press, 2001.

Bernstein, Richard. *Beyond Objectivism and Relativism.* Philadelphia: University of Pennsylvania Press, 1983.

Bordo, Susan. *Unbearable Weight: Feminism, Western Culture, and the Body.* Berkeley: University of California Press, 1993.

Brennan, Tad. *The Stoic Life.* Oxford: The Clarendon Press, 2005.

Brown, Wendy. "Feminist Hesitations, Postmodern Exposures." *differences* 3 (1991): 63–84.

——, and Joan W. Scott, "Power." In *Critical Terms for the Study of Gender*, edited by Catharine R. Stimpson and Gilbert Herdt, 335–57. Chicago: University of Chicago Press, 2014.

Butler, Judith. *The Psychic Life of Power: Theories in Subjection.* Stanford: Stanford University Press, 1997.

Chodorow, Nancy. *The Reproducton of Mothering.* Berkeley: University of California Press, 1978.

Cicero. *De Officiis* (On Obligations). Translated by P. G. Walsh. Oxford: Oxford University Press, 2000.

Clark, Maudemarie. *Nietzsche on Truth and Philosophy.* Cambridge: Cambridge University Press, 1990.

Clegg, Stewart R. *Frameworks of Power.* London: Sage, 1989.

Cudd, Ann. *Analyzing Oppression*. Oxford: Oxford University Press, 2006.

Dahl, Robert A. "The Concept of Power." *Behavioral Science* 2 (1957): 201–15.

Digeser, Peter. "Forgiveness and Politics: Dirty Hands and Imperfect Procedures." *Political Theory* 26 (1998): 700–24.

Dovi, Suzanne. "Guilt and the Problem of Dirty Hands." *Constellations* 12 (2005): 128–46.

Epictetus. *Discourses: Book 1*. Translated with an introduction by Robert Dobbin. Oxford: The Clarendon Press, 1998.

———. *Manual for Living (Encheiridion)*. Translated with an introduction by Sharon Lebell. New York: HarperCollins, 1994.

Everitt, Anthony. *Cicero*. New York: Random House, 2001.

Femia, Joseph, V. *Gramsci's Political Thought*. Oxford: Clarendon Press, 1981.

Finnis, John. "Practical Reasoning, Human Goods, and the End of Man,. *Proceedings of the American Catholic Philosophical Association* 58 (1985): 23–36.

Fish, Stanley. "Does Philosophy Matter? *New York Times*, The Opinion Pages, August 1, 2011.

Flynn, Thomas. "Foucault as Parrhesiast." In *The Final Foucault*, edited by James Bernauer and David Rasmussen. Cambridge: The MIT Press, 1988.

Foot, Philippa. *Virtues and Vices and Other Essays in Moral Philosophy*. Oxford: Oxford University Press, 1979.

Foucault, Michel. "Disciplinary Power and Subjection." In *Power*, edited by Steven Lukes. New York: New York University Press, 1986.

———. *The History of Sexuality*, vol. 1: *An Introduction*. Translated by Robert Hurley. New York: Pantheon Books, 1978.

———. *The History of Sexuality*, vol. 2: *The Use of Pleasure*. Translated by Robert Hurley. New York: Pantheon Books, 1978.

———. "How Much Does It Cost for Reasons to Tell the Truth." In *Foucault Live: Interviews, 1966–1984*, edited by Sylvere Lotringer. New York: Semiotexte, 1989.

———. "How Power Is Exercised." In Afterword to Hubert L. Dreyfus and Paul Rabinow. *Michel Foucault: Beyond Structuralism and Hermeneutics*, 2nd edition. Chicago: University of Chicago Press, 1983.

———. "Interview." In *The Final Foucault*, edited by James Bernauer and David Rasmussen. Cambridge: The MIT Press, 1988.

———. *Power/Knowledge: Selected Interviews and Other Writings, 1972–1977*. Edited by Colin Gordon. New York: Pantheon Books, 1980.

———. "Prison Talk." In *Power/Knowledge: Selected Interviews and Other Writings, 1972–1977*, edited by Colin Gordon. New York: Pantheon Books, 1980.

———. *Society Must Be Defended: Lectures at the College De France, 1975–76*. Edited by Mauro Bertani and Alessandro Fontana. New York: Picador, 1997.

———. "The Subject and Power." Afterword to Hubert L. Dreyfus and Paul Rabinow, *Michel Foucault: Beyond Structuralism and Hermeneutics*, 2nd edition. Chicago: University of Chicago Press, 1983.

————. "Truth and Power." In *Power/Knowledge: Selected Interviews and Other Writings, 1972–1977*, edited by Colin Gordon. New York: Pantheon Books, 1980.

————. "Two Lectures." In *Power/Knowledge: Selected Interviews and Other Writings, 1972–1977*, edited by Colin Gordon. New York: Pantheon Books, 1980.

————. "Why Study Power?" Afterword to Hubert L. Dreyfus and Paul Rabinow, *Michel Foucault: Beyond Structuralism and Hermeneutics*, 2nd edition. Chicago: University of Chicago Press, 1983.

Fraser, Nancy. "Foucault on Modern Power: Empirical Insights and Normative Confusions." *Praxis International* 1 (1981): 272–87.

————. *Unruly Practices*. Minneapolis: University of Minnesota Press, 1989.

Fyre, Marilyn. *The Politics of Reality*. Freedom, CA: The Crossing Press, 1983.

Germino, Dante. "Second Thoughts on Leo Strauss's Machiavelli." *Journal of Politics* (1966): 794–817.

Gilbert, Felix. "On Machiavelli's Idea of *Virtù*." *Renaissance News* 4 (1951): 53–55.

Gillan, Garth. "Foucault's Philosophy." In *The Final Foucault*, edited by James Bernauer and David Rasmussen. Cambridge: The MIT Press, 1988.

Goldman, Alvin I. "On the Measurement of Power." *The Journal of Philosophy* 71 (1974): 231–52.

————. "Power, Time, and Cost." *Philosophical Studies* 26 (1974): 263–270.

————. "Toward a Theory of Social Power." *Philosophical Studies* 23 (1972): 221–67.

Gottlieb, Roger S. "The Contemporary Critical Theory of Jürgen Habermas." *Ethics* 91 (1981): 280–95.

Gramsci, Antonio. *Selections from the Prison Notebooks*. Edited and translated by Quinton Hoare and Geoffrey Nowell-Smith. London: Lawrence and Wishart, 1971.

Griffin, James. *Well-Being*. Oxford: Clarendon Press, 1986.

Habermas, Jürgen. "A Reply." In *Communicative Action*, edited by Axel Honneth and Hans Joas. Cambridge: MIT Press, 1991.

————. *Between Facts and Norms*. Cambridge: The MIT Press, 1998.

————. *Communication and the Evolution of Society*. Boston: Beacon Press, 1979.

————. "Discourse Ethics." In *Moral Consciousness and Communicative Action*, translated by Christian Lenhardt and Shierry Weber Nicholson. Cambridge: The MIT Press, 1990.

————. "Hannah Arendt's Communication Conception of Power." *Social Research* 44 (1977): 3–23.

————. *The Inclusion of the Other*. Edited by Ciaran Cronin and Pablo De Greiff. Cambridge: Polity Press, 1998.

————. *Knowledge and Human Interests*. Boston: Beacon Press, 1968.

————. *Legitimation Crisis*. Boston: Beacon Press, 1975.

————. "Moral Development and Ego Identity." In *Communication and the Evolution of Society*. Boston: Beacon Press, 1979.

————. "The Postnational Constellation and the Future of Democracy." In *The Postnational Constellation*. Oxford: Polity Press, 2001.

————. *Theory and Practice*. Boston: Beacon Press, 1973.

————. *The Theory of Communicative Action*, vol. 1. Boston: Beacon Press, 1985.

Hartsock, Nancy. "Community/Sexuality/Gender: Rethinking Power." In *Revisioning the Political: Feminist Reconstructions of Traditional Concepts in Western Political Theory*, edited by Nancy J. Hirschmann and Christine Di Stefano. Boulder: Westview, 1996.

————. *Money, Sex, and Power*. New York: Longman, 1983.

Haugaard, Mark. "Power: A 'Family Resemblance' Concept." *European Journal of Cultural Studies* 13 (2010): 419–38.

————, ed. *Power: A Reader*. Manchester: Manchester University Press, 2002.

Hegel, Georg. *Phenomenology of Spirit*. Translated by A. V. Miller. Oxford: Oxford University Press, 1977.

————. *Philosophy of Mind*. Translated by William Wallace and A. V. Miller. Oxford: Clarendon Press, 1971.

Heidegger, Martin. *Being and Time*. Translated by John Macquarrie and Edward Robinson. New York: Harper and Row, 1962.

Held, Virginia. *Feminist Morality*. Chicago: University of Chicago Press, 1993.

Hoagland, Sarah Lucia. *Lesbian Ethics*. Palo Alto: Institute of Lesbian Studies, 1988.

Holland, Tom. *Rubicon*. New York: Doubleday, 2003.

Hollis, Martin. "Dirty Hands." *British Journal of Political Science* 12 (1982): 385–98.

Howard, W. Kenneth. "Must Public Hands Be Dirty?" *Journal of Value Inquiry* 11 (1977): 29–40.

Hurka, Thomas, *Perfectionism*. New York: Oxford University Press, 1993.

Ingram, David. "Foucault and Habermas on the Subject of Reason." In *The Cambridge Companion to Foucault*, edited by Gary Gutting. Cambridge: Cambridge University Press, 1994.

Inwood, Brad. *Reading Seneca*. Oxford: The Clarendon Press, 2008.

Isaac, Jeffrey C. *Power and Marxist Theory*. Ithaca: Cornell University Press, 1987.

Jaggar, Alison. *Feminist Politics and Human Nature*. Totowa, NJ: Rowman and Allanheld, 1983.

Jessop, Bob. "From Micro-powers to Governmentality." *Political Geography* 26 (2007): 34–40.

Kahn, Robbie Pfeufer. "The Problem of Power in Habermas." *Human Studies* 11 (1988): 361–87.

Kant, Immanuel. *Critique of Practical Reason and Other Works on the Theory of Ethics*. Ttranslated by T. K. Abbot. London: Longmans, Green Publishers, 1926.

————. *Critique of Pure Reason*. Translated by J. M. D. Meiklejohn. New York: John Wiley, 1943.

————. *Lectures on Ethics*. Translated by Louis Infield. New York: Harper and Row, 1963.

————. *The Metaphysics of Morals*. Edited and Translated by Mary Gregor. Cambridge: Cambridge University Press, 1996.

Kaufmann, Walter. *Nietzsche: Philosopher, Psychologist, Antichrist*, 4th ed. Princeton: Princeton University Press, 1974.

Kekes, John. *The Examined Life*. University Park: The Pennsylvania State University Press, 1992.

———. "Morality and Impartiality." *American Philosophical Quarterly* 18, no. 4 (1981): 295–303.

Kraut, Richard. *What Is Good and Why: The Ethics of Well-Being*. Cambridge: Harvard University Press, 2007.

Larrain, Jorge. "Base and Superstructure." In *A Dictionary of Marxist Thought*, edited by Tom Bottomore. Cambridge: Harvard University Press, 1983.

Long, A. A. *Epictetus: A Stoic and Socratic Guide to Life*. Oxford: The Clarendon Press, 2002.

———. *From Epicurus to Epictetus*. Oxford: The Clarendon Press, 2006.

Lukes, Steven. *Power: A Radical View*, 2nd ed. New York: Palgrave MacMillan, 2005.

———, ed. *Power*. New York: New York University Press, 1986.

Machiavelli, Niccolò. *The Art of War*. Edited and translated by Neal Wood. Cambridge, MA: Da Capo Press, 1965.

———. *Discourses on the First Decade of Titus Livius ("The Discourses")*. In *The Chief Works and Others*, edited and translated by Allan H. Gilbert. Durham: Duke University Press, 1989.

———. *Discourses on the First Decade of Titus Livius ("The Discourses")*. In *Selected Political Writings*, edited and translated by David Wootton. Indianapolis: Hackett, 1994.

———. *Florentine Histories*. Edited and translated by Laura F. Banfield and Harvey C. Mansfield. Princeton: Princeton University Press, 1988.

———. *Machiavelli and His Friends: Their Personal Correspondence*. Edited and translated by James B. Atkinson and David Sices. DeKalb: Northern Illinois University Press, 1996.

———. *The Prince*. In *Selected Political Writings*, edited and translated by David Wootton. Indianapolis: Hackett, 1994.

MacKinnon, Catharine A. "Feminism, Marxism, Method, and the State: An Agenda for Theory." *Signs* 7 (1982): 515–44.

Mansfield, Harvey C. "Strauss's Machiavelli." *Political Theory* 3 (1975): 372–84.

Marx, Karl. "Contributions to the Critique of Hegel's Philosophy of Law." In Marx and Engels, *Collected Works*, vol. 3. New York: International Publishers, 1976.

———. "Critique of Hegel's Doctrine of the State." In *Early Writings*, translated by Rodney Livingstone and Gregor Benton. New York: Penguin Books, 1992.

———. "Economic and Philosophic Manuscripts of 1844." In Marx and Engels, *Collected Works*, vol. 3. New York: International Publishers, 1976.

———. *Das Kapital*. Translated by Samuel Moore. Seattle: Pacific Publishing Studio, 2010.

May, J. A. "The 'Master-Slave' Relation in Hegel's 'Phenomenology of Spirit' and in the Early Marx." *Current Perspectives in Social Theory* 5 (1984): 225–66.

McCarthy, Thomas. "The Critique of Impure Reason." In *Rethinking Power*, edited by Thomas E. Wartenberg. Albany: State University of New York Press, 1992.

McKeon, Richard. "Introduction to the Philosophy of Cicero." In Marcus Tullius Cicero, *Selected Works*, translated by Hubert M. Poteat. Chicago: University of Chicago Press, 1950.

Miller, Jean Baker. "Women and Power." In *Rethinking Power*, edited by Thomas E. Wartenberg. Albany: State University of New York Press, 1992.

Moravia, Alberto. "Portrait of Machiavelli." *Partisan Review* 22 (1955): 357–71.

Morriss, Peter. *Power: A Philosophical Analysis*, 2nd ed. Manchester: Manchester University Press, 2002.

Murphy, Arthur E. "The Common Good." *Proceedings and Addresses of the American Philosophical Association* 24 (1950): 3–18.

Nehamas, Alexander. *Nietzsche: Life as Literature*. Cambridge: Harvard University Press, 1985.

Neuhouser, Frederick. "Desire, Recognition, and the Relation between Bondsman and Lord." In *The Blackwell Guide to Hegel's Phenomenology of Spirit*, edited by Kenneth Westphal. Oxford: Wiley-Blackwell, 2009.

Nietzsche, Friedrich. *Beyond Good and Evil*. Translated by Walter Kaufmann. New York: Vintage Books, 1966.

———. *The Birth of Tragedy*. Translated by Walter Kaufmann. New York: Random House, 1967.

———. *Ecce Homo*. Translated by Walter Kaufmann and R. J. Hollingdale. New York: Random House, 1967.

———. *The Gay Science*. Translated by Walter Kaufmann. New York: Random House, 1967.

———. *On the Genealogy of Morals*. Translated by Walter Kaufmann and R. J. Hollingdale. New York: Vintage Books, 1967.

———. *Thus Spoke Zarathustra*. Translated by Walter Kaufmann. In *The Portable Nietzsche*. New York: Viking Press, 1954.

———. *Twilight of the Idols*. Translated by Walter Kaufmann. In *The Portable Nietzsche*. New York: Viking Press, 1954.

———. *Untimely Meditations*. Translated by R. J. Hollingdale. Cambridge: Cambridge University Press, 1986.

Nozick, Robert. "Coercion." In *Philosophy, Politics, and Society*, edited by Peter Laslett, W. G. Runciman, and Quentin Skinner. Oxford: Oxford University Press, 1972.

———. *The Examined Life: Philosophical Meditations*. New York: Simon and Schuster, 1989.

———. *Philosophical Explanations*. Cambridge: Harvard University Press, 1981.

Nussbaum, Martha C. *Women and Human Development*. New York: Cambridge University Press, 2000.

Okin, Susan Moller. *Justice, Gender, and the Family*. New York: Basic Books, 1989.

O'Mahony, Patrick. "Habermas and Communicative Power." *Journal of Power* 3 (2010), 53–73.

O'Neill, John, ed. *Hegel's Dialectic of Desire and Recognition*. Albany: State University of New York Press, 1996.

Parsons, Talcott. "On the Concept of Political Power." In *Political Power: A Reader in Theory and Research*, edited by Roderick Bell, David V. Edwards, and R. Harrison Wagner. New York: Free Press, 1969.

Pateman, Carole. *The Sexual Contract*. Stanford: Stanford University Press, 1988.

Plato. *Collected Dialogues*, 7th ed. Edited by Edith Hamilton and Huntington Cairns. Princeton: Princeton University Press, 1973.

———. "Gorgias," translated by W. D. Woodhead. In *Plato: Collected Dialogues*, 7th ed., edited by Edith Hamilton and Huntington Cairns. Princeton: Princeton University Press, 1973.

———. "The Republic," translated by by Paul Shorey. In *Plato: Collected Dialogues*, edited by Edith Hamilton and Huntington Cairns. Princeton: Princeton University Press, 1973.

Plutarch. *The Lives of the Noble Grecians and Romans*. Translated by John Dryden. Edited and revised by Arthur Hugh Clough, volumes 1 and 2. New York: The Modern Library, 1992.

Poggi, Gianfranco. *Forms of Power*. Cambridge: Polity Press, 2001.

Powell, J. G. F. *Cicero the Philosopher*. Oxford: The Clarendon Press, 1999.

Prezzolini, Giuseppe. "The Christian Roots of Machiavelli's Moral Pessimism." *Review of National Literatures* 1 (1970): 26–37.

Price, Russell. "The Senses of *Virtù* in Machiavelli." *European Studies Review* 3 (1973): 315–45.

———. "The Theme of *Gloria* in Machiavelli." *Renaissance Quarterly* 30 (1977): 588–631.

Radford, Robert T. *Cicero*. Amsterdam: Editions Rodopi, 2002.

Rawls, John. *A Theory of Justice*. Oxford: Clarendon Press, 1972.

Richardson, John. *Nietzsche's System*. Oxford: Oxford University Press, 1996.

Rouse, Joseph. "Power/Knowledge." In *The Cambridge Companion to Foucault*, edited by Gary Gutting. Cambridge: Cambridge University Press, 1994.

Russell, Bertrand. *Power*. New York: W. W. Norton, 1983.

Saar, Martin. "Power and Critique." *Journal of Power* 3 (2010): 7–20.

Sawicki, Jana. *Disciplining Foucault: Feminism, Power, and the Body*. New York: Routledge, 1991.

Schmitt, Richard. *Marx and Engels: A Critical Reconstruction*. Boulder: Westview, 1987.

Schopenhauer, Arthur. *The World as Will and Idea*, 3 vols. Translated by R. B. Haldane and J. Kemp. London: Routledge and Kegan Paul, 1948.

Scott, John C. *Domination and the Arts of Resistance*. New Haven: Yale University Press, 1990.

———. *Power*. Cambridge: Polity Press, 2001.

Sellars, John. *Stoicism*. Berkeley: University of California Press, 2006.

Stimpson, Catharine R., and Gilbert Herdt, eds. *Critical Terms for the Study of Gender*. Chicago: University of Chicago Press, 2014.

Strauss, Leo. *Thoughts on Machiavelli*. Chicago: University of Chicago Press, 1958.

Taylor, Charles. *Hegel*. Cambridge: Cambridge University Press, 1977.

Tilley, Charles. "Domination, Resistance, Compliance . . . Discourse." *Sociological Forum* 6 (1991): 593–602.

Trebilcot, Joyce, ed. *Mothering*. Totowa, NJ: Rowman and Allanheld, 1983.

Wagner, Gerhard, and Heinz Zipprian. "Habermas on Power and Rationality." *Sociological Theory* 7 (1989): 102–109.

Walzer, Michael. "Political Action: The Problem of Dirty Hands." *Philosophy and Public Affairs* 2 (1973): 160–80.

Wartenberg, Thomas E. *The Forms of Power*. Philadelphia: Temple University Press, 1990.

———, ed. *Rethinking Power*. Albany: State University of New York Press, 1992.

West, David. "Power and Formation: New Foundations for a Radical Conception of Power." *Inquiry* 30 (1987): 137–54.

White, D. M. *The Concept of Power*. Morristown, NJ: General Learning Press, 1976.

White, Stephen A. "Cicero and the Therapists." In *Cicero: The Philosopher*, edited by J. D. Powell. Oxford: Clarendon Press, 1999.

Williams, Roger R. "Hegel and Nietzsche: Recognition and Master/Slave." *Philosophy Today* 45 (2001): 164–79.

Wrong, Dennis. *Power: Its Forms, Bases, and Uses*. Oxford: Blackwell, 1979.

Yeatman, Anna, "Feminism and Power." In *Reconstructing Political Theory*, edited by Mary Lyndon Shanley and Uma Narayan. University Park: The Pennsylvania State University Press, 1997.

Young, Iris Marion. "Five Faces of Oppression." *The Philosophical Forum* 19 (1988): 270–90.

———. "Five Faces of Oppression." In *Rethinking Power*, edited by Thomas E. Wartenberg. Albany: State University of New York Press, 1992.

———. *Justice and the Politics of Difference*. Princeton: Princeton University Press, 1990.

About the Author

Raymond Angelo Belliotti is SUNY Distinguished Teaching Professor of Philosophy at the State University of New York at Fredonia. He received his undergraduate degree from Union College in 1970, after which he was conscripted into the United States Army, where he served three years in military intelligence units during the Vietnamese War. Upon his discharge, he enrolled at the University of Miami where he earned his Master of Arts degree in 1976 and Doctorate in 1977. After teaching stints at Florida International University and Virginia Commonwealth University, he entered Harvard University as a law student and teaching fellow. After receiving a Juris Doctorate from Harvard Law School, he practiced law in New York City with the firm of Barrett Smith Schapiro Simon & Armstrong. In 1984, he joined the faculty at Fredonia.

Belliotti is the author of 17 other books: *Justifying Law* (1992); *Good Sex* (1993); *Seeking Identity* (1995); *Stalking Nietzsche* (1998); *What Is the Meaning of Human Life?* (2001); *Happiness is Overrated* (2004); *The Philosophy of Baseball* (2006); *Watching Baseball Seeing Philosophy* (2008); *Niccolò Machiavelli* (2008); *Roman Philosophy and the Good Life* (2009); *Dante's Deadly Sins: Moral Philosophy in Hell* (2011); *Posthumous Harm: Why the Dead Are Still Vulnerable* (2011); *Shakespeare and Philosophy* (2012); *Jesus or Nietzsche: How Should We Live Our Lives?* (2013); *Jesus the Radical: The Parables and Modern Morality* (2014); *Machiavelli's Secret: The Soul of the Statesman* (2015); and *Why Philosophy Matters: 20 Lessons on Living Large* (2015).

Good Sex was later translated into Korean and published in Asia. *What Is the Meaning of Human Life?* was nominated for the *Society for Phenomenology and Existential Philosophy*'s Book of the Year Award. He has also published seventy articles and twenty-five reviews in the areas of ethics, jurisprudence, sexual morality, medicine, politics, education, feminism, sports, Marxism, and legal ethics. These essays have appeared in scholarly journals based in Australia, Canada, Great Britain, Italy, Mexico, South Africa, Sweden, and the United States. Belliotti has also made numerous presentations at philosophical conferences, including the 18th World Congress of Philosophy in England, and has been honored as a featured lecturer on the *Queen Elizabeth-2* ocean liner.

While at SUNY Fredonia he has served extensively on campus committees, as the chairperson of the Department of Philosophy, as the chairperson of the University Senate, and as Director of General Education. Belliotti also served as United University Professions local Vice President for Academics. For six years he was faculty advisor to two undergraduate clubs: the Philosophical Society and *Il Circolo Italiano*. Belliotti has been the recipient of the SUNY Chancellor's Award for Excellence in Teaching, the William T. Hagan Young Scholar/Artist Award, the Kasling Lecture Award for Excellence in Research and Scholarship, and the SUNY Foundation Research & Scholarship Recognition Award. He is a member of the SUNY Distinguished Academy Visiting Scholars Program and was also a member of the New York State Speakers in the Humanities Program for eight years.

Index